HONEST JEFF
&
DISHONEST ABE

BOOKS BY AWARD-WINNING AUTHOR LOCHLAINN SEABROOK

A Rebel Born: A Defense of Nathan Bedford Forrest - Confederate General, American Legend (winner of the 2011 Jefferson Davis Historical Gold Medal)

Everything You Were Taught About the Civil War is Wrong, Ask a Southerner! - Correcting the Errors of Yankee "History"

Nathan Bedford Forrest: Southern Hero, American Patriot - Honoring a Confederate Icon and the Old South

Abraham Lincoln: The Southern View - Demythologizing America's Sixteenth President

The Quotable Nathan Bedford Forrest: Selections From the Writings and Speeches of the Confederacy's Most Brilliant Cavalryman

The Quotable Robert E. Lee: Selections From the Writings and Speeches of the South's Most Beloved Civil War General

Honest Jeff and Dishonest Abe: A Southern Children's Guide to the Civil War

The Unquotable Abraham Lincoln: The President's Quotes They Don't Want You To Know!

Lincolnology: The Real Abraham Lincoln Revealed in His Own Words - A Study of Lincoln's Suppressed, Misinterpreted, and Forgotten Speeches and Writings

The Quotable Jefferson Davis: Selections From the Writings and Speeches of the Confederacy's First President

Give 'Em Hell Boys! The Complete Military Correspondence of Nathan Bedford Forrest

The Quotable Alexander H. Stephens: Selections From the Writings and Speeches of the Confederacy's First Vice President

The Old Rebel: Robert E. Lee As He Was Seen By His Contemporaries

The Constitution of the Confederate States of America: Explained

The Quotable Edward A. Pollard: Selections From the Writings of the Confederacy's Greatest Defender

Encyclopedia of the Battle of Franklin - A Comprehensive Guide to the Conflict that Changed the Civil War

Carnton Plantation Ghost Stories: True Tales of the Unexplained from Tennessee's Most Haunted Civil War House!

The McGavocks of Carnton Plantation: A Southern History - Celebrating One of Dixie's Most Noble Confederate Families and Their Tennessee Home

The Caudills: An Etymological, Ethnological, and Genealogical Study - Exploring the Name and National Origins of a European-American Family

The Blakeneys: An Etymological, Ethnological, and Genealogical Study - Uncovering the Mysterious Origins of the Blakeney Family and Name

Britannia Rules: Goddess-Worship in Ancient Anglo-Celtic Society - An Academic Look at the United Kingdom's Matricentric Spiritual Past

UFOs and Aliens: The Complete Guidebook

Christmas Before Christianity: How the Birthday of the "Sun" Became the Birthday of the "Son"

The Book of Kelle: An Introduction to Goddess-Worship and the Great Celtic Mother-Goddess Kelle, Original Blessed Lady of Ireland

The Goddess Dictionary of Words and Phrases: Introducing a New Core Vocabulary for the Women's Spirituality Movement

SEA RAVEN PRESS

Thought Provoking Books For Smart People
www.SeaRavenPress.com

HONEST JEFF
&
DISHONEST ABE

A Southern Children's Guide to the

CIVIL WAR

LOCHLAINN SEABROOK
WINNER OF THE JEFFERSON DAVIS HISTORICAL GOLD MEDAL

First Civil War Sesquicentennial Edition

FOREWORD BY AL BENSON JR.

SEA RAVEN PRESS, FRANKLIN, TENNESSEE, USA

HONEST JEFF & DISHONEST ABE
A Southern Children's Guide to the Civil War

FOR AGES EIGHT TO TWELVE • SECOND TO SIXTH GRADES

Published by
Sea Raven Press, P.O. Box 1054, Franklin, Tennessee 37065-1054 USA
www.SeaRavenPress.com • searavenpress@nii.net

Copyright © 2012 Lochlainn Seabrook
in accordance with U.S. and international copyright laws and regulations, as stated and protected under the Berne Union for the Protection of Literary and Artistic Property (Berne Convention), and the Universal Copyright Convention (the UCC). All rights reserved under the Pan-American and International Copyright Conventions.

First Sea Raven Press Civil War Sesquicentennial Edition: March 2012
ISBN: 978-0-9838185-9-5
Library of Congress Catalog Number: 2012932247

This work is the copyrighted intellectual property of Lochlainn Seabrook and has been registered with the Copyright Office at the Library of Congress in Washington, D.C., USA. No part of this work (including text, covers, drawings, photos, illustrations, maps, images, diagrams, etc.), in whole or in part, may be used, reproduced, stored in a retrieval system, or transmitted, in any form or by any means now known or hereafter invented, without written permission from the publisher. The sale, duplication, hire, lending, copying, digitalization, or reproduction of this material, in any manner or form whatsoever, is also prohibited, and is a violation of federal, civil, and digital copyright law, which provides severe civil and criminal penalties for any violations.

Honest Jeff and Dishonest Abe: A Southern Children's Guide to the Civil War / by Lochlainn Seabrook. Foreword by Al Benson Jr. Includes an index and bibliographical references.

Front and back cover design, interior book design and layout, by Lochlainn Seabrook
Typography: Sea Raven Press Book Design
Front cover image: "The True Issue," 1864, Library of Congress
Sketch of the author on "Meet the Author" page © Tracy Latham
All images are from 19th-Century public domain sources, unless otherwise indicated

The views on the American "Civil War" documented in this book *are* those of the publisher.

The paper used in this book is acid-free and lignin-free. It has been certified by the Sustainable Forestry Initiative and the Forest Stewardship Council and meets all ANSI standards for archival quality paper.

PRINTED & MANUFACTURED IN OCCUPIED TENNESSEE, FORMER CONFEDERATE STATES OF AMERICA

Dedication

To all Southern children: May you grow up with affection for your culture, pride in your heritage, and a love of your history.

Epigraph

"[After the Civil War] . . . there emerged as the years went by a condition and a necessity which had not been anticipated. With utmost difficulty the schools of the South had been re-established, and seminaries and colleges had been re-opened, in the faithful effort to preserve the intelligence and character of the generation of sons and daughters rising up through the land.

"It was discovered with a shock of pain and indignation that the great body of the youth of the land were being fed with a literature created by alien authors. Histories, biographies, readers, issued by publishers whose one purpose was to secure the great market now opening in every school district far and wide over the South, were found to be replete with error and misrepresentation. Consciously or unconsciously, the aims of the people of the South, and of their State governments were falsified, and the characters of great and good men were belittled and defamed.

"The poison of unjust accusation was carried to the minds of all the children of the Southland, and already a generation was growing up with conceptions of the motives of their fathers, and the causes of the war between the sections which were not only mistaken, but altogether dishonorable. The youth of the whole South were being stealthily robbed of an heritage glorious in itself and elevating and ennobling to themselves and all who came after them.

"It was a condition and a process which could not be consented to for a moment. There was no surrender at Appomattox, and no withdrawal from the field which committed our people and their children to a heritage of shame and dishonor. No cowardice on any battlefield could be as base and shameful as the silent acquiescence in the scheme which was teaching the children in their homes and schools that the commercial value of slavery was the cause of the war, that prisoners of war held in the South were starved and treated with a barbarous inhumanity, that Jefferson Davis and Robert E. Lee were traitors to their country and false to their oaths, that the young men who left everything to resist invasion, and climbed the slopes of Gettysburg and died willingly on a hundred fields were rebels against a righteous government.

"The State Camp of Virginia of Confederate Veterans rose promptly and vigorously to resist another invasion, which would have turned the children against their fathers, covered the graves of patriots and heroes with shame and made the memory of the Confederacy and its sacrifices and struggles a disgrace in all coming history. The camps throughout the South had a new task given them. They were to meet the threatening evil at the door of every school house in the land.

"All that was, or is now, desired [by the South] is that error and injustice be excluded from the text-books of the schools and from the literature brought into our homes; that the truth be told, without exaggeration and without omission; truth for its own sake and for the sake of honest history, and that the generations to come after us be not left to bear the burden of shame and dishonor unrighteously laid upon the name of their noble sires."

Confederate Reverend James P. Smith, 1907

CONTENTS

Notes to Parents - 11
Foreword, by Al Benson Jr. - 15
Parents' Introduction - 18
A Note to Young Readers - 21
Children's Introduction - 25

SECTION 1
THE CAUSES OF THE CIVIL WAR

Chapter 1: The Origins of American Slavery - 33
Chapter 2: The Origins of Southern Slavery - 37
Chapter 3: The Origins of the American Abolition Movement - 40
Chapter 4: The Yankee Abolitionists' Assault on the South - 42
Chapter 5: The Truth About Southern "Slavery" - 47
Chapter 6: Igniting the Embers of the Civil War - 54
Chapter 7: Holding a Wolf By the Ears! - 57
Chapter 8: A Yankee Madman Named John Brown - 61
Chapter 9: Dishonest Abe: A Dictator in the White House! - 63
Chapter 10: A Lesson in Politics & American History - 66
Chapter 11: States' Rights & Governmental Powers - 72
Chapter 12: Secession: The Southern States Leave the Union! - 76
Chapter 13: Liberals, Dictators, Thought Police, & Empires - 82

SECTION 2
THE WAR FOR SOUTHERN INDEPENDENCE: 1861-1865

Chapter 14: Lincoln Launches His War at Fort Sumter - 95
Chapter 15: Lincoln Tries to Hurt the South & Her People - 103
Chapter 16: Battles: 1861- 110
Chapter 17: Battles: 1862 - 112
Chapter 18: The Emancipation Proclamation: 1863 - 120
Chapter 19: Lincoln & Black Colonization - 128
Chapter 20: Battles: 1863 - 134
Chapter 21: The Gettysburg Address: 1863 - 139
Chapter 22: Battles: 1864 - 144
Chapter 23: The Final Battle & Surrender: 1865 - 152

SECTION 3
THE TRUTH ABOUT DISHONEST ABE
Chapter 24: The Man Our Southern Ancestors called "Stinkin' Lincoln" - 157

SECTION 4
LIFE IN THE CONFEDERATE ARMY
Chapter 25: The World of the Confederate Soldier - 167
Chapter 26: Confederate Implements of War - 178

SECTION 5
FORBIDDEN FACTS THEY DON'T TEACH YOU IN SCHOOL
Chapter 27: The Hidden Truth About the Civil War - 191
Chapter 28: Cabinets, Soldiers, & An Unfair Fight - 197
Chapter 29: Our Multi-Colored Confederates Armies - 203
Chapter 30: Black, Indian, Jewish, & Latino Confederate Soldiers - 210
Chapter 31: Women, Horses, Beards, & Music - 215

SECTION 6
IMPORTANT FACTS YOU NEED TO KNOW
Chapter 32: Important Facts About the Civil War - 223
Chapter 33: Important Facts About Jefferson Davis - 228
Chapter 34: Important Facts About Abraham Lincoln - 231
Chapter 35: Important Facts About Robert E. Lee - 238
Chapter 36: Important Facts About Nathan Bedford Forrest - 241
Chapter 37: The South & the Confederacy Today - 245

Appendix A (For Children): Other names for the "Civil War" - 252
Appendix B (For Parents): An Early Attempt to Prevent the Northernization of Our Schools - 254
Glossary - 256
Bibliography - 261
Index - 305
Meet the Author - 313

Jefferson Davis, "Honest Jeff," was the Confederacy's first president. As the Confederacy's leading Founding Father, we will honor President Davis for all time as a great Southern man and an American hero.

NOTES TO PARENTS

☞ *Honest Jeff and Dishonest Abe* was written for eight to twelve year olds; that is, for second graders to sixth graders. This may seem to cover an overly large age group, but the span is intentional.

Parents can read aloud to the younger ones, those in second grade (seven and eight year olds). For those in third and fourth grades (eight to ten year olds), parents and children can read together. Fifth and sixth graders (ten through twelve year olds) will be able to, and will probably want to, tackle this book on their own.

One is never too young to get started on the topic of authentic Southern history.

☞ All quotes by individuals such as Jefferson Davis or Abraham Lincoln have been taken verbatim from their original sources. However, in order to make them more understandable to children, I have paraphrased them (unless otherwise indicated).

☞ In any study of the "Civil War" it is vitally important to keep in mind that the two major political parties were then the opposite of what they are today. The Democrats of the mid 19th Century were conservatives, akin to the Republican Party of today, while the Republicans of the mid 19th Century were liberals, akin to the Democratic Party of today. Thus the Confederacy's Democratic president, Jefferson Davis, was a conservative (with libertarian leanings); the Union's Republican president, Abraham Lincoln, was a liberal (with socialistic leanings).

☞ As I very much dislike the inaccurate, Yankee-invented phrase, the "Civil War" (for the reasons given in Chapter 1 of my book *Everything You Were Taught About the Civil War is Wrong, Ask a Southerner!*), its use as part of the title of this book deserves an explanation.

Today America's entire literary system refers to the conflict of 1861 using the Northern term the "Civil War," whether we in the South like it or not. Thus, as all book searches by readers, libraries, and retail outlets are now performed online, and as all bookstores categorize works from this period under the heading "Civil War," book publishers and authors who deal with this particular topic have little choice but to use this term themselves. If I were to refuse to use it, as some of my Southern colleagues have suggested, few people would ever find or read my books.

Add to this the fact that scarcely any non-Southerners have ever heard of the names we in the South use for the conflict, such as the "War for Southern Independence"—or my personal preference, "Lincoln's War." It only makes sense then to use the term "Civil War" in most commercial situations.

We should also bear in mind that while today educated persons, particularly educated Southerners, all share an abhorrence for the phrase "Civil War," it was not always so. Confederates who lived through and even fought in the conflict regularly used the term throughout the 1860s, and even long after.

Among them were Confederate generals such as Nathan Bedford Forrest, Richard Taylor, and Joseph E. Johnston, not to mention the Confederacy's vice president, Alexander H. Stephens. Even the Confederacy's highest leader, President Jefferson Davis, used the term "Civil War," and in one case at least, as late as 1881—the year he wrote his brilliant exposition, *The Rise and Fall of the Confederate Government*.

☞ The Civil War, especially the Southern version of the Civil War, is often not an easy subject, even for adults. Lincoln's cold-hearted brutality, along with the countless outrages committed by his soldiers on our people and homeland between 1861 and 1865, are almost beyond comprehension to the modern reader. As such, I have done my best to "childrenize" the stark realities of the War while retaining the authentic facts. Still, I advise parents to read this book in order to determine if it's suitable for your child.

☞ Because this is a children's book, there are no footnotes. But rest assured that every statement made has been thoroughly researched and documented. This is a work of historical fact, after all, not a collection of fairy tales based on subjective bias, as you will find in most pro-North books.

☞ For those parents who are interested in studying the source material for most of the information in *Honest Jeff and Dishonest Abe*, and who also want to learn more about genuine Southern history as opposed to the pseudo-histories of anti-South writers, see my books:

Everything You Were Taught About the Civil War is Wrong, Ask a Southerner! - Correcting the Errors of Yankee "History"
A Rebel Born: A Defense of Nathan Bedford Forrest
Nathan Bedford Forrest: Southern Hero, American Patriot - Honoring a Confederate Icon and the Old South
The Quotable Nathan Bedford Forrest: Selections From the Writings and Speeches of the Confederacy's Most Brilliant Cavalryman
Give 'Em Hell Boys! The Complete Military Correspondence of Nathan Bedford Forrest
The Quotable Jefferson Davis: Selections From the Writings & Speeches of the Confederacy's First President
The Quotable Robert E. Lee: Selections From the Writings and Speeches of the South's Most Beloved Civil War General
The Old Rebel: Robert E. Lee As He Was Seen By His Contemporaries
Abraham Lincoln: The Southern View - Demythologizing America's Sixteenth President
Lincolnology: The Real Abraham Lincoln Revealed in His Own Words - A Study of Lincoln's Suppressed, Misinterpreted, and Forgotten Speeches and Writings
The Unquotable Abraham Lincoln: The President's Quotes They Don't Want You to Know!
The Constitution of the Confederate States of America: Explained
Encyclopedia of the Battle of Franklin: A Comprehensive Guide to the Conflict that Changed the Civil War
The McGavocks of Carnton Plantation: A Southern History - Celebrating One of Dixie's Most Noble Confederate Families and Their Tennessee Home
Carnton Plantation Ghost Stories: True Tales of the Unexplained from Tennessee's Most Haunted Civil War House!

☞ A word to Northern parents who may be bothered by the contents of this work: this book is not *for* you.

14 🔫 Honest Jeff & Dishonest Abe

FOREWORD

An Authentic History Book for the Southern Home School Movement

At this late date it should come as no surprise to Southerners that they and their children have been lied to about their history and heritage. Unfortunately, this is not a new thing. It has been going on since the Yankee government forced "reconstruction" on the Southern states after the War of Northern Aggression. The public school system in the South was part and parcel of "reconstruction" and was instituted, according to author John Chodes "to teach the rebel's children 'respect for national authority.'" If successive generations of Southern children could be properly indoctrinated via public education, they could be taught to never again have the courage and principles to stand up for their God-given rights. That's what public education was and is all about.

If Southerners are ever to find the truth they must be able to begin to look beyond the Yankee textbooks that are the bedrock of the public education system and must learn to find other more reliable sources for their information. Not only that, they must begin to re-educate their children, lest they continue to believe the lies they have been taught. This would seem to be a Herculean task, given almost 150 years of Yankee/socialist indoctrination that has been forced down their throats. Nonetheless, in recent years, a beginning has been made. Within the past decade or so several books have been published that have presented the Southern perspective about the War and the real reasons for it, and people have been enabled to start reading and learning. We have a long way to go yet.

One area very little has been done in is accurate history books for young folks. My wife and I (we home schooled our children) used to go to various home school book fairs. The first thing I always checked out was the history books. Most of these, sadly, were virtual carbon copies of what was being used in public schools, with a few Bible verses sprinkled over them. So, even with the growing home schooling

16 Honest Jeff & Dishonest Abe

movement our children were still not learning much real history. Thankfully, that is now beginning to change.

Award winning Southern historian Lochlainn Seabrook has set out to remedy this situation with *Honest Jeff and Dishonest Abe: A Southern Children's Guide to the Civil War*. This is a non-fiction book for children ages 8-12 and it is over 300 pages long. When I first saw the length of the book I thought "No youngster that age in our day is ever going to read 300 pages." I soon realized that this is a children's *history* book and as I scanned through parts of it I began to see that, yes, with the proper guidance and instruction, many youngsters this age will get through this book—and they will learn something much more true and accurate than anything they will ever receive from public school "history" texts. This should be a history book for the home school movement in the Southern states. I wish I had been able to have this for my grandchildren, who are mostly past this age now.

Mr. Seabrook deals with subjects in this book that students today are routinely lied to about regarding historical events. He deals with the origins of American slavery. It started in the North, not in the South, and for decades Yankee slave traders made lots of money in the slave trade. He talks about the origins of the American abolitionist movement (it actually started in the South). Yet all the history books mention are the abolitionist radicals of the William Lloyd Garrison stripe from New England. You never hear about the responsible Southern abolitionists who were not radicals. He has a chapter on John Brown, who most students today are encouraged to idolize. I've read a bit about John Brown over the years. He was nothing more than a 19th century terrorist, and Mr. Seabrook gives the youngsters the truth about John Brown in language they can understand.

He has a chapter in this book called "Dishonest Abe: A Dictator in the White House." Is that ever the truth! Something else the vast majority of the "history" books don't bother to include. Lincoln has become, thanks to clever propagandists, sort of a secular deity in this country that people have been taught to impute only noble and virtuous motives to. In real life this was hardly the case. Lincoln was a completely pragmatic politician that believed in the Marxian concept that the ends justify the means, and that's all he was. Our young folks, at an early age, need to begin to learn the truth about Mr. Lincoln, and Mr. Seabrook gives them a good primer here.

They need to begin, again, at an early age, to learn the real reasons for the War (slavery was the least of them). They need to begin to learn about secession, the rights of the individual states, Lincoln's views about black people, and why he wanted them all shipped out of the country. There is a section in the book called "Forbidden Facts They Don't Teach You in School." More of what you will never read in public school "history" books.

In short, Mr. Seabrook gives children, in age-appropriate language, historical truths they are not very likely to come across today in too many places, if at all. Interestingly enough, the totalitarian intellects that control the public education system in this country want to be able to reach our children at an even earlier age. Some of them want kids in public schools as early as age three. We need to resist this indoctrination by giving Southern youngsters the truth at an earlier age also. Eight years old is not too young to begin.

Let's face it, with the exception of a really dedicated history teacher here and there in public schools, our kids are never going to get the truth about their history at any age.

With *Honest Jeff and Dishonest Abe* Lochlainn Seabrook is giving you the chance to reverse that trend. If you are a home schooler or even have your children in a private Christian school, this book should be on your book shelf. If you have your youngsters in public school then you really need this book to combat the lies they will be told about their history and heritage.

AL BENSON JR.
Sterlington, Louisiana

Publisher of *The Copperhead Chronicle*, former editor of *The Christian Educator*, and author of *Lincoln's Marxists* (with Walter D. Kennedy)

PARENTS' INTRODUCTION

For those parents who are from traditional Southern homes, much of the contents of this book will be familiar. For those parents who are from outside the South, and in particular from the North where anti-South bias is at its most severe, some of this material may be surprising, even shocking.

For those in the latter category, rest assured that this is not a fictitious story fabricated to entertain children. *Honest Jeff and Dishonest Abe* tells the true story of the American South and what we call the War for Southern Independence. As my exhaustive bibliography illustrates, it is the result of many years of in-depth research, study, and writing, distilled from thousands of books—over a dozen which I myself, a Southern historian, have authored over the past decade.

Still, some may be asking: why do we need "A *Southern Children's Guide to the Civil War*"? What's wrong with the information that has always been presented in our schools?

This question can be best answered by a conversation that took place on the popular TV program, "The O'Reilly Factor" on Fox News, January 16, 2012, Martin Luther King Day. Northerner Bill O'Reilly was interviewing Southerner Richard Harpootlian:

> HARPOOTLIAN: The Republicans have injected race [into the presidential contest] by Newt Gingrich and [Rick] Santorum saying "this will be the most important election since 1860." Now what happened in 1860?
> O'REILLY: We elected Abraham Lincoln.
> HARPOOTLIAN: In 1860 we elected a president who passed the Emancipation Proclamation.
> O'REILLY: And they [Gingrich and Santorum] say this was the most important election since 1860.
> HARPOOTLIAN: Why 1860? I don't get it.
> O'REILLY: Because that's Lincoln coming in to try to

> keep the Union together. That's what happened in 1860. Surely you know that.
> HARPOOTLIAN: Well, the Union didn't stay "together." We in the South have a little different version of what happened in 1860.

If you read this entire book alone or with your child, and I highly recommend that you do one or the other, you will indeed discover that there is a *Southern* version of Lincoln's War, one that is quite different from the one long espoused by the North.

Being a Southerner I am, of course, predisposed to embrace the Southern version. However, unlike many in the North, I have taken the time to study both versions, and after years of diligent work on the subject there is only one logical conclusion a reasoning person can come to.

The Northern version of the Civil War turns out to be a sinister concoction of anti-South lies, hyperbole, distortions, misrepresentations, misinformation, disinformation, and outright slander, all of it purposefully manufactured by Lincoln's wartime anti-South propaganda machine. Lincoln's purpose? To fan the flames of sectional hatred and racial bigotry (long two of the liberal's trademark tactics), maintain Northern support for his War, and curry votes for his 1864 reelection campaign.

Despite the obvious demagoguery and political expediency behind the Northern version of the War, this is the one that is being taught in our children's schools. And it is over 150 years old!

Do we really want the next generation to grow up thinking that the Civil War was fought over slavery when both Lincoln and Davis said it wasn't? Do we really want our kids thinking Lincoln was the "Great Emancipator" when he was the Civil War generation's most aggressive advocate of black deportation (known in the 1800s as "colonization")? Do we really want our sons and daughters thinking that Lincoln "preserved the Union" and "freed the slaves" when he did neither?

Do we really want them to become adults believing that because the South lost the War, Southerners are "bad" people and Northerners are "good" people? Do we want our Southern children growing up associating the label "slavery" with the South, when we know full well that American slavery got its start in the North and that the American abolition movement got its start in the South? Do we want them to feel shame toward their Southern heritage when the South has not only never done anything to be ashamed of, but has done many things to be proud of?

The answer to all of these questions is a resounding "no!" And I am sure that after reading this book, you will agree.

Because the true story of the Civil War, that is the Southern version, has been banned from our schools by the liberal establishment that runs them, a faithful and accurate account of the conflict has been desperately needed. *Honest Jeff and Dishonest Abe* was written to fill that need, and it is my hope that parents, wherever they are from, will use this book to properly educate their children in both authentic American and Southern history. This is a great and solemn responsibility, and one of the most important tasks you will ever fulfill as a parent.

The liberal left is hellbent on eradicating Southern culture, and with it, our heritage, symbols, stories, customs, heroes, traditions, and most importantly, our history. Giving your child *Honest Jeff and Dishonest Abe* is one of the best things you can do to put a stop to this nefarious process of cultural genocide. And in doing so, you will help insure that one day they will pass this book onto their children.

May my work bring many years of education and enjoyment to your family. God bless the South!

LOCHLAINN SEABROOK
Franklin, Williamson County, Tennessee, USA
March 2012, Civil War Sesquicentennial

A NOTE TO YOUNG READERS

In 1861, Americans went to war with each other. The people in the Northern states, known as Yankees, decided they should tell the people in the Southern states how to live their lives.

Southerners said "We know what's best for ourselves. Please leave us alone!" But the Yankees wouldn't listen. Instead, they sent armed soldiers into Dixie to try and force Southerners to behave the way they wanted them to.

Southerners had no choice but to fight back. The result is what Yankees still call the "Civil War." But we in the South call it the "War for Southern Independence," because we only wanted to be free.

Like you, I'm a Southerner. This book tells the story of the War that the Yankees fought against our people.

I wrote this book for you because most schools don't teach the true history of the "Civil War" anymore. Teachers only want you to know the Yankee version.

But we Southerners have our own version of the War, one that's based on facts, not on silly stories made up to make the South look bad! This book is about how we here in the South see the "Civil War," and in it you'll learn the truth about what really happened.

You are a child of the South. This is *your* history. Be proud of it, and share it with everyone you know!

"Our Heroes and Our Flags" was printed in 1896 to honor our Southern heritage and promote Confederate pride. Every Southern child should know the names of these men on sight. In the center are full-length portraits of (left to right) Stonewall Jackson, Pierre Gustave Toutant Beauregard, and Robert E. Lee. These three men are surrounded by four different Confederate flags. Top left: First National (the "Stars and Bars") . Top right: Battle Flag (the "Soldier's Flag"). Bottom left: Second National (the "Stainless Banner"). Bottom right: Third National (the "Blood Stained Banner"). Starting at the top center and going counterclockwise, the surrounding outer men are: Jefferson Davis, Pierre Gustave Toutant Beauregard, Braxton Bragg, John Bell Hood, Ambrose Powell Hill, James Longstreet, John Brown Gordon, Wade Hampton, Albert Sidney Johnston, John Hunt Morgan, Edmund Kirby Smith, Joseph Eggleston Johnston, James Ewell Brown "Jeb" Stuart, William Joseph Hardee, Leonidas Polk, Sterling Price, Stonewall Jackson, and Alexander Hamilton Stephens.

Honest Jeff
&
Dishonest Abe

A Southern Children's Guide to the Civil War

CHILDREN'S INTRODUCTION

THE WAR THAT DIVIDED AMERICA

In 1861, the War for Southern Independence, or what Yankees call the "Civil War," divided America right across the middle with the South on one side and the North on the other. These weren't just two different regions of America, as they teach you in school. The War was fought between two truly separate countries.

Our people in the South belonged to the Confederate States of America, the C.S.A. for short. We sometimes also call it the "Confederacy," or "Dixie." Our president at the time was a sincere, brave, Christian man named Jefferson Davis, who I've nicknamed "Honest Jeff." Our soldiers were mainly farm boys, and wore gray, or sometimes light brown "butternut," uniforms.

Most of our soldiers were country boys, farmers, and plantation owners.

The people in the North, the Yankees, belonged to the

United States of America, the U.S.A. for short. It's also sometimes known as the "Union." Their president was a deceptive cowardly anti-Christian man name Abraham Lincoln, who I've nicknamed "Dishonest Abe." Yankee soldiers were mostly city boys, and wore blue uniforms.

The "Civil War" was a very bitter conflict, one that not only divided America, but also split individual states and towns in two. In Kentucky, for example, my home state, half of the people sided with the C.S.A., the other half with the U.S.A. In Tennessee, where I now live, the eastern side went mainly over to the North, while the western side went mainly with the South.

The Civil War was a painful and unnecessary conflict that separated South from North.

NORTHERN MEN WHO SWITCHED SIDES
When the War started, a great many really smart Yankees turned their backs on the North and fought for the Confederacy; men like Confederate Generals:

- Zebulon York (from Maine)
- William Steele (from New York)
- Josiah Gorgas (from Pennsylvania)
- Daniel Ruggles (from Massachusetts)
- Franklin Gardner (from New York)
- Arnold E. Jones (from Maryland)
- John C. Pemberton (from Pennsylvania)
- John H. Winder (from Maryland)

- Walter H. Stevens (from New York)
- William McComb (from Pennsylvania)
- Robert H. Hatton (from Ohio)
- Samuel G. French (from New Jersey)
- Lloyd Tilghman (from Maryland)
- John Slidell (from New York)
- William C. Quantrill (from Ohio)
- Danville Leadbetter (from Maine)
- Francis A. Shoup (from Indiana)
- Richard Griffith (from Pennsylvania)
- Lawrence S. Ross (from Iowa)
- Daniel M. Frost (from New York)
- Otho F. Strahl (from Ohio)
- Martin L. Smith (from New York)
- William S. Walker (from Pennsylvania)
- Claudius W. Sears (from Massachusetts)
- Richard S. Ewell (from Washington, D.C.)
- Clement H. Stevens (from Connecticut)

General John C. Pemberton was a Northerner who joined the Confederate army.

SOUTHERN MEN WHO SWITCHED SIDES

Sadly, there were a few very confused Southerners who turned their backs on the South and fought for the Union. These men were sometimes known as "homemade Yankees," or worse, "galvanized Yankees," because they betrayed the Southern Cause. Some of these Union Generals were:

- Samuel P. Carter (from Tennessee)
- Philip St. George Cooke (from Virginia)
- John B. McIntosh (from Florida)
- Stephen G. Burbridge (from Kentucky)
- Jacob Ammen (from Virginia)
- James A. Williamson (from Kentucky)

- David B. Birney (from Alabama)
- Cassius M. Clay (from Kentucky)
- William D. Porter (from Louisiana)
- Thomas L. Crittenden (from Kentucky)
- Joseph R. West (from Louisiana)
- Jeremiah T. Boyle (from Kentucky)
- David G. Farragut (from Tennessee)
- Joseph A. Cooper (from Kentucky)
- John Buford (from Kentucky)
- Louis Marshall (from Virginia)
- Francis P. Blair, Jr. (from Kentucky)
- Robert Anderson (from Kentucky)
- William B. Campbell (from Tennessee)
- William T. Ward (from Virginia)
- Augustus L. Chetlain (from Missouri)
- George H. Thomas (from Virginia)
- Edward R. S. Canby (from Kentucky)
- William Birney (from Alabama)
- Thomas T. Crittenden (from Alabama)
- Napoleon B. Buford (from Kentucky)

General George H. Thomas was a Southerner who joined the Union army.

THE SCALLYWAG

There are those who call these Southerners "traitors," and that would be true. But we have our own name for these particular people. We call them "scallywags," a word that means "a Southerner who turns against his own people."

There are still scallywags in the South today, even 150 years after the "Civil War." You can always tell a scallywag from a true Southerner: a true Southerner defends the South and the Confederacy; the scallywag says mean and untrue things about them!

THE BROTHERS' WAR

The "Civil War" was a very bad time for our people. The division between individuals of the same states caused a lot of suspicion and distrust between neighbors.

Even families split up over the War, with cousins taking opposite sides, and often even fathers fighting against their sons. Worse still, brothers sometimes took different sides and shot at each other across the battlefield. This is why the War is sometimes called "the Brothers' War."

What would cause not only entire states and towns, but neighbors, friends, and even families to pick up guns and fight against each other?

To understand what caused the War for Southern Independence we must travel back in time many hundreds of years; long before there was either a Confederate States of America or a United States of America. This time period is called the "Colonial Period," because back then there were no states. There were only small groups of Europeans who had moved to America and formed what are known as "colonies."

The Civil War pitted families against one another, and so is sometimes called the Brothers' War.

The first Europeans to form a colony in America were Southerners, because, in 1607, they landed in what we now call the state of Virginia, where they formed a famous settlement called "Jamestown."

But this is not where the "Civil War" got it's start. To find the birthplace of the Brothers' War we must travel North to New England, the home of the Yankee.

Confederate brass mountain Howitzers.

Section 1

THE CAUSES OF THE CIVIL WAR

CHAPTER 1

THE ORIGINS OF AMERICAN SLAVERY

MASSACHUSETTS & THE AMERICAN SLAVE TRADE

Four hundred years ago, in the 1630s, a white Yankee ship captain from the state of Massachusetts sailed to Africa and traded rum, gunpowder, and cloth for dozens of African men and women.

The men and women didn't want to come to America, but they were already slaves in Africa: cruel African chiefs had captured them and forced them into slavery. When the Yankee ship captain came ashore, he purchased these slaves with his goods, put them in shackles, and sailed them all the way back to America. This ship captain was called a "slave trader."

Africans were enslaving one another thousands of years before the arrival of Yankee slave traders from America.

This was the first American to trade goods for slaves. And so we know exactly when and where the American slave trade began: it started in Massachusetts in 1638, the year the ship captain returned home with his cargo of human slaves from Africa.

MASSACHUSETTS & AMERICAN SLAVERY

Now that slaves were in Massachusetts, Yankee farmers began to buy them to work on their plantations. Rich Yankee families bought African slaves to do their housework, to cook their meals, and to help raise their children.

There were so many slaves in Massachusetts by the year 1640, that the state's leaders had to make a law saying it was okay to buy and keep slaves. And so, we know exactly when and where American slavery began: it started in Massachusetts in 1641, the year white Americans made slavery legal for the first time.

Yankee slave captains purchased black men and women who had already been made slaves in their own native country by cruel power-hungry African chiefs.

SLAVERY EXPANDS ACROSS THE NORTH

As the years passed, Yankee slavery became very popular: Yankees liked having black servants do their work for them. And so slavery spread quickly all across the Northern states. As it spread, it grew and grew, until there were thousands and thousands of slaves.

It became so popular that in cities like Perth Amboy, New Jersey, nearly every white person owned at least one slave. By the early 1700s, nearly half of all New York homes had slaves, and in the Narragansett region of Rhode Island alone, 50 percent of the citizens were black African slaves.

To keep up with the Yankee demand for slaves, more and more ship

The South never traded in slaves. Slave trading was strictly a Yankee enterprise.

captains turned to slave trading. It was a lucrative business, and many Yankees became extremely wealthy selling African slaves to other Yankees.

AMERICA'S FIRST SLAVE PORTS OPEN IN THE NORTH
In order to get as many slaves into the North as fast as possible, Yankees opened up dozens of seaports so that their slave ships would have someplace to unload their human cargo.

Some of the biggest slave ports were in the cities of Boston, Massachusetts; Providence, Newport, and Bristol, Rhode Island; Baltimore and Annapolis, Maryland; and Philadelphia, Pennsylvania.

SLAVERY IN OUR NATION'S CAPITAL
One of the largest and richest slave ports was in our nation's capital city: Washington, D.C. Slaves were bought and sold at markets located near the Capitol, where slave traders set up their slave pens and auction blocks.

As this old illustration from 1830 clearly shows, the slave trade once flourished in Washington, D.C., well within sight of the U.S. Capitol (upper right corner).

It was these same slaves who were used to build most of the U.S. government's buildings and roads in Washington during the late 1700s and early 1800s, including the White House and the U.S. Capitol.

NEW YORK CITY: AMERICA'S SLAVE TRADE CENTER
America's largest slave port by far was in New York City. Countless Yankee slave trading ships sailed in and out of the New

36 Honest Jeff & Dishonest Abe

York Harbor everyday, bringing in millions of dollars for the wealthy Yankee businessmen who owned the shipping companies. Slavery became so common in New York that in boroughs like Kings, Queens, Richmond, and Westchester, slaves made up 25 percent of the population.

Today New York City is only America's richest and biggest city because of its earlier ties to slavery, and because the rich men connected to the slave trade invested so much of their money in the town.

Among the many powerful New Yorkers who profited from Northern slavery were the Lehman Brothers, John Jacob Astor, Pierpont Morgan, Charles Tiffany, and Archibald Gracie. These names are still well-known in New York City.

A Typical slave market in New England, only one of many. All American slaves were brought here by Yankee slave ships, that were owned by Yankee ship captains, who were funded by Yankee businessmen. These same slaves were then sold by Yankee slave traders to other Yankees. Our nation's biggest slave ports were in Massachusetts, Rhode Island, Maryland, and Pennsylvania. New York City had the largest slave port of all and was America's slave capital for many decades. New York City is the biggest and richest city in the United States today only because of the money and power she obtained from the Yankees' "peculiar institution": the Northern slave trade.

CHAPTER 2

THE ORIGINS OF SOUTHERN SLAVERY

YANKEES DECIDE THEY DON'T LIKE BLACK PEOPLE

Slavery continued to expand across the North throughout the 1700s and early 1800s, with hundreds of huge slave plantations developing from New England down into New York.

But about this time, a major change began to take place. Yankees discovered that they didn't like African people very much after all. They enjoyed having them do their laundry and take care of their crops, for example, but they found that they didn't really like to be around blacks themselves.

We don't know exactly why this is, but we do know from the books and letters and laws they created in the 1800s that many Yankees believed African people were inferior; that were not as attractive, as smart, as ambitious, or as creative as white people.

Northern slaves at their house on one of the thousands of Yankee plantations that dotted the Northern states in the 1700s and 1800s.

NORTHERN WEATHER & SOIL

And there was something else going on at the same time.

Yankee plantation owners were discovering that the Northern growing season was too short and too cold, and that the ground was too sandy and rocky, to produce large harvests. They were losing money each year, and lots of it. Something had to change.

YANKEES BEGIN TO PUSH SLAVERY ON THE SOUTH

And so Northern farmers and slave traders turned to the South. Why? First of all, they knew that white Southerners didn't mind living around and with black people, for, unlike white Northerners, white Southerners had a reputation for being more tolerant of other races.

Yankees eventually discovered that their climate wasn't right for slavery, and that they didn't particularly like black people. So they decided to push slavery southward, where the weather was nicer and the people were more tolerant. In this way, Yankees could still make money from slavery without having to live side by side with blacks.

But there was something else that interested Yankees even more: the South had a longer, warmer growing season and much more fertile soil. These factors made the South very appealing to Northerners. For if Southerners could be convinced to take the North's slaves, Yankees could continue to make money from slavery without having to deal directly with the slaves themselves.

HOW SOUTHERNERS REACTED TO SLAVERY

When the South was approached with this idea in the late 1700s, they didn't like the idea of slavery at all. Southerners like U.S. Presidents George Washington, Thomas Jefferson, and James Madison had been trying to rid the country of slavery for decades, without success. Now the North wanted to move their slaves to Dixie!

But despite this, Southerners did like the promise of increasing their incomes. And since they enjoyed the company of black people, white Southerners agreed to the plan, and the Yankees slowly but surely sold their slaves southward.

MONEY & THE COTTON TRIANGLE

At first everything went smoothly, for under the U.S. Constitution slavery was now legal in all of the Northern states and in all of the Southern states. Southern slaves planted and harvested their owners' cotton, then the owners sold this cotton to Northern businessmen.

Yankees created the "Cotton Triangle," which involved a three step process of selling slaves to the South, buying the cotton picked by the slaves, and selling the textiles made from the cotton to finance more trips to Africa.

The Northern businessmen made clothing from the cotton, then used the money they earned from selling the clothing to make more trips to Africa, where they traded goods for more slaves. This three-part process, invented by Yankees, was called the "Cotton Triangle."

SOUTHERNERS BELIEVED SLAVERY WAS IMMORAL

Everybody was making money, it's true. But people knew that slavery was wrong. For one thing, it went against Thomas Jefferson's famous line from the Declaration of Independence, which states that "all men are created equal."

More importantly, slavery went against the Bible and Christian teaching. Some 2,000 years ago Jesus said: "This is my commandment, that you love one another."

CHAPTER 3

THE ORIGINS OF THE AMERICAN ABOLITION MOVEMENT

THE AMERICAN ABOLITION MOVEMENT IS BORN

As a result of this concern, a great movement started in the South made up of Southerners who hated slavery. They called themselves abolitionists, from the word abolition: which means "to destroy completely." They wanted to completely destroy slavery, and so their efforts became known as the "American Abolition Movement."

Now you know where and when America's first abolition societies started: in the South; and more specifically, in the state of Virginia. But this movement eventually branched out into *all* of the Southern states.

The American Abolition Movement got its start in the South, not in the North. The Southern Founding Fathers were the first to call for freeing the slaves and getting rid of the entire institution of slavery.

THE FIRST AMERICAN ABOLITION LEADERS

We have already mentioned some of the leaders of America's first abolition movement, Virginians like George Washington, Thomas Jefferson, and James Madison. But there were thousands of others too.

And it wasn't just Southern men who wanted to get rid of slavery. Southern women did too, women like Sarah and Angela Grimké, were anxious to abolish the institution in Dixie.

Southern abolitionists wrote articles and books and gave lectures around the country, hoping to the change the laws so that slavery would end and the slaves could be set free.

While he was president of the United States, Thomas Jefferson pushed through a bill that prohibited the slave trade after 1808. But the law was completely ignored by Yankee slavers, who refused to stop the evil business or support the idea of abolition. As a result, the Northern slave trade continued right up to and into the Civil War, when Lincoln had New York ship captain Nathaniel Gordon hanged for the crime of slave trading in February 1862.

This false and ridiculous pro-North illustration portrays Lincoln as the "Great Emancipator." Actually, Lincoln stalled abolition for as long as possible, blocked black advancement, campaigned to have all blacks deported, and refused to issue the Emancipation Proclamation until he was forced to; and even then it was only because he needed more soldiers and wanted the abolitionists' vote for his reelection in 1864. It would be more appropriate to call Lincoln the "Great Procrastinator"!

CHAPTER 4

THE YANKEE ABOLITIONISTS' ASSAULT ON THE SOUTH

YANKEES LIKE THE SOUTHERN IDEA OF ABOLITION

Soon the idea of abolition caught on in the North as well. Some Yankees thought it was a good idea to end slavery. But there was a difference.

In the South, white people wanted to abolish slavery because they knew it was wrong, and because they liked blacks and wanted them to be free, like they were.

In the North, however, white people wanted to abolish slavery because black people made them uncomfortable. They thought that abolition was a good way to get rid of people of African heritage: once the slaves were freed, they could be deported; meaning, they could be sent out of the country.

Most white Northerners preferred living in an all white America. This type of racism was far less common in the South, as Alexis de Tocqueville and many others observed during their travels through the United States in the 1800s.

YANKEES & BLACK COLONIZATION

This idea of freeing then deporting black people, was called "black colonization," or "colonization" for short. Yankees who liked the idea were called "colonizationists."

By 1816, there were so many of them in the North that Yankees started a large organization in New Jersey called the "American Colonization Society." It's ultimate goal was to make America "white from coast to coast."

The colonizationists collected money from their supporters and used it to buy land in other countries, mainly in Africa. On this land they constructed settlements, or colonies, where the members of the American Colonization Society intended to send the slaves after they were freed.

YANKEES CREATE LIBERIA FOR AMERICAN SLAVES

The most famous of these was an African colony called "Liberia," a name that comes from the word liberate, meaning "to set free."

Actually, for the colonizationists the name Liberia had two meanings: they wanted blacks to think they were going to a place specifically made for "liberated" slaves. But they knew full well what the real meaning was: the North would be "liberated" from all black people.

A YANKEE NAMED WILLIAM LLOYD GARRISON

One of the many early Yankee supporters of colonization was a man named William Lloyd Garrison, from

Liberals tell us that the North was the abolition capital of the U.S., but this is false. When Virginia slave Anthony Burns ran away to Boston, Massachusetts, in 1853, for example, New England Yankees quickly captured him and had him arrested, thrown in prison, tried, and sent back to the South.

Newburyport, Massachusetts. Garrison was an abolitionist and a colonizationist. This means he liked the idea of freeing the slaves then sending them to another country.

He eventually gave up on black colonization, probably because he knew it would never work. But he remained an abolitionist for the rest of his life, and worked hard to end slavery.

For this we can certainly thank him.

But he did something else that was not very nice, something that hurt the South and all Southern people, including Southern black people. What he did was so bad, it helped lead to the "Civil War."

GARRISON STIRS UP TROUBLE!

In 1831, Garrison began publishing his own abolitionist newspaper. He called it *The Liberator* because it was dedicated to "liberating" the slaves and sending them to the colony of Liberia.

Like so many other Yankees, Garrison didn't like the South or Southern people anymore than he liked black people. So he decided to use his newspaper to try and hurt white Southerners' feelings.

The front page of The Liberator *looked like this. At the center of the illustration is the figure of Jesus. Why? There was nothing Christlike about Garrison's words and actions! Only a few people read his guileful little newspaper, but because of the mean spirited articles he wrote and printed, it caused a firestorm of controversy—even leading to riots and murders throughout the U.S.*

He began printing articles demanding that Southerners "give up slavery immediately"; he started calling slavery a "horrible sin" and a "terrible crime"; and he began calling slave owning Southerners "criminals," and said they should be punished for their "evildoing."

No one had ever spoken like this about slave owners before, either Northern or Southern ones. Up until then, abolitionists had only criticized slavery. So this was something new; something untruthful, spiteful, and cowardly.

Newspaper vendors, like this one, sold Garrison's paper, The Liberator, in cities across the U.S.

What Garrison *didn't* print was that slavery started in his home state of Massachusetts, and that it was his own people, the Yankees, who pushed slavery down South when they found black people disagreeable and slavery unprofitable!

He also forgot to tell his readers that under the Constitution, slavery was still legal in the North at the time as well!

Garrison and other Yankees unfairly criticized Southerners for owning slaves: American slavery had started in Garrison's home state of Massachusetts. And besides, it was still legal across the entire U.S.!

Trouble making abolitionist and Yankee busybody William Lloyd Garrison of Newburyport, Massachusetts. Garrison's preposterous and misleading attacks on the South helped lead our country into the bloodiest and most unnecessary war ever fought on American soil. Here in the South, 150 years later, we're still trying to recover.

CHAPTER 5

THE TRUTH ABOUT SOUTHERN "SLAVERY"

THERE WERE VERY FEW SOUTHERN SLAVE OWNERS

There was something else Garrison also ignored, something very important that you will never learn in school: very few white Southerners actually owned slaves. In 1860, for example, only 4.8 percent, or slightly less than five out of every 100 people, owned a black servant.

This is about the same number of people who have red hair in the United States today. How many kids do you know who have red hair? Not very many! It's a beautiful but very rare hair color. Yet Garrison called *all* white Southerners "evil slave owners." This wasn't fair!

Apparently, Yankees like Garrison believed that *all* or at least most Southerners owned slaves. But we can prove this is not true.

Only a tiny fraction of Southerners owned slaves. This was in part because each one cost the modern equivalent of $50,000, more than twice as much as the average American today makes in one year. So only the wealthiest men could afford them.

ONLY THE VERY RICH OWNED SLAVES

Slaves were very expensive. This means that only the rich could afford them. Most Southerners, however, were poor farmers.

So, it's obvious that very few Southerners owned slaves. As we just saw, only a tiny fraction, just 4.8 percent of the total population, owned slaves. Earlier, the figure was even lower: in 1850 only 2.3 percent of Southerners owned slaves!

YANKEE LIES ABOUT "SLAVE ABUSE" IN THE SOUTH

Garrison and his supporters also made up stories about how "cruel" Southern slave owners were. They told how our people beat and whipped our slaves on a daily basis, kept them in chains, neglected them, starved them, imprisoned them, and yelled at them all the time.

This picture of a white owner whipping his slave is a fantasy created by the anti-South movement. In fact, whipping was almost unheard of in the Old South. Not only was it inhumane and un-Christian to hurt one's servants, but it was also both bad business and against the law. Those few ignorant owners who broke this law were usually reported to the sheriff by concerned neighbors. The outlaw was then arrested, tried, and imprisoned. In some cases exceptionally cruel slave owners were hanged.

None of this was true, but it didn't stop the Yankees from spreading these fairy tales around, pretending they were facts. They're still telling these same lies even today!

YANKEES LIE ABOUT "WHITE RACISM" IN THE SOUTH

Worst of all, Northerners called white Southerners "racists." A racist is someone who dislikes someone else because of the color of their skin.

Unfortunately there are many people today who think that only whites are racists. But this is false. There are also black (African) racists, brown (Hispanic) racists, red (Native-

American) racists, and yellow (Asian) racists.

Actually, most white people in the South, where religion is so important, have always greatly disliked racism. This is because the Bible teaches us not to judge other people by their skin color. Here in the South we like to say that "God is color blind." And those who believe in Him are too. That includes most of us here in Dixie!

THE TRUTH ABOUT SOUTHERN SLAVERY

The truth is that white and black Southerners got along very well in the 1800s. White slave owners considered their slaves personal friends, and in most cases treated them like members of their own family. White children loved their family's slaves so much they called them "Uncle" and "Aunty," and spent as much time with them as possible.

In fact, the child of a slave owner was usually raised, not by his or her own mother, but by a well respected slave woman known as the "Mammy."

The Mammy had lots of power and authority around the Big House, the owner's home. She fed, bathed, and dressed the children, told them bedtime stories, rocked them to sleep, and scolded them

This old photo shows a Southern Mammy affectionately holding one of her owner's children. White children often grew up feeling closer to their mammies than to their real mothers.

when they were bad. Many white children grew up with very fond memories of the Mammy, and she of them.

SOUTHERN SLAVES WERE WELL TAKEN CARE OF!
Did you know that the slave owner also paid all of his slaves' bills, protected them from danger, and took care of all their physical wants and needs for their entire lives? It's a fact!

In return the slave "worked at his or her job," whether it be tilling the soil, harvesting crops, and doing laundry, or mucking out stalls, shoeing horses, and building barns and houses.

This illustration depicts something you'll never hear about in school: the friendly relations between whites and blacks in the Old South. Here, a white family stops to talk with a free black family living in the same neighborhood.

Whatever their occupation, in most cases slave owners and their slaves considered it a fair exchange: work for free room and board. And that isn't all.

THE RIGHTS OF SOUTHERN SLAVES
Southern slaves themselves had numerous legal rights, and were allowed to marry, have children, live in their own homes, run their own businesses, earn extra income, grow their own crops, hire themselves out to other employers, sell their own products, take time off, attend church, celebrate holidays, and hunt, fish, and hold parties. They could also save up their money, buy themselves, and set themselves free!

Free black people and slaves were so accepted across the South that they mingled quite freely with whites in nearly every area of life. They could walk through town with whites, ride on trains with whites, attend the same churches, and be cared for in the same hospitals.

After death a Southern black person was treated with just as much respect as when he or she was alive: in almost every case they were given a proper funeral and buried near their white owner, something unheard of in the North at the time.

SOUTHERN "SLAVERY" WAS ACTUALLY SERVITUDE

Southern slavery was so mild that Southerners didn't even think of it as actual slavery, which is true. This is why it was called "servitude" in the South, and this is why Southern slave owners called their black workers "servants," not "slaves."

To this day Northerners continue to call it "slavery," but it wasn't real slavery, and here's why: true slaves have *no* rights of any kind and cannot buy themselves and set themselves free. Only servants have these kinds of rights.

In the Old South, slaves had hundreds of rights, were well respected and even loved by their owners, and were often treated like members of the family. In this illustration, fun-loving servants attend a weekly dance on the plantation known as a "slave ball."

WHY YANKEES LIED ABOUT SOUTHERN SLAVERY

So where did Yankees get the idea that Southerners "abused"

their slaves? They made it all up to anger us, embarrass us, and make us look bad in the eyes of the world. It was all part of the same argument that Northerners and Southerners had been having with each other for so many years!

THE NORTH WAS MORE RACIST THAN THE SOUTH

The fact is that studies show that there was far more racism in the North than in the South in the 1800s. And it had been this way from the very beginning.

A famous Frenchman named Alexis de Tocqueville, for instance, traveled across the United States in the 1830s and wrote a book about it. One of the things he mentioned over and over was how intolerant white Northern people were toward blacks and how tolerant white Southern people were.

This preserved well built "slave cottage" in Mississippi is typical of how many Southern servants lived. The reality is that this house was far nicer than what many white people could afford back then—and even now! In many parts of the U.S. this attractive middle class home would be worth hundreds of thousands of dollars today.

Another man, a New Yorker named Frederick Law Olmsted (who designed New York City's Central Park), toured the South in the mid 1800s and was horrified to see whites and blacks talking, laughing, and mingling together in the streets, in shops, and on trains. He was shocked because this kind of friendship and affection between whites and blacks was something he rarely saw up North where he lived.

Around the same time, an Englishman named Edward Dicey visited New York City and was stunned, as he wrote, to

How did Lincoln and his Union soldiers treat Southern slaves after he "freed" them? The above illustration tells it all! This is what the Yanks called a "contraband camp," but which we Southerners call a "slave prison." Since, for some unknown reason, Lincoln never made any plans for what to do with the South's slaves after emancipating them, he simply stuck them in huge filthy U.S. government military camps, where they were forced to do slave like work for their new "owners": white Yankee officers. Once, when someone asked Lincoln how he planned on helping the slaves after they were freed, he compared them to farm animals and coldly replied: "Let them root, pig, or perish." Abolitionists rightly called Lincoln and the Union officials who ran these squalid contraband camps "racists," and charged them with sending liberated slaves "back into slavery." After seeing what Northerners actually thought of black people, many slaves quickly fled back to the safety, comfort, warmth, peace, and love of their Southern homes.

discover that "everywhere and at all times black people form a completely separate community. In the public streets you hardly ever see a colored person with a white person—unless he or she is a slave."

YANKEES & THEIR BLACK CODES

White Northerners had hundreds of laws called "Black Codes," that restricted African-Americans at the time. This was almost the opposite of what one found in the South, where the racial atmosphere was much more lenient and accepting.

But up North, because of the Black Codes, blacks were not allowed to sit on a train next to a white person; they were not allowed in the same hospitals or churches; and when they died, they had to be buried far away from any white person.

Northern blacks were not even allowed to walk on the same sidewalks as whites.

CHAPTER 6
IGNITING THE EMBERS OF THE CIVIL WAR

GARRISON & STOWE ANGER THE SOUTH

Despite these facts, Garrison and other Yankee abolitionists kept on criticizing white Southerners, knowing full well that their stories were completely untrue. Garrison had never even visited a Southern plantation. How would he know what Southern slavery was really like?

Another Yankee who never stepped foot in the South was Connecticut novelist Harriet Beecher Stowe. Yet she wrote a fictitious book called *Uncle Tom's Cabin* that pretended to be factual, and which made all slave owners look like horrible people.

Now you might think that Stowe's make-believe novel and Garrison's little fabricated abolition newspaper, *The Liberator*, wouldn't have had much of an effect on people. After all, *The Liberator* in particular was read by only a few thousand black people and only a handful of white

Although Yankee novelist Harriet Beecher Stowe knew absolutely nothing about Southern slavery, she wrote a fictional tale about it that made all slave owners look like brutal beasts. It caused an international uproar. In the South, parents wouldn't let their children read her books. South Carolina author Mary Chesnut accused Stowe of "imagining facts." Southern newspapers angrily called Stowe's book a "dang Yankee lie." It was!

abolitionists.

But Garrison's articles were so unusually mean, and Stowe's book seemed so realistic, that they both became big news, and eventually everybody heard about them.

When Garrison's and Stowe's words reached the South, they had a *huge* impact. They hurt Southerners' feelings. Not so much because they were rude. Over the years Southerners had grown accustomed to rude Yankees! It was because their words were untrue.

How would you feel if someone said something about you that was not only hateful, but false as well? You wouldn't like it, and Southerners didn't like it either.

But worse was to come.

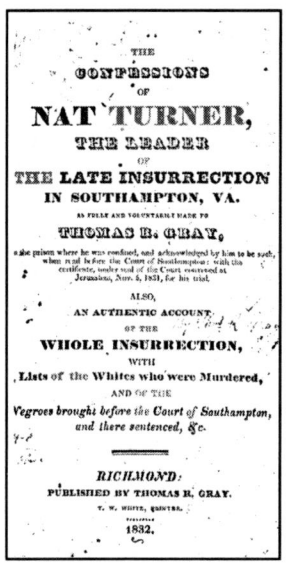

THE NAT TURNER REBELLION

In 1831, a Virginia slave named Nat Turner got a hold of a copy of Garrison's newspaper. In it he read how white Southerners were "abusive monsters"; how they beat and whipped their black slaves everyday; and how brutal they were to black women and children.

Turner knew that none of this was true, for he was a Southern slave himself, one who had numerous freedoms and rights. But being mentally deranged, he got angry anyway and decided to do something about it.

In August of 1831, in Southampton County, Virginia, Turner

Shortly before his execution, Turner confessed his many appalling crimes to attorney Thomas R. Gray, who published them in this book.

secretly gathered together about sixty of his black friends from other plantations. Using knives and axes (so as not to wake anyone), they roamed around at night killing dozens of innocent white people, most who did not even own slaves.

The gang of escaped slaves managed to outrun the police, but they were eventually caught, and Turner was hanged for his many foul deeds.

THE IMPACT OF TURNER, STOWE, & GARRISON

"The Nat Turner Rebellion," as it was called, along with Stowe's book and Garrison's newspaper, all had major consequences in the South and in the North, especially for black people.

White Southerners got scared that other slaves might do what Turner did. So during the 1830s and 1840s, they made up new laws that placed greater restrictions on their black servants. They did this not just for themselves, but for blacks too: whites cared about them and their welfare, and didn't want to see them get into trouble with the police, like Turner did. So the new stricter laws protected both whites and blacks equally.

Nat Turner's arrest in the Fall of 1831. By murdering at least 60 innocent non-slave owning whites, Turner did far more damage to the cause of abolition than good. In the ensuing mayhem that followed, 100 blacks also died, the South enacted new laws that restricted slaves, and the bad feelings between South and North greatly intensified.

Meanwhile, Garrison was so detested across the South that a price was placed on his head: the state of Georgia offered a reward to anyone who could bring the meddlesome abolitionist in alive!

CHAPTER 7

HOLDING A WOLF BY THE EARS!

A WAR OF WORDS & MONEY

Unfortunately, in the North, Yankees didn't understand the new slave laws that were enacted here in the South. They believed that we were treating our slaves worse than ever. So they began criticizing us more than ever.

They called Southerners "dumb," "backwards," and "lazy," and drew cartoons of us to try and make our people look silly. We were no longer considered respectable fellow Americans. Instead they called us "uneducated hayseeds," "drunken hillbillies," and "good-for-nothin' rednecks."

Southerners didn't think much of Yankees either. They saw

We Southerners have always been a smart, civilized, highly cultured people. But in the 1800s, Northerners thought they could make themselves look better than us by calling us names. This fooled no one and only led to more bad feelings between the South and the North.

Northerners as greedy, loud, impatient snobs, who would do anything to make money; nosey people who meddled in the South's business, and pretended to know what was best for us.

It was like a brother (the South) and a sister (the North)

having an argument: even though they were both from the same family (America), they couldn't get along. So they yelled back and forth and called each other names.

This argument between the South and the North went on for many years, and only got more severe as time went by. Yankees punished the South by raising taxes on us, and we punished them back by raising the price of cotton so high they couldn't afford it. But they needed our cotton to make textiles to trade for slaves in Africa, and we needed the North's money to buy slaves from them. So everybody lost. It was not a good situation for a country to be in.

This drawing of a manacled slave was made up out of the imaginations of South-hating abolitionists who wanted to turn the world against us. The truth is that this terrible scene was rarely if ever witnessed in the South, where servants were not only protected by law, but were treated respectfully and even lovingly, and were legally registered in court as members of the owner's family.

TRYING TO FIGURE OUT HOW TO END SLAVERY

The problem was made worse by the fact that even though nearly everyone, both South and North, wanted to end slavery, no one really knew how to do it.

Northern abolitionists and colonizationists told Southerners that they should immediately set their slaves free. But it wasn't as simple as that. In fact, many people, even in the North, understood that *immediate* abolition would cause problems that were far worse than slavery itself—and they were right.

For example, as legal family members, not only were slaves the private property of their owners, they were also extremely valuable, with each servant being worth about $50,000 in today's currency. Those few rare, very wealthy slave owners possessed dozens and even hundreds of slaves. For an owner like this it meant that his slave force was literally worth tens of millions of dollars! If he set his slaves free, who would pay him back for all of the money he had invested and then lost?

Setting the South's 3.5 million slaves free all at the same time would have caused a nationwide crisis, which is why Southern leaders wanted to go slowly and figure out all of the details first. This was their legal right under the U.S. Constitution, which protected slavery and slave owners at the time. Yankee abolitionists thought they knew better, however. All they were concerned with was emancipation itself, so they wanted our Southern slaves liberated immediately. They didn't care what happened to either the slave owners or the slaves after they were set free!

There were other problems too. The slave owners took care of every need of their slaves. Yes, the slaves often worked hard, but in return they were given a nice house to live in, a garden, a horse and buggy, and free food, free clothing, and free health care from birth to death. When they grew too old to work any longer, they were allowed to "retire," and do whatever they wanted for the rest of their lives—all without a care in the world.

Now if their owners set all their slaves free at once, where would they go? How would they earn money? What would they do for work? Where would they live? How would they buy food and where would they get their clothing? Who would take care of them when they got sick or too old to look after themselves?

Think about this: in the early 1800s there were 3.5 million slaves in the South. There were at least another 1 million in the North. That's nearly 5 million slaves, about the same number of people who today live in Houston, Texas; or Philadelphia, Pennsylvania; or San Francisco, California.

A wolf is an extremely dangerous animal. President Thomas Jefferson ingeniously compared slavery to holding a wolf by the ears!

Can you imagine one day if every single person in one of these cities was thrown out into the street with no home, no job, no money, no car, no food, no clothing, and no medical care? It would disrupt our entire country and cause widespread chaos!

This is the same problem that Southerners faced in the early 1800s.

President Thomas Jefferson came up with a clever way of understanding the dilemma. He said that slavery was like holding a wolf by the ears: you can't hang onto it and you can't let it go, because either way you'll get hurt!

CHAPTER 8

A YANKEE MADMAN NAMED JOHN BROWN

THE HARPERS FERRY RAID

All through the 1840s and 1850s, both Southerners and Northerners struggled to figure out how to end slavery without disrupting the nation. And while this was going on, the argument between the two regions continued to worsen.

The North kept putting pressure on the South to immediately free her slaves; the South kept telling the North to mind her own business. The North kept raising taxes on the South; the South kept resisting.

The psychotic Yankee abolitionist and murderer, John Brown.

Then, on October 16, 1859, a truly unfortunate event occurred. An insane Yankee murderer and fugitive from Connecticut named John Brown, decided that he would liberate all of America's slaves and take revenge on the South for practicing slavery!

Claiming that God was "directing" him, Brown and 18 of his friends captured the arsenal at Harpers Ferry, Virginia, then took several townspeople hostage. His goal was to free then enlist thousands of black slaves, arm them with guns from the armory, and take over the South. The whole plan was ridiculous, not to mention impossible! But this didn't stop him from going forward.

The next day, October 17, U.S. troops stormed the arsenal, captured Brown, and released the hostages. Brown's attempt to abolish slavery in the South *and* penalize the South for practicing slavery came to an abrupt end: not a single Southern slave joined his band of renegades, a number of innocent people were killed, and Brown and six of his fellow gangsters were convicted of "treason, murder, and fomenting insurrection," and hanged on December 2.

Despite Brown's failed plot and his grisly execution, when it came to the brewing squabble between the South and the North, his raid on Harpers Ferry was like pouring gasoline on a fire!

U.S. Marines were easily able to overtake John Brown and his gang of thugs at the Harpers Ferry Arsenal on October 17, 1859.

Brown had been supported by many Northern abolitionists, all who felt like he did. They believed that Southern slavery needed to end immediately, even by violence if necessary. These particular Yankees gave Brown money to fund his unlawful plan, and called him a "hero," a "saint," and a "crucified martyr."

Our Southern ancestors, however, saw it quite differently! It was obvious to them that the North was prepared to do whatever it would take to get rid of Southern slavery, even send armed civilians into Dixie to kill innocent men, women, and children. This not only showed a complete disregard for life, the Constitution, and states' rights, but a total lack of respect and understanding of the South and her people, as well.

It was 1860, and our feud with the North was now at the boiling point. Everyone was fed up and ready for change.

CHAPTER 9

DISHONEST ABE: A DICTATOR IN THE WHITE HOUSE!

THE CROOK WHO DIDN'T WANT TO BE PRESIDENT

It was during this atmosphere of discontent, mutual hostility, and sectional bitterness that the 1860 presidential election was held.

On November 6 of that year, Northerners voted in a relatively unknown politician named Abraham Lincoln, a deceptive and cunning man I call "Dishonest Abe." He managed to win even though he didn't want to be president, and even though he said that people shouldn't vote for him!

Here is how Mr. Lincoln responded once when he was asked to run for president: "Personally I don't feel that I'm fit to be president of the United States. Can you imagine a dummy like me running the country?" That's not how a future U.S. president should talk about himself. But those were his exact words!

Abraham Lincoln, the man I've nicknamed "Dishonest Abe," became the sixteenth U.S. president in 1860 with only 6 percent of the total American vote!

MOST AMERICANS DIDN'T WANT LINCOLN

Even stranger is the fact that Lincoln won in 1860 even though the majority of Northerners didn't vote for him, not a single Southerner voted for him, and no women or slaves voted for him (neither group was allowed to vote that year). Only adult white Northern males voted in the 1860 election.

To put it another way, that year only 39 percent of Yankees wanted him to be president, and 0 percent of Southerners wanted him to be president. In fact, only 1 in 17 (or about 6 percent) of all Americans voted for him! So how did he win?

President Lincoln and his son Thomas posed for this photo on February 5, 1865. You would never know by looking at this quaint family portrait that Lincoln was a mentally disturbed dictator who stomped on the Constitution, started an illegal war with the South, and was responsible for the suffering of millions of Americans, both South and North.

Lincoln was made president because of something called the electoral college: a select group of men and women called "electors," who actually elect the president and the vice president.

So in 1860, we got a president who didn't want to be president, and who most Americans didn't want to be president. All of this was a bad sign of things to come!

LINCOLN: SOUTHERNER TURNED NORTHERNER

Abraham Lincoln was born in 1809 in Kentucky. This makes him a Southerner. But his family didn't like the South. They wanted to live in a Yankee state.

So when he was still a child, his father moved the family to Illinois. This is where Lincoln grew up, this is the place he considered his home state, and this is where he lived until he became president and moved into the White House in early 1861.

After Southerners learned that Abraham Lincoln had been made president of the United States that year, they got very scared and upset. Why? Because politically speaking, Lincoln was a liberal who didn't like the South.

Yankee President Abraham Lincoln was a big government liberal. Most Southerners, however, were small government conservatives. It was clear from the start that the two regions would never be able to live in peace together with a man like this in the White House.

Now most Southerners were conservatives who didn't like the North. It was like trying to mix oil and water together. It can't be done. So this was not a good situation for anyone, whether they lived in the South or in the North.

CHAPTER 10

A LESSON IN POLITICS & AMERICAN HISTORY

UNDERSTANDING LIBERALS

What is a political liberal? A liberal is an idealist who thinks the U.S. government in Washington should be big and powerful and should take care of everyone. A liberal believes in heavily taxing the people, then using this money to give education, housing, and health care to everyone "for free."

A liberal thinks that the government knows better than we do what is best for us. Liberals think the bigger and more powerful the government is, the better life will be for the nation's citizens.

Lastly, liberals like change and constant progress in everything. They don't like the original U.S. government or the U.S. Constitution as they were created by the Founding Fathers. In other words, they don't like the past or tradition. They think everything needs constant "improving," even if it's working perfectly well!

Our 32nd president, Franklin Delano Roosevelt, was one of our most liberal leaders. His 1930s socialistic "New Deal" program was named after liberal Lincoln's socialistic domestic policies, which were known as the "New Deal" in 1865. Both Lincoln and Roosevelt helped turn the United States into an enormous welfare "nanny" state, the opposite of what the Southern Founding Fathers intended.

UNDERSTANDING CONSERVATIVES

Our 40th president, Ronald Reagan, was a wonderful example of a conservative politician. Unlike Lincoln, Reagan supported states' rights and, as he put it, "individual liberty, self-government, and free enterprise." President Reagan had a lot in common with our Southern Founding Fathers.

What is a political conservative? A conservative is a realist who thinks the U.S. government in Washington should be small and weak and that people should take care of themselves by working hard. A conservative believes in lightly taxing the people, and that education, housing, and health care should be earned, not handed out by the government like candy.

A conservative believes that we the people know better than the government what is best for us. Conservatives think the tinier and more powerless the government is, the better life will be for the nation's citizens.

Lastly, conservatives like to keep things the way they've always been. They love the original U.S. government and the U.S. Constitution as they were created by the Founding Fathers. They respect the past and tradition, and believe that if something works, it's best not to try to "improve" it.

UNDERSTANDING SOCIALISM

No doubt the biggest difference between a liberal and a conservative is that a liberal prefers a type of government called "socialism," while a conservative prefers a type of government called a "confederate republic," or a "confederacy" for short.

Socialism is where the government owns, operates, and

controls everything, including transportation, agriculture, business, health care, education, housing, food and nutrition, the military, and so on. With the public dependent on the government, they're easier to control!

In a socialist country the people and the states have almost no power and no rights. The government tells people what they can and can't do. In some ways a socialist country is similar to a monarchy, which has a king and queen who control every aspect of life and strictly rule over the people.

UNDERSTANDING CONFEDERACY

A confederate republic is where the government plays a very small role, controlling the least possible, usually just the military. In a confederacy the people are completely free, and are in charge of their own transportation, agriculture, business, health care, education, housing, food and nutrition, and so on.

German philosopher Karl Marx was a famous socialist who detested capitalism, states' rights, and private property. He believed that the government should run and control everything. Lincoln and Marx had similar views. This is why, after all, Marx wrote Lincoln a letter in November 1864 congratulating him on his reelection, and it's why President Lincoln surrounded himself with socialists, and it's why he was loved and supported by a group of radical socialists called the "Forty-Eighters."

In a confederacy the individual states operate as small independent nations, with full rights to do as they please. These rights are called "states' rights" and are silently guaranteed in the U.S. Constitution under the Tenth Amendment.

A confederacy is the opposite of a monarchy: in a

confederacy the power is in the people and in their states; in a monarchy the power is in the government and its rulers.

THE UNITED STATES BEGAN AS A CONFEDERACY

What you need to know is this: when the Founding Fathers created the United States in 1776 they created it to be a confederate republic. In fact, between the years 1781 and 1789 the U.S. was literally called "the Confederacy" by the Fathers, and our first constitution was called the "Articles of Confederation."

The Thomas Jefferson Memorial in Washington, D.C. President Jefferson, of Virginia, helped create the first U.S. Confederacy in the late 1700s. He's still considered an American hero by traditional Southerners and lovers of liberty around the world.

This tells us that the last thing the Founders would have wanted the U.S. to be or become is a socialist government, like a monarchy. This is why our early American ancestors broke away from England to begin with: England at the time was a monarchy that was unfairly dominating American life and overly taxing Americans.

THE SOUTHERN FOUNDING FATHERS

Here's something else you need to know: the most important Founding Fathers were all Southerners! Among them were:

- John Smith, from England, established the first permanent English settlement in North America in 1607 at Jamestown, Virginia. This not only makes him the first true white Southerner, but it makes the South—not New England—the true birthplace of the United States of America!

- Patrick Henry, from Virginia, wrote the Virginia Stamp Act Resolutions in 1765, which helped inspire the American Revolutionary War—the conflict that allowed Americans to separate from England and form their own country, the U.S.A.
- George Mason, from Virginia, wrote our country's first state constitution (for Virginia) in 1776, and along with another Virginian, James Madison, was instrumental in the creation of the Bill of Rights in 1789 (which was based on Virginia's constitution).
- Charles Pinckney, from South Carolina, asked Congress to revise the Articles of Confederation in 1786, which led to the creation of the U.S. Constitution.
- George Washington, from Virginia, was our first president, from 1789 to 1797.
- Thomas Jefferson, from Virginia, wrote the Declaration of Independence, and served as our third president, from 1801 to 1809.
- James Madison, also from Virginia, wrote the U.S. Constitution *and* the Bill of Rights, and served as our fourth president, from 1809 to 1817.

Southerner Patrick Henry was one of Founding Fathers who insisted that the U.S. be set up as a confederacy.

So it was mainly Southerners who created the United States of America, men we call the "Founding Fathers of the American Confederacy." And because they were conservatives, they intentionally designed our country to be a confederate republic: a small weak government with powerful independent states.

You can see from this how different liberals and conservatives are! And you can see why the conservative South was so concerned when liberal Lincoln was made president in 1860.

The official Seal of the Confederate States of America features Southern Founding Father and first U.S. President George Washington in the center on horseback. The Confederate government was even established on Washington's birthday in 1862: February 22. Why the focus on Washington? Because the Southern Confederacy was intentionally patterned by the Confederate Founding Fathers on the original U.S. Confederacy, which was created by men like Washington. This proves once and for all that when the Southern Confederacy was formed in 1861, it was only trying to maintain the original government as it had been set up by the Founders, not "destroy the United States government," as Lincoln falsely claimed.

CHAPTER 11

STATES' RIGHTS & GOVERNMENTAL POWERS

LINCOLN WANTED TO CHANGE THE U.S.

Even before he was elected, Lincoln had been talking about all of the changes he wanted to make to the United States, to the government, to the Constitution, and to our way of life. He wanted to create a "new United States" based on liberal socialist ideas: big government, high taxes, and free handouts.

Of course, this is what one would expect from a liberal. But the conservative South wanted to keep things just as they were. They liked the Constitution and the confederate government exactly the way the Founding Fathers had created them in 1776. They couldn't understand why anyone would want to change them.

UNDERSTANDING SECESSION
Now you can see why, less than a month after Lincoln was elected in November 1860, the Southern states began talking about leaving the United States and forming their own country. They didn't want to wait around and watch as Lincoln destroyed the most wonderful confederate republic in the history of the world.

Confederate Memorial Monument at Montgomery, Alabama, honoring the 122,000 men from the Yellowhammer state who fought for the Constitution and personal liberty, 1861 to 1865.

So even though they still

loved the old United States, the one originally created by the Founding Fathers, they felt they had no choice but to break away and become independent.

When a state leaves its parent country it's called "secession." The right of secession is a natural states' right that was taken for granted by the Founding Fathers, and by all Americans at the time. Everyone assumed that if a state could join the United States voluntarily, a right called "accession," then it could leave the United States voluntarily ("secession"). And they were correct!

The rights of accession and secession were never spelled out clearly in the Constitution. Why? Because the Founding Fathers believed that they were so commonly understood and accepted by Americans, that they didn't need to be. So they just included both rights "silently" in the Tenth Amendment, which reads:

The U.S. Capitol Building, today the seat of our country's power in Washington, D.C. The Founders, however, intended that nearly all governmental power be "inherent in the people" and the individual states.

> "The powers that have not been given to the United States government by the Constitution or the states belong to the people."

UNDERSTANDING U.S. GOVERNMENTAL POWERS
What exactly were the "powers" that were originally given to the

United States government by the people? These are spelled out in Article 4, Section 4 of the Constitution, which reads:

> "The U.S. government guarantees that every state in the Union will have a republican form of government [that is, it will be an independent confederate republic], and that it will protect them from foreign invasion and domestic violence."

This tells us that the Founding Fathers only gave the U.S. government two powers: the power to make sure each state remains free and independent, and the power to use military force to protect each state from invasion from outside the U.S. and from violent people inside the U.S.

The White House, the president's home in Washington, D.C. The Founding Fathers didn't want our president to have the powers of a king. They wanted him to be a "servant of the people." Lincoln, however, and other liberal socialistic presidents since him—such as Barack Obama—have behaved more like crowned royals heading a monarchy! This is unconstitutional and therefore illegal.

WHY THE FOUNDERS LIMITED THE GOVERNMENT

Sadly, the Confederate Republic that the Founding Fathers created in 1776—with its small weak government and all-powerful free states—no longer exists. It was already beginning to disappear when Lincoln was elected in 1860: liberal politicians before him had started to make the influence of the government bigger and stronger and the influence of the states smaller and weaker. Why?

It's a known fact that when you give people a little power, they usually want more. It's just part of human nature. So almost everyone we elect to help run our country starts to want more power as soon as they get into office.

And this is exactly why the Founding Fathers tried so hard to limit the size and power of the government when they wrote the Constitution in 1787: they knew that future politicians would try to enlarge the government and weaken the states. They understood that many of the people who would eventually run the U.S. government would want to turn the entire country into a socialist-like monarchy.

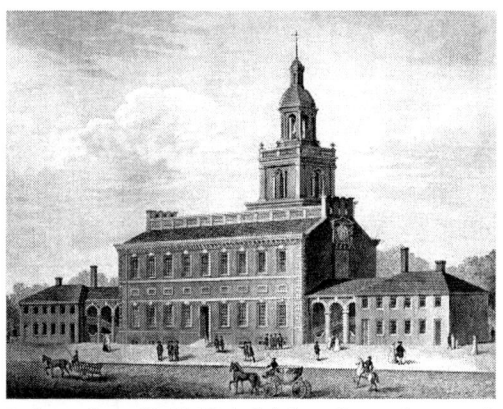

Independence Hall, Philadelphia, Pennsylvania. It was here that the Declaration of Independence, the Articles of Confederation, and the U.S. Constitution were debated and approved. In other words, it was at Independence Hall that the U.S. was created as a confederacy, the same confederacy that was carried on by the Southern states when they seceded from the U.S. beginning in December 1860.

Remember that in socialism the government controls everything, and in a monarchy the country is run by a single person, a king or queen. The Founding Fathers intended for the U.S. to be the opposite of a socialist nation or a monarchy. They wanted a type of government and country known as a "confederacy," where all of the power was controlled by the people of each individual state.

CHAPTER 12

SECESSION: THE SOUTHERN STATES LEAVE THE UNION!

LINCOLN DIDN'T LIKE THE CONSTITUTION

As we mentioned a moment ago, even before Lincoln got into the White House he was talking about changing the United States, beginning with the Constitution. Here is what he told a group of men in February 1861, just a few weeks before he was officially made president:

"I will take an oath to the best of my ability to preserve, protect, and defend the Constitution . . . even though it is not the Constitution as I would like to have it . . ."

Dishonest Abe, our 16th president, greatly disliked the U.S. Constitution, and said so!

Yes, Lincoln said that he did not like the Constitution! But he's not the only president who has disliked our country's most sacred document. Another one of our many liberal big government presidents, Barack Obama, said much the same thing: "The U.S. Constitution is an imperfect document," he once told the American people. And all throughout his presidency, Obama tried—just like Lincoln—to change the Constitution and enlarge the government!

THE FIRST SOUTHERN STATE SECEDES

It should be very clear now why the conservative South wanted to break away from the United States after liberal Lincoln was elected in November 1860. In fact, it didn't take long for the first state to say "goodbye."

This occurred on December 20, 1860, when South Carolina became the first Southern state to secede from the United States, or "Union," as it was known back then. The state wrote up a document called the "South Carolina Secession Ordinance," which officially severed all ties between South Carolina and the U.S. Here's what it said:

The December 22, 1860, issue of Harper's Weekly *announced the secession of the first Southern state, South Carolina, with this cover showing the state's delegation.*

> "This is a new rule ending the union between the State of South Carolina and other States united with her under the agreement known as 'The Constitution of the United States of America.'
>
> "We, the people of the State of South Carolina officially declare that the law adopted by us May 23, 1788, when the Constitution of the United States of America was ratified, is now canceled and thrown out; and that the union now

existing between South Carolina and other States, under the name of the 'United States of America,' is dissolved.

"This ordinance of secession was signed into law at Charleston, South Carolina, December 20, 1860."

SIX MORE SOUTHERN STATES LEAVE THE UNION

A few days after South Carolina left the Union, some of the other Southern states followed her out as well:

On January 9, 1861, Mississippi seceded from the Union.
On January 10, 1861, Florida seceded from the Union.
On January 11, 1861, Alabama seceded from the Union.
On January 19, 1861, Georgia seceded from the Union.
On January 26, 1861, Louisiana seceded from the Union.
On February 1, 1861, Texas seceded from the Union.

Legally operating under the Tenth Amendment of the Constitution, seven Southern states were now out of the Union, and well on their way to forming their own country.

THE BEGINNING OF THE SOUTHERN CONFEDERACY

In February 1861, at Montgomery, Alabama, these seven states set up a temporary government and officially named our new Southern country "The Confederate States of America."

But they had an informal name

The new Confederacy had its own song. Known as the National Confederate Anthem, *it was Dixie's Star Spangled Banner.*

for it as well: the "Confederacy." This wasn't an accident. The name was the same one used by the Founding Fathers for the original United States between 1781 and 1789.

Why was this so important to the men who created the Confederate States of America, the C.S.A., in 1861?

With liberal Lincoln now president of the U.S.A., the South knew that he would change both the Constitution and the government to something the Founding Fathers didn't want. He was going to try and "improve" them! But they didn't need improving or changing.

So the conservative Southern states decided it was better to leave the Union and create a new country in which they could preserve the traditional conservative values of the Founding Fathers. This is why they nicknamed it the "Confederacy."

The first official flag of the Confederacy had 7 stars representing the 7 Southern states that had left the Union at the time. It was called the First National Flag, and was nicknamed the "Stars and Bars."

THE FOUNDING FATHERS OF THE CONFEDERACY

After the first seven Southern states seceded from the Union, a temporary constitution was drawn up and a temporary cabinet was elected:

- Jefferson Davis (Honest Jeff) was made president.
- Alexander H. Stephens was made vice president.
- Robert A. Toombs was made secretary of state.
- Christopher G. Memminger was made secretary of the

Treasury.
- LeRoy Pope Walker was made secretary of war.
- Stephen R. Mallory was made secretary of the navy.
- Judah P. Benjamin was made attorney general.
- John H. Reagan was made postmaster general.
- Robert E. Lee was made general-in-chief of Confederate forces.

We call these men the "Founding Fathers of the Southern Confederacy," because they all helped formulate the new country known as the Confederate States of America. There were many others too, of course, who aren't listed here.

Our Confederate Founding Fathers: President Davis and his cabinet in 1861. From left to right: Stephen Russell Mallory (secretary of the Navy), Judah Philip Benjamin (attorney general), LeRoy Pope Walker (secretary of war, standing), Jefferson Davis (president), Robert Edward Lee (general-in-chief of Confederate forces), John Henninger Reagan (postmaster general), Christopher Gustavus Memminger (secretary of the Treasury), Alexander Hamilton Stephens (vice president, sitting), Robert Augustus Toombs (secretary of state).

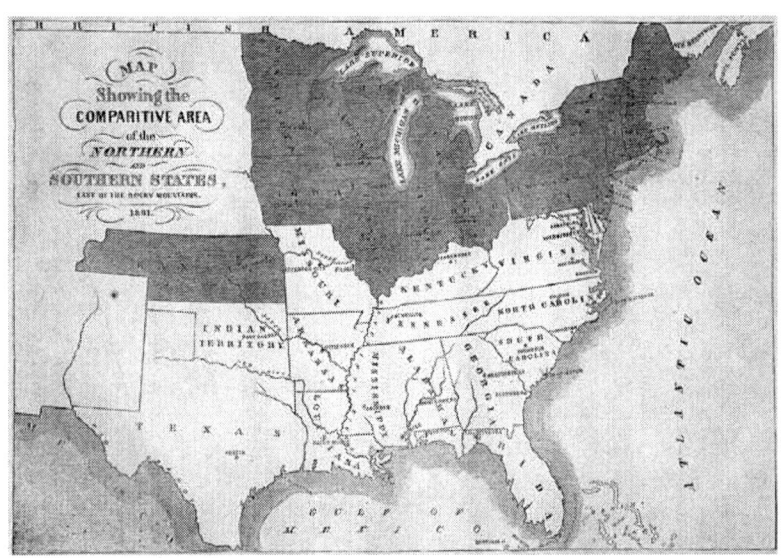

An 1861 map of two countries, totaling 34 states: The Confederate States of America (C.S.A.), with 13 states, is the un-shaded section at the bottom. The United States of America (U.S.A.), with 21 states, is the shaded section at the top. Lincoln's election in 1860 caused the (legal) secession of the Southern states and the (constitutional) formation of the Confederacy, which divided the nation in two. America was still a young country, so looking to the left you'll notice that most of the Western states had not been created yet. During the Civil War, two more states were added to the Union: West Virginia (in 1863) and Nevada (in 1864). Thus, by the end of the War, the U.S.A. had 23 states.

CHAPTER 13

LIBERALS, DICTATORS, THOUGHT POLICE, & EMPIRES

SECESSION ANGERED & EMBARRASSED LINCOLN

Lincoln became furious when he found out the Southern states wanted to get out of the Union.

That February, in 1861, as the South was busy minding its own business and setting up its own legally formed government, President Lincoln was back at the White House in Washington, D.C., hopping mad!

He couldn't believe that the Southern states were leaving the Union. He was not only angry, but he was embarrassed, because he knew that they were only leaving because he had been elected president.

But why would Lincoln care if the Southern states split away or stayed with the Union? Why didn't he just let them go in peace? After all, as we've seen, secession is one of the states' rights and is legal under the U.S. Constitution. The South then was perfectly free to go her own way and form her own country.

POWER HUNGRY LINCOLN

There were several reasons Lincoln didn't want the South to become a free and independent nation.

First, Lincoln had an adult mental illness called "megalomania" that makes a person power hungry. A megalomaniac is an emotionally immature and psychologically disturbed person with a huge ego, one who believes that he's extremely important—though he isn't; who thinks everyone loves him—when they don't; who assumes he's better than everyone else—when he isn't; and who feels he has unlimited powers—though he doesn't.

Megalomania is natural, and even accepted, in very young children. But in normal kids, as they get older, they mature and naturally outgrow the childish beliefs that they're superior to others and that they can do anything they want. This is a natural part of growing up and maturing, and we all go through it.

But some children, mainly those who have terrible childhoods, never outgrow their megalomania, and take it into adulthood with them. When an adult has megalomania it's considered a "psycho-pathological illness"; that is, a mental disease that's both unnatural and unhealthy. In fact, as we're about to see, adults with megalomania can be very dangerous, especially if they're in positions of power like Lincoln was!

LEFT-WING LIBERAL LINCOLN

The second and more important reason Lincoln didn't want to let the South go free was that he was a left-wing liberal. For as long as they've been around, liberals—or lefties as they're also called—have liked to control the thoughts, behavior, and lives of other people. To do this they create lots of unnecessary rules and regulations that others have to live by.

Like all liberals, Lincoln was more concerned with principles than with practicality.

Liberals don't like the idea of freedom of expression. They believe that everyone should think the way they do, and that their ideas are the only "politically correct" ones.

This is why liberals love to censor other people's thoughts: they are mind and speech controllers, people we call "thought police." If they don't agree with an idea, they label it "politically incorrect," then they try to suppress it; that is, they ban the idea from as many places as they can, or bury it under a mountain of rules so that no one can find it!

Nearly all of America's schools are run by liberal thought police who don't want you to know the truth about Lincoln and his "Civil War." This is why I wrote this book for you. If I hadn't written it, you would never know the truth. The liberals who run our schools would never allow the information in this book to be taught by their teachers, and they would certainly never allow this book into their school libraries.

Liberals would like us all to be dependent on the government. Why? Because this makes it easier for them to control our thoughts and behavior! Sometimes when liberal leaders don't get their way, like Lincoln, they'll violate the Constitution and send in armed soldiers to force everyone to do what they want. This is why Lincoln started the "Civil War" with the South.

Instead, because the truth about the "Civil War" goes against their personal ideals and makes them uncomfortable, they would call my book "politically incorrect." Then they'd ban it from being read by you or any other students at your school. This is not only unfair, it's a violation of your First Amendment rights as promised in the Constitution!

Because Lincoln was a liberal thought policeman, if he were alive today he would do the same thing: he would make a law saying that no one could read this book. He would have probably even had me illegally arrested and put in jail for writing something he didn't like—just as he actually did to tens of thousands of people during the 1860s!

SOUTHERN CONSERVATISM
Now here in the South, we're mainly a conservative region. As conservatives, we may not like what someone else writes or says or thinks, but we would never create a law to try and stop someone from expressing these ideas. Southern conservatives respect the Constitution and believe strongly in obeying the First Amendment, which guarantees "the freedom of speech."

This is one of the many differences between a liberal and a conservative, and in the 1800s, this was one of the primary differences between the Southern people (who were mainly conservative), and the Northern people (who were mainly liberal). Southern conservatives, like Honest Jeff, loved and obeyed the Constitution, and still do. Northern liberals, like Dishonest Abe, disliked and disobeyed the Constitution, and still do!

Our beloved President Jefferson Davis was a conservative. This is why he followed the Constitution and respected the rights of the Southern people.

CLEARING UP SOME POLITICAL CONFUSION

You may be wondering about something: today Republicans are considered conservatives and Democrats are considered liberals. So how could Abraham Lincoln, who was a Republican, be a liberal, and Jefferson Davis, who was a Democrat, be a conservative?

This is because in the mid 1800s the ideas of the two parties, known as "platforms," were the opposite of what they are today.

To make this perfectly clear then:

- The Republicans of today are conservatives, but the Republicans of the Civil War era were liberals.
- The Democrats of today are liberals, but the Democrats of the Civil War era were conservatives.

This is why, even though Lincoln was a Republican, he was considered a liberal; and this is why, even though Davis was a Democrat, he was considered a conservative.

Proof of this is that the people in Lincoln's Republican party called themselves "liberals," while the people in Davis' Democratic party called themselves "conservatives."

Just remember that today, the ideas, or platforms, of the two parties are the reverse of what they were during the "Civil War."

KING ABRAHAM: TYRANNICAL DICTATOR

Now what do you get when you combine a liberal with a megalomaniac? You get a tyrant and a dictator! And this is exactly what Lincoln was. Here was a man who thought of himself, not as a "servant of the people," as our president is supposed to, but rather as a sort of king. "King Abraham" wanted full control of as many people, as much territory, as many soldiers, as many businesses, and as much money as possible.

Men like this are called "dictators" because they insist on dictating the lives of their country's citizens. They can't tolerate the idea of people being free. A dictator always wants to be in complete control, make up all the rules, and tell other people what to do, what not to do, and how to live their lives down to the smallest detail.

SOME FAMOUS EMPIRES

To achieve this type of complete control, the dictator creates a "dictatorship," or what's also known as an "empire." You've probably heard about or read about some of these empires:

In a monarchy, the king rules over the people. But in a confederate republic, like the U.S., the people are supposed to rule over the president!

- the Roman Empire
- the Persian Empire
- the Byzantine Empire
- the Russian Empire
- the Ottoman Empire
- the Austrian Empire
- the Spanish Empire
- the Sikh Empire
- the German Empire
- the Mongol Empire

Probably the best known modern one is the British Empire.

Empires, and the dictators who rule them, like to force their ideas on other people, and on other nations. Again, this is why they're called dictators: they like to "dictate" or control the world around them, usually for riches and power.

The Circus Maximus ("Big Circle"), a chariot racing arena in ancient Rome. About 1,500 years ago, ancient Rome was a Republic, similar to the Confederate Republic we Americans had from 1781 to 1789. During the time of Jesus, however, the Roman Republic was overthrown and turned into a dictatorship known as an "empire." The new leader was an authoritarian dictator called an "emperor." Like all dictatorships, the Roman Empire eventually crumbled and disappeared. Why? Because the Roman people wanted to be free to think, talk, and act however they wanted to. This is exactly how the Southern people felt when Abraham Lincoln was elected president in November 1860: knowing he would try to assume dictatorial powers and force the Southern states into an unconstitutional empire, Southerners broke away to try and preserve the freedoms they had enjoyed under the Confederate Republic of the Founding Fathers. But being a dictator, Emperor Lincoln didn't like that idea. So he started the "Civil War" to try and make the Southern states remain in the Union!

AMERICA WAS BUILT ON THE IDEA OF FREEDOM

In America, the "home of the free," dictators have always been greatly disliked. Why? Because the very idea of a dictator ruling over an empire goes completely contrary to the liberty loving tradition of the United States. One of the first sentences in our Declaration of Independence reads:

"We hold these truths to be self-evident, that all men are created equal, that they are endowed by their Creator with certain unalienable Rights, that among these are Life, *Liberty* and the pursuit of Happiness."

The Liberty Bell is a famous American symbol of freedom that most liberal's have forgotten about.

So the very foundation of our country was built on the assumption that people have the right to be free and control their own lives.

In an empire, however, there are few freedoms. This is because the dictator, a type of liberal thought policeman, only allows people to do what he wants. These are usually things that only benefit him!

SOME FAMOUS DICTATORS

Among the world's most well-known dictators we have:

- Adolf Hitler (Germany)
- Benito Mussolini (Italy)
- Joseph Stalin (Soviet Union)

- Fidel Castro (Cuba)
- Vladimir Ilich Lenin (Soviet Union)
- Saddam Hussein (Iraq)
- Francisco Franco (Spain)
- Josip Tito (Yugoslavia)
- Kim Jong-il (North Korea)
- Robert Mugabe (Zimbabwe)

There have been thousands of others. As we're about to see, Abraham Lincoln was also a member of the "Dictators' Club"!

LINCOLN & THE AMERICAN SYSTEM

Now we have a clearer idea of why Lincoln was so upset when the Southern states seceded from the U.S. For when he was elected a few months earlier, in November 1860, he had planned on "ruling" over the entire United States, including all of the Southern states. He had had big plans for the U.S. back then, one of which was to install what was called the "American System."

The American System was a program in which the U.S. president was to act as a dictatorial ruler with all-encompassing powers. Under this presidential dictator, the U.S. government would become a consolidated superpower in control of the nation's people and their money. Worst of all, the states were to be stripped of their independence and their

Like Karl Marx, another famous socialist, Nazi dictator Adolf Hitler, also adored Lincoln, and even promoted Lincoln's anti-states' rights views in his 1925 autobiography Mein Kampf *("My Struggle"). The ideas of Marx, Hitler, and Lincoln are not at all what the Founding Fathers had in mind for the United States!*

individual rights, and placed under the complete domination of the U.S. government.

The South was, and still is, mainly an agricultural region built around farming. The North was, and still is, mainly an industrial region built around business.

As part of his American System, however, Lincoln wanted to "Northernize" the South; that is, he wanted to make the South just like the North. He thought Southerners would be better off if they got rid of their farms and became businessmen, like Yankees!

WHY LINCOLN DIDN'T WANT THE SOUTH TO GO
Understandably, Southerners didn't like one single bit of President Lincoln's American System, and they let him know it by leaving the Union. But this went against Lincoln's plan to enlarge the U.S. government, take over the nation's banks, and "Northernize" the South. In fact, he couldn't install the American System successfully without the Southern states.

The South was loaded with wealth. There were, for instance, her wonderful natural resources (fertile crop lands, wide river ways, mineral laden mountains, and virgin forests), and her valuable farm products (like potatoes, oats, corn, and wheat). There were also her 12 million people (8 million whites and 4 million blacks), most of them hard working, tax paying individuals—*very* important to money hungry Lincoln!

Most importantly, the South's 3.5 million slaves picked the cotton that supported the Northern slave trade. If all of this was taken away, the Northern states would lose their main source of income and they would go bankrupt.

Lincoln, as a Northerner, felt that he had to get the Southern states back into the Union—no matter what. And there was no time to lose.

King Abraham said he fought the South to "preserve the Union." What he meant to say was, to "preserve big government"!

Section 2

THE WAR FOR SOUTHERN INDEPENDENCE 1861-1865

CHAPTER 14

LINCOLN LAUNCHES HIS WAR AT FORT SUMTER

LINCOLN THREATENS VIOLENCE ON THE SOUTH

As more and more of the Southern states broke away to become part of the Southern Confederacy, it was clear to Lincoln that mere talk was not enough to accomplish his plan. So, he secretly decided he would make the Southern states come back into the Union by using *physical force*. In other words, he would send thousands of U.S. soldiers into the Confederacy and shoot Southern men, women, and children if they refused to rejoin the United States!

Are you shocked by this? Of course! And you can believe that Southerners, and even many Northerners, were upset by Lincoln's war threats as well.

South Carolina's flag with the state seal on it. Surrounding the famous palmetto tree symbol is the state motto in Latin: *Animis Opibusque Parati*, meaning "Prepared in Mind and Resources."

But the Yankee president had a problem: he knew if he attacked the South first, history would always view him and the North as the "bad guy." So instead, he thought up an evil plan to make the South look like the villain instead. He would trick

Southerners into firing the first shot of the war he so desperately wanted!

A TINY GARRISON CALLED FORT SUMTER

Lincoln waited and waited for his opportunity, and it finally came on April 12, 1861, at a little garrison located on a little island in the middle of Charleston Harbor, South Carolina. It was called "Fort Sumter."

Before Lincoln was elected president, Fort Sumter had belonged to the United States of America, which stationed some of its soldiers there to protect the U.S. coastline. But after South Carolina seceded in December 1860, Fort Sumter became the property of the Confederate States of America. For South Carolina was no longer part of the U.S.A. She was now part of the C.S.A.

Contrary to what Lincoln believed, after South Carolina seceded from the Union in December 1860, Fort Sumter—located in Charleston Harbor—became the legal property of the Confederacy.

It just so happened that in April 1861, there was still a small group of U.S. soldiers stationed at Fort Sumter. President Davis, Honest Jeff, had decided to leave them alone, hoping that they would eventually leave and go back North on their own.

The Union commander at Fort Sumter was Robert

Anderson, a Kentuckian who had switched sides and become a Yankee officer. Despite this, he still loved the South and didn't want any trouble with his old friends. He, like the rest of his men, just wanted to leave the island peacefully and go home.

Unfortunately for everyone, Lincoln ordered Anderson to stay. Why? Because the little Yankee unit was to become a pawn in his military chess game. His secret goal? To launch a war with the South, but make the South look like the aggressor!

LINCOLN'S FORT SUMTER LIE

In early April, Lincoln began publicly spreading the lie that his soldiers at Fort Sumter were "starving." He promised to evacuate the men soon, but first he wanted to send a U.S. supply ship to the island to deliver food to them.

We know that none of this was true because the friendly and generous people of Charleston had been giving food to Lincoln's soldiers for many weeks. The men were far from starving, and, in fact, were fat and well fed!

Breaking all of his earlier promises to evacuate Fort Sumter, Lincoln ordered warships from New York City to sail right up to the outskirts of Charleston Harbor in an attempt to scare the Confederates into firing their guns first.

Despite this, Lincoln carried on with his devilish plan, and the South was about to be pulled right into his trap!

HOW LINCOLN TRICKED THE SOUTH

When Lincoln said he was going to send a supply ship to Fort

Sumter, the South said: "Absolutely not. Fort Sumter is the property of the Confederacy now. Please remove your troops and leave us alone, and everything will be fine."

Naturally, Lincoln ignored this order, and on April 12 he proceeded to send in his supply ship, knowing full well that the South would consider this a "hostile act." To make sure the South "got the message," Lincoln also had a fleet of huge, well armed U.S. warships sail right up to the edge of Charleston Harbor, where they would be in full view.

In one of the most tragic moments in world history, the South fell for Lincoln's trickery. Thinking that South Carolina was about to be attacked by the North, Confederate soldiers on the shore began firing at Fort Sumter to try and drive the U.S. soldiers off the island.

THE BATTLE OF FORT SUMTER

As battles go, the Battle of Fort Sumter was very small and no one was even hurt. Yet it was significant in that Lincoln used it as an excuse to start the "Civil War."

The Battle of Fort Sumter, as it's called, lasted only a day or so, and not a single person on either side was killed or even injured.

The next morning, Anderson and his men surrendered and President Davis kindly allowed them to travel back to the North. All across the South, there was great relief: war with the United States had been avoided, the U.S. troops were gone, no one had been hurt, and Fort Sumter was now back in possession of the Confederacy.

LINCOLN DECLARES WAR!

But things were far from over. Lincoln's plan to make the South look like the "bad guy" had worked: the South had "fired the first shot" against an "innocent starving garrison of U.S. soldiers." Lincoln made things worse by telling his people in the North that this was an "assault on the U.S. flag," an "act of war" that had to be responded to.

Lincoln's "response" was to "declare war" on the South and send out a call for 75,000 Northern men to join the U.S. military. And so began the American "Civil War"!

But it was all illegal, immoral, unnecessary, and illogical.

WHY LINCOLN'S WAR WAS ILLEGAL

After Fort Sumter, Lincoln ordered 75,000 Yankee soldiers to attack the South. For what? She had done nothing wrong!

First, Lincoln declared war. According to the U.S. Constitution (Article 1, Section 8, Clause 11), only Congress has this power. This makes Lincoln an outlaw and a corrupt politician.

Second, Lincoln lied to the American public in order to initiate his war, even going against the advice of his own cabinet members and military officers. This makes Lincoln a liar and a cheat.

Third, when the Southern states seceded, Lincoln sent his armies into Dixie and killed 2 million of our people over the next four years. This is not the response of a civilized leader. It's the response of a wicked dictator. This makes Lincoln a very bad man, *and* a war criminal.

HOW LINCOLN SHOULD HAVE RESPONDED

You might be asking yourself, if Lincoln did the wrong thing, *how* then should he have handled the situation?

The answer is this: when a state secedes from its parent country, the lawful and correct reaction is to let the state go in peace. If the parent country doesn't want it to leave, the next step would be to invite the leaders of the departing state to a discussion and settle the matter calmly, diplomatically, and legally. Either way, under the U.S. Constitution (Tenth Amendment), secession is the legal right of every state.

The Union we call the United States of America was meant to be a "*voluntary* agreement between friendly states." The Founding Fathers never meant for the states to be permanently held together, especially by military force and threats of physical violence.

Southern Founding Father Thomas Jefferson said that the United States is a "voluntary union," and therefore a state has the right to leave if it wants to.

In fact, they took it for granted that because a state could enter the Union voluntarily (accession), that it could leave voluntarily (secession). This is why the rights of accession and secession are not specifically mentioned in the Constitution. They were assumed!

Now for those who claim that there is no proof of this, and that secession is illegal, the South would like you to point out where in the Constitution it says that "secession is against the law." There is no such statement because secession is legal.

The trouble with Lincoln is that he chose neither of the two moral and legal options he had when he was faced with the secession of the Southern states: let them go or hold a meeting. Instead, he chose the worst possible option: full scale war!

LINCOLN'S LIES ABOUT THE CAUSE OF HIS WAR

Even when President Davis sent numerous "peace commissions" to Washington to try and end the war, Lincoln ignored them. Why? Because he wasn't interested in peace. He was interested in power! And without the Southern states, he had only half the power he planned on having when he was elected president. Now you know the real reason Lincoln went to war against the South.

Confederate President Davis, Honest Jeff, sent countless Southern diplomats to Washington, D.C. to talk with Lincoln, in the hopes that the Civil War could be brought to an end. But Lincoln would not meet with them, for his goal wasn't peace. It was domination!

This reason is so selfish, so sinister, and so absurd, that Lincoln would never admit it. So he had to make up a fake reason for going to war.

The first one he came up with was this: "We are waging war against the South to preserve the Union," he told the U.S.

Congress on July 4, 1861. And this was the lie he told over and over, right up until the day he died four years later.

As we'll discuss shortly, about half way through the "Civil War," in early 1863, Lincoln tried to alter the purpose of his war from "preserving the Union" to "abolishing slavery."

But this too was just another lie. Both were merely meant to hide the real reason for sending Yankee troops into the South to slaughter hundreds of thousands of innocent law abiding Southerners: Lincoln's love of power, money, and control!

Liberal Lincoln made up lies to hide the real cause of his War: his socialistic obsession with controlling the U.S. government and the American people.

CHAPTER 15

LINCOLN TRIES TO HURT THE SOUTH & HER PEOPLE

MORE SOUTHERN STATES SECEDE

Following the Battle of Fort Sumter on April 12, 1861, the Confederate capitol was moved from Montgomery, Alabama, to Richmond, Virginia, and four more of the Southern states that were still part of the United States quickly seceded:

On April 17, 1861, Virginia seceded from the Union.
On May 6, 1861, Arkansas seceded from the Union.
On May 20, 1861, North Carolina seceded from the Union.
On June 8, 1861, Tennessee seceded from the Union.

LINCOLN ILLEGALLY CREATES WEST VIRGINIA

In the Summer of 1861, the people living in the western part of Virginia were still undecided as to whether they should join the Confederacy or stay with the United States.

    Nosey Lincoln butted in and "strongly encouraged" them to secede from the state of Virginia and form a new state, to be called "West Virginia." Keep in mind that he did this at a time when he was brutally killing people in the other Southern states for seceding from the Union!

    His double standard didn't seem to bother him though. And the fact that what he did was illegal also didn't seem to bother him. Article 4, Section 3, Clause 1 of the U.S. Constitution clearly states:

"New states may be admitted by the Congress into this Union; but no new state will be formed within the territory of any other state, or be formed by combining two or more states, without the approval of the legislatures of those states and of the Congress."

Though West Virginia was declared a separate state on June 20, 1863, Lincoln never got the approval of Virginia to allow its western section to break away and form its own state. But he permitted it anyway!

To this day, West Virginia is still not a constitutionally formed state, nor is it a legal part of the United States. Technically it's still the western section of Virginia. This is just another one of the many crimes Lincoln committed while he was president!

West Virginia has an official state seal, but because of Lincoln it's not an official state!

WHY LINCOLN CREATED WEST VIRGINIA

Why did Lincoln push so hard to illegally create the "state" of West Virginia?

Because it would give him several more electoral votes in the 1864 election. You'll remember that he won the 1860 election, not by the popular vote of the people, but because of the electoral college. So he wanted to have as many electoral votes as possible for his reelection campaign in 1864.

LINCOLN BLOCKED STATES FROM SECEDING
Two Southern states wanted to secede but never did. Why? Because Lincoln sent soldiers in and prevented them from leaving the Union! These two states were Maryland and Delaware.

LINCOLN CLAMPS DOWN ON MARYLAND
In Maryland, in particular, Lincoln acted like a ruthless dictator, arresting and jailing the entire state legislature and replacing the men with his own hand-picked politicians—men who supported *him*, of course!

Then Lincoln had the entire state of Maryland placed under martial law. This means that civilians were no longer allowed to control their own state. He gave complete control over everything to his military, and ordered his soldiers to make sure no one said anything bad about him.

Every day citizens, newspaper editors, and even clergymen in Maryland who spoke out against Lincoln were promptly arrested. Many of these innocent people—every one of them who was speaking legally under the protection of the First Amendment of the Constitution—were treated very viciously by Lincoln and his soldiers. Some were kept in prison for the entire length of the War (four years). Others were tortured. Some died or were even killed due to the cruelty they had to endure at the hands of the Yankee soldiery.

In Dixie Southerners wore this secession rosette and badge, with Jefferson Davis' picture on it, to celebrate their new country: the C.S.A.

None of them had committed any real crimes. They were only crimes in Lincoln's mind. This is one of the things that made the mentally ill Yankee president such a scary and dangerous man.

These types of crimes certainly didn't win Lincoln any friends. In fact, there were so many Northerners who didn't like him that he eventually placed many other states under martial law, including the state of New York, where he committed the same kinds of atrocities.

It was said that Lincoln's right-hand man, William H. Seward, could ring a little bell and make someone "disappear." With a dictator like Lincoln in the White House, these were indeed very frightening times!

Lincoln used this man, his secretary of state, William H. Seward, to arrest, imprison, kidnap, and even torture Northerners who wanted to make peace with the South.

MISSOURI & KENTUCKY

Two other Southern states, Missouri and Kentucky, also talked about seceding. But half of their citizens wanted to remain in the U.S., while the other half wanted to leave and join the C.S. So only parts of these two states left the Union:

On October 31, 1861, a section of Missouri seceded from the Union.

On November 20, 1861, a section of Kentucky seceded from the Union.

Because they were located between the borders of the Confederate states and the United States, and because their entire states didn't join the Confederacy, Missouri and Kentucky were called "Border States."

There were several other Border States as well: Maryland, Delaware, and West Virginia. If all five of the Border States had *fully* sided with the Confederacy, there is no doubt that the South would have won the War. We only wish they had!

LINCOLN ISSUES AN ILLEGAL NAVAL BLOCKADE

On April 19, 1861, as the Southern states were busy leaving the United States as fast as they could, Lincoln committed another one of his hundreds of war crimes: he issued a naval blockade all the way around the Southern coastline. This was illegal for a number of reasons:

- Blockades are only legal during a war between two *different* countries. But Lincoln never considered the C.S.A. a separate nation.

Lincoln's naval blockade of the South's coast was illegal. This is just one of the many reasons his War itself was illegal.

- The War itself was illegal because, as we've seen, Lincoln declared war without the approval of Congress.
- International maritime law requires that for a naval blockade to be legitimate, *every* mile of coastline must be patrolled. Lincoln and his navy never came close to patrolling the entire 3,549 miles of the South's coast.
- International maritime law also requires that for a naval blockade to be "lawful and effective," every inch of

coastline must be blocked so that no ship can get in or out without being seen. Lincoln never blocked every inch of the Southern coast, and in fact, right through to the end of the War, thousands of Confederate ships came and went through Lincoln's marine barricade.

It was because of these many violations that Lincoln's naval blockade was nicknamed a "paper blockade" by Southerners. It was only realistic on paper, not in real life!

THE CONFEDERACY IS COMPLETE

Despite Lincoln's many criminal actions to try and prevent the legal right of secession, by November 1861, thirteen states were finally able to secede from the United States of America and join the Confederate States of America. They were, in order of their secession:

1. South Carolina
2. Mississippi
3. Florida
4. Alabama
5. Georgia
6. Louisiana
7. Texas
8. Virginia
9. Arkansas
10. North Carolina
11. Tennessee
12. Missouri
13. Kentucky

After all 13 states had seceded in November 1861, the Confederate Congress issued the First National Flag of the Confederate States of America with 13 stars, representing the 13 states of the Confederacy.

Now you know why the Confederate Flag has thirteen stars.

Each one stands for one of the thirteen states that joined the Confederacy.

This is the same number of stars that were put on the first U.S. flag in 1777, representing the original Thirteen Colonies that existed during the first American Revolutionary War. In this way the Confederate Flag mirrored the symbolism of the first U.S. flag, a fact which we Southerners have always been very proud of.

In fact, just as the 1775 war for independence from England was called the first American Revolutionary War, here in Dixie we often refer to the 1861 Civil War as the "second American Revolutionary War." Why?

Because it was fought to win our independence from the United States. These similarities make us feel a powerful kinship with our Revolutionary War ancestors, the colonial men and women who we have so much in common with.

In 1775 our Revolutionary War ancestors risked their lives for independence from the English monarchy under King Charles. In 1861 our Confederate ancestors risked their lives for independence from the U.S. monarchy under King Abraham.

The early American leaders of these courageous people, of course, were the Founding Fathers, among the best and the brightest who were Southerners!

CHAPTER 16

BATTLES
1861

TEN THOUSAND BATTLES!

Though the Battle of Fort Sumter on April 12, 1861, was the *first* battle of the War, it was a small one in comparison to what was to come.

In fact, over the next four years, from 1861 to 1865, there would be some 10,455 battles, skirmishes, and other various types of engagements between the C.S. military and the U.S. military.

All of them were important in their own way. However, if we talked about each one of these, this book would be thousands of pages long! So we'll just focus on some of the big war-changing battles, and some of the prominent features and events of the conflict.

THE BATTLE OF FIRST MANASSAS: 1861
Just four months after the little Battle of Fort Sumter, the first major battle of Lincoln's War was fought. It was called the Battle of First Manassas, and it took place on July 21, 1861, in Fairfax and Prince William Counties, Virginia.

The main Confederate commanders were Brigadier Generals Joseph E. Johnston and Pierre Beauregard, leading some 32,000 men. The main Union commander was Brigadier General Irvin McDowell, leading some 28,000 men.

It was here, at First Manassas, that the Confederates won their first big victory, and it's also here that General Thomas J.

Jackson earned the nickname "Stonewall Jackson." He was standing tall and bravely in the midst of the fighting, when one soldier said to another: "Don't he look just like a stonewall standin' there?" The nickname stuck, and to this day we Southerners still love to call him "Stonewall"!

Yankee General McDowell did such a bad job of directing his troops against our brave Rebel soldiers at First Manassas that Lincoln had him "relieved" from his command.

McDowell was then replaced by an equally unfit Yankee officer: Major General George B. McClellan, the man pictured on the cover of this book standing in between Honest Jeff and Dishonest Abe.

Lincoln disliked McClellan so much that he soon relieved him of his command as well. But McClellan got back at him later on: in 1864 he ran for president against Lincoln on an antiwar platform, and caused him a lot of problems!

The Battle of First Manassas was the first major Confederate victory of Lincoln's War.

You should know that Northerners have different names for many of the battles of the "Civil War." And the Battle of First Manassas is one of them. Northerners still call it the "Battle of First Bull Run." But we traditional Southerners don't use Yankee battle names here in the South. That wouldn't be right. That would be disrespectful of our Southern heritage.

CHAPTER 17
BATTLES
1862

THE BATTLE OF FORT DONELSON: 1862

The Battle of Fort Donelson took place from February 11 to February 16, 1862, in Stewart County, Tennessee.

The main Confederate commanders were Brigadier General John B. Floyd, Brigadier General Gideon Pillow, and Brigadier General Simon B. Buckner, leading 15,000 men. The main Union commanders were Brigadier General Ulysses S. Grant and Flag-Officer Andrew Hull Foote, leading 25,000 men.

After a few days of heavy skirmishing, Grant was able to back the Rebels into a corner. Most of the senior Confederate officers decided to surrender. But Rebel officer Nathan Bedford Forrest thought it was unnecessary, and rode out at night through a hole in the Union lines with over 1,000 men.

Forrest's superiors should have listened to him: the loss of Fort Donelson was a disaster for the South. It meant that Yankees had now trapped Kentucky in the Union, and that all of

If the Confederate commanders at Fort Donelson had kept fighting, as General Nathan Bedford Forrest had urged them to do, the entire outcome of the War might have been different.

western and central Tennessee was vulnerable to attack.

Worse yet, because of his victory, not only did Yankee General Grant avoid being arrested by Union military authorities for "insubordination," but he was promoted to major general and turned into a Civil War hero. After the War, because of Grant's celebrity, he was elected U.S. president twice (1869-1877), during which time he continued to punish and abuse the South.

It was at the Battle of Fort Donelson that Grant earned his lifelong nickname: "Unconditional Surrender," said to match his initials: U. S. Grant.

THE BATTLE OF HAMPTON ROADS: 1862

Despite its name, the Battle of Hampton Roads was actually a sea battle, and it's of interest to us because it was the first fight between two ironclads: specially made heavily armored ships.

This marine duel was fought from March 8 to March 9, 1862, in a harbor in Virginia known as Hampton Roads. The main Confederate commanders were Captain Franklin Buchanan and Lieutenant Catesby R. Jones. The main Union commander was Lieutenant John L. Worden.

At the Battle of Hampton Roads, the Confederate ship Virginia *went up against the Union ship* Monitor. *The deadly fight was the first battle between two ironclad ships in world history.*

On March 8, the Confederates steamed their ironclad ship the CSS *Virginia* (a converted Yankee ship originally named the USS *Merrimac*) from Norfolk into Hampton Roads. Here she sank the USS *Cumberland* and ran the USS *Congress* aground.

The next day, March 9, the Yankees' own ironclad ship, the tiny USS *Monitor*, steamed into Hampton Roads and fought violently with the much larger *Virginia*. Even after numerous broadsides from their enormous cannons, neither was able to sink the other, and the battle was considered a draw (no one won).

The Confederates made fun of the Yankees's little ship *Monitor*, and called it a "cheese box on a raft." The Battle of Hampton Roads is sometimes called the Battle of the Ironclads.

THE BATTLE OF SHILOH: 1862

The Battle of Shiloh was fought from April 6 to April 7, 1862, in Hardin County, Tennessee.

The main Confederate commanders were General Albert S. Johnston and General Pierre Beauregard, leading the Army of Mississippi with 45,000 men. The main Union commanders were Major General Ulysses S. Grant and Major General Don Carlos Buell, leading the Army of the Tennessee and the Army of the Ohio with 65,000 men.

At the Battle of Shiloh we lost one of our finest generals: Albert Sidney Johnston, a native Kentuckian and a West Point graduate.

After much fierce fighting, Confederate General Johnston was killed and his army was so severely weakened that it had to retreat to Corinth, Mississippi. Confederate General Nathan Bedford Forrest, however, was able to force the Yankees back to

Pittsburg Landing.

Still, the Union had scored another victory under General Grant. Northerners call this conflict the Battle of Pittsburg Landing.

THE BATTLE OF SEVEN DAYS: 1862

The "Battle" of Seven Days was actually six smaller battles that took place from late June to early July 1862 across eastern Virginia. They were the Battles of Oak Grove (June 25), Beaver Dam Creek (June 26), Gaines' Mill (June 27), Savage's Station (June 29), Glendale/White Oak Swamp (June 30), and Malvern Hill (July 1).

The main Confederate commanders were General Robert. E. Lee, Major General Stonewall Jackson, and Major General John Magruder. The main Union commanders were Major General George B. McClellan, Brigadier General Fitz John Porter, Major General Edwin Sumner, and Major General William Franklin.

After a week of heavy fighting and losses, our Confederate boys managed to win the Battle of Seven Days.

The Confederates won at Gaines' Mill; the Yankees won at Beaver Dam Creek and Malvern Hill; and no one won the Battles of Oak Grove, Savage's Station, and Glendale/White Oak Swamp.

Despite the South's heavier losses, McClellan's approach

was typically unimpressive and indecisive. The entire week long conflict ended with Lee driving the Yanks back down the Virginia peninsula, making the overall campaign a Confederate win.

The Battle of Oak Grove is also called the Battle of French's Field or King's School House. The Battle of Beaver Dam Creek is also called the Battle of Mechanicsville or Ellerson's Mill. The Battle of Gaines' Mill is also called the Battle of First Cold Harbor.

The Battle of Glendale/White Oak Swamp is also called the Battle of Nelson's Farm, Frayser's Farm, Charles City Crossroads, White Oak Swamp, New Market Road, and Riddell's Shop. And the Battle of Malvern Hill is also called the Battle of Poindexter's Farm.

THE BATTLE OF SECOND MANASSAS: 1862

The Battle of Second Manassas was fought from August 28 to August 30, 1862, in Prince William County, Virginia.

The main Confederate commanders were General Robert E. Lee and Major General Stonewall Jackson. The main Union commander was Major General John Pope.

At the Battle of Second Manassas, the Rebels beat the Yanks and inflicted major damage on the Union armies.

At one point in the conflict, Confederate General James Longstreet sent 28,000 Rebel soldiers up against Yankee General Fitz John Porter, resulting in the biggest simultaneous mass assault of the entire War. The Yanks lost a total of some 23,000 men, and Lee and his men scored a major victory.

The Battle of Second Manassas is called the Battle of Second Bull Run by Northerners, but is also known as the Battle of Manassas Plains, the Battle of Groveton, the Battle of Gainesville, and the Battle of Brawner's Farm.

THE BATTLE OF SHARPSBURG: 1862

The Battle of Sharpsburg was fought from September 16 to September 18, 1862, in Washington County, Maryland.

The main Confederate commander was General Robert E. Lee. The main Union commander was Major General George B. McClellan.

Though the Confederates came out ahead at the Battle of Sharpsburg, Lincoln lied and told the world that the North won. Then he used the imaginary "victory" as an excuse to issue his racist Preliminary Emancipation Proclamation on September 22.

This conflict produced some of the most savage and bloody fighting of Lincoln's War. The Rebels were greatly outnumbered, with the Yanks having a force twice their size. Still, as usual, McClellan lacked initiative, using less than 75 percent of his soldiers. This allowed Lee to gain the upper hand momentarily and finally withdraw to safety over the Potomac River.

There were a massive number of casualties (wounded, missing, captured, and dead) on both sides, with a total of at least 23,000. Though Lee actually escaped with his army, most historians consider the battle a draw.

Northerners call the Battle of Sharpsburg the Battle of Antietam.

THE PRELIMINARY EMANCIPATION PROCLAMATION

On September 22, 1862, Yankee President Abraham Lincoln issued his Preliminary Emancipation Proclamation, to see what kind of reaction he'd get before issuing his Final Emancipation Proclamation. The response wasn't good!

It's true that in this particular document the ultra racist leader, America's sixteenth president, asked for the destruction of slavery. However, he didn't request this for the benefit of blacks. He wanted it for the benefit of whites! How do we know this?

Because he included a clause in the Preliminary Emancipation Proclamation calling for the deportation of

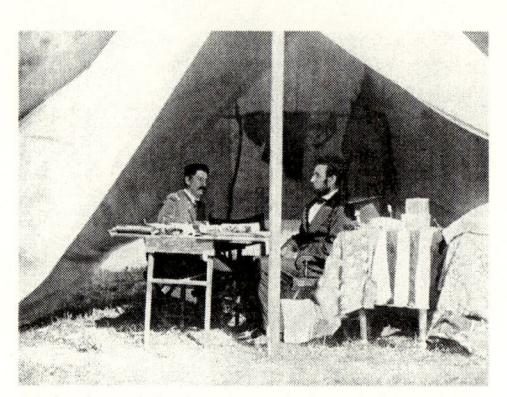

Nobody liked Lincoln's Preliminary Emancipation Proclamation, especially Union General George B. McClellan, seen here talking with the president at Antietam, Maryland, in the Fall of 1862.

all blacks out of the country as soon as possible. He even asked Congress to give him money to pay for the enormous cost!

Both white and black abolitionists were furious at Lincoln. Even his own cabinet members began calling him "that idiot in the White House!" Lincoln's secretary of war, Edwin M. Stanton, nicknamed Lincoln "the original gorilla," while Yankee

General George B. McClellan referred to the president as a "teller of low stories" and a "well meaning baboon."

THE BATTLE OF MURFREESBORO: 1862-1863

The Battle of Murfreesboro was fought from December 31, 1862, to January 2, 1863, in Rutherford County, Tennessee.

The main Confederate commander was General Braxton Bragg, leading the Army of Tennessee and 37,000 men. The main Union commander was Major General William S. Rosecrans, leading the Army of the Cumberland and 44,000 men.

The Rebels fought furiously for their freedom at the Battle of Murfreesboro, but in the end they were outnumbered and outgunned.

Although at one point the Rebels drove the Yanks back over McFadden's Ford, they lacked artillery support, so the Union troops were able to regain their ground. The Yanks suffered 13,000 casualties, the Rebs about 10,000.

After the intense three day fight, Bragg withdrew to Tullahoma, Tennessee. The Union army had chalked up another win. All in all, it was a terrible and decisive blow against the Confederacy.

Yankees call the Battle of Murfreesboro the Battle of Stones River, a name that should never be used anywhere in the South!

CHAPTER 18

THE EMANCIPATION PROCLAMATION 1863

LINCOLN DIDN'T WANT TO ISSUE IT

On January 1, 1863, two years *after* his War started, Lincoln reluctantly issued his fourth and last version of the Emancipation Proclamation. For this reason it was called the Final Emancipation Proclamation. This document is so important that we need to devote an entire chapter to it!

Why do I say that he issued it "reluctantly"?

Because abolitionists had been begging him, pushing him, and harassing him for two years to do something about freeing the slaves. In fact, he was so slow in finally issuing the Emancipation Proclamation, that his party members began calling him the "tortoise president."

Why did he wait so long?

WHY LINCOLN FINALLY ISSUED IT

Lincoln saw freeing the slaves not as something that would benefit *them*, but as something that would benefit *him*: he thought that freed slaves would make good workers in his armies, and that they could do the hard dull type of work that his white soldiers didn't want to do. So he decided that he wouldn't free the slaves until there was a "military necessity," as he put it.

Throughout 1861 and 1862, Lincoln lost thousands of his white soldiers to disease, desertion, and death. By the end of 1862, it was clear that he'd need more men to replace those he'd lost. This is the main reason that he waited two years, until January 1, 1863, to issue his Emancipation Proclamation. And this is why he referred to it, not as a *"civil rights* emancipation," but as a *"military* emancipation"!

EMANCIPATION & GRUNT WORK

It's obvious then why he issued the Emancipation Proclamation: he needed new common workers to build forts, dig trenches, do guard duty, and keep his naval ships clean.

This type of labor is called "grunt work." White Civil War soldiers disliked grunt work because it was boring, difficult, and often dangerous. Lincoln thought he would help his white soldiers by making blacks do this kind of labor. Here's what the president said in a letter to James C. Conkling on August 26, 1863, about his proclamation:

Lincoln put "freed" slaves to work doing the same labor they had formally done as slaves! In this illustration, "emancipated" blacks are loading Southern cotton onto boats for shipment to the Northern states. Many "freed" blacks had hoped that Lincoln would allow them to fight in the Union army, but the racist president refused, saying, in his Emancipation Proclamation, that he only wanted them to do construction work and guard forts.

> "I thought that whatever negroes could be got to do as soldiers, leaves just so much less for our white soldiers to do . . ."

In the proclamation itself, Lincoln actually spelled out what he expected of the slaves after he freed them and put them into his army. He expected them to do grunt work:

> "As president of the United States I order that all strong and healthy freed slaves be put into the armed service, to guard forts, positions, stations, and other places, and to man all types of ships in the military."

LINCOLN DISLIKED THE EMANCIPATION

Here's something else you should know: in this version, the Final Emancipation Proclamation, Lincoln's cabinet members forced him to remove the original clause about "shipping all blacks back to Africa," for fear that he would lose the abolitionist vote in his upcoming bid for reelection in November 1864.

What does this mean? It means that the Final Emancipation Proclamation was *not* the one Lincoln wanted to issue. It was the one he was forced to issue out of political necessity. The version he wanted everyone to read was the Preliminary Emancipation Proclamation, the one he had issued earlier on

According to former Northern slave Sojourner Truth, Lincoln once told her that if the South hadn't seceded, he would have never issued the Emancipation Proclamation.

September 22, 1862, because it included his black colonization clause!

But his final verison had lots of problems too. In fact, it had so many things wrong with it that no one ended up liking it, especially African-Americans.

THE EMANCIPATION WAS ILLEGAL
First, it was illegal. The leader of one country can't pass laws in another country. Yet, this is exactly what Lincoln did: as president of the United States of America (U.S.A), he was telling the people of the Confederate States of America (C.S.A.) what to do.

However, the C.S.A. was a constitutionally formed country that was now completely separate and independent from the U.S.A. So Lincoln had no authority to try and issue his Emancipation Proclamation there.

THE EMANCIPATION FREED NO SLAVES
Secondly, his Emancipation Proclamation actually didn't free any slaves at all. Lincoln cleverly worded the document so that slaves in those parts of the South that *hadn't* been captured by his troops were to be freed, while slaves in those parts of the South that *had* been captured by his troops were "for the present to be left precisely as if this

Because it didn't free slaves in either the South or the North, Lincoln's illegal Emancipation Proclamation actually had no effect on slavery. The document literally says that slavery would be allowed to continue in all of the Northern states and in parts of the Southern states "precisely as if this proclamation were not issued."

Emancipation Proclamation had never been issued."

In other words, Lincoln abolished slavery in the parts of the (free) South where he had no legal authority, while allowing slavery to continue in the (captured) parts of the South where he did have control. He doesn't even mention the many slaves still in the North. All in all, this means that no slaves were actually freed by Lincoln's Final Emancipation Proclamation!

Afterward, Lincoln's own secretary of state, a disappointed William H. Seward, wrote sourly:

> "We show our sympathy with slavery by emancipating slaves where we cannot reach them, and holding them in bondage where we can set them free."

Why did Lincoln do this? As always, he was thinking ahead about his reelection in 1864. By pretending to free slaves in the South he would please the small minority of angry Northern abolitionists. But by not actually freeing any slaves, he would please the vast majority of Northerners who didn't care about slavery, or who actually owned slaves and didn't want the institution to be destroyed.

In the South whites and blacks had much friendlier relations than in the North, where racists like Lincoln lived.

THE EMANCIPATION GAVE NO RIGHTS TO BLACKS

A third problem was that Lincoln's Final Emancipation

Proclamation didn't give "freed" blacks any civil rights, which was one of the primary goals of white and black abolitionists. In his document, Lincoln said nothing about allowing blacks to vote, hold political office, sit on juries, or marry whites, all rights that Yankees in the North had long been denying African-Americans.

THE EMANCIPATION DIDN'T MAKE BLACKS SOLDIERS

A fourth problem was that there was absolutely nothing in the Final Emancipation Proclamation about blacks serving as real armed soldiers. This was another strong desire of both blacks and abolitionists: they wanted black slaves to be freed, then be able to serve as genuine soldiers in Lincoln's army.

But Dishonest Abe didn't think blacks were capable of handling guns and combat. He didn't think they were smart enough or brave enough. He believed that if he gave guns to blacks, that they'd get scared when our Southern boys started firing at them, and that they'd run away and lose their weapons as they fled.

Lincoln didn't issue the Emancipation Proclamation until he was forced to, and he didn't allow blacks to enlist or be armed soldiers until he was forced to!

Obviously this is wrong: it's just another racist belief that Lincoln and many other Northern whites had at the time.

The truth is that black soldiers turned out to be just as good as white soldiers, and in some cases, even better. But Lincoln didn't like black people, so he never admitted this. Instead, he spent the rest of his life blocking the advancement of blacks in almost every way that he could!

Here's an example. On September 13, 1862, when someone asked him about freeing blacks and giving them guns to fight in the Union armies, he replied:

> "It's true that we'd get some additional military strength if we did that. It's also true that this would weaken the Confederates by stealing away their main source of labor (slaves)—which is of great importance to us. But I am not so sure we would accomplish much by putting blacks into our Union army. If we give them guns, I fear that in a few weeks the guns would be lost, and that they'd find their way into the hands of the Rebels. We don't even have enough guns for our white soldiers. So I would really prefer not to put blacks into my armies."

Now you understand why the entire world scoffed at Lincoln's Emancipation Proclamation: it was a deceitful and unlawful document written by a hypocrite and a criminal!

Southern newspapers quickly exposed the Emancipation Proclamation for what it was. The *Richmond Examiner*, for example, called it "the most startling political crime in American history."

Europeans saw through the appalling document as well. Here's what some of the English and Irish newspapers said about it:

- "The Emancipation Proclamation was intentionally written to deceive England and Europe." — the London *Standard* (England)
- "It's a very sad document and a hypocritical sham." — the London *Spectator* (England)
- "The Emancipation Proclamation is the latest and foulest crime perpetuated by the Lincoln administration." — the *Belfast News* (Ireland)
- "It's nothing but the wretched makeshift of a pettifogging lawyer, one who is doing his best to excite a servile war in the States he cannot occupy with his armies." — the London *Times* (England)

Here, President Lincoln is reading his deceitful, phoney, and unlawful Emancipation Proclamation to his cabinet members. From left to right: Edwin M. Stanton, Salmon P. Chase, Abraham Lincoln, Gideon Welles, (seated in front) William H. Seward, (standing in back) Caleb B. Smith, (standing in back next to Smith) Montgomery Blair, and (seated far right), Edward Bates. No one liked everything about the Emancipation Proclamation, and most people disliked all of it, particularly abolitionists and blacks—the very people it was supposed to please the most!

CHAPTER 19

LINCOLN & BLACK COLONIZATION

LINCOLN CALLED BLACKS AN "INFERIOR RACE"

It's clear that Lincoln had a very low opinion of black people. This is, after all, why he often referred to them as an "inferior race" in his letters and speeches.

It's a strange fact that, even today, Northerners believe that Lincoln not only loved African-Americans, but wanted them to have equal rights with European-Americans (white people). But we in the South know the truth about Lincoln and blacks, because we actually read the speeches and letters he wrote in the 1800s. We wish that all those who idolize Dishonest Abe would do the same!

In his public speeches President Lincoln spoke openly about "getting rid" of black people. Like all racists, he believed there was a "race problem." Unlike most other racists, however, he had an unusual solution. As he put it to a large crowd at Ottawa, Illinois, on August 21, 1858: "My first impulse would be to free all the slaves, then send them back to their own native land."

HOW LINCOLN REALLY FELT ABOUT BLACK PEOPLE

Here's another example of how Lincoln really felt about African-

Americans and equal rights. He spoke these words on October 16, 1854, during a speech at Peoria, Illinois. Someone in the crowd asked Lincoln about ending slavery and freeing black slaves, to which he said:

> "If we do that, what next? Should we then make blacks our political and social equals? I can't accept this, and if I can't, then I know that most other white people won't either. My feelings on this matter have nothing to do with justice.
> "In fact, justice has nothing to do with this question at all. A feeling held by so many white people, whether it's right or wrong, can't be ignored. The bottom line is that we simply cannot make whites and blacks equals."

During the same speech Lincoln went on to say:

> "Don't let anyone tell you that I'm fighting to establish political and social equality between white people and black people. I've said over and over again that I'm not, and that I have no plans to do so."

Four years later, on July 10, 1858, at Chicago, Illinois, Lincoln gave the following a speech:

> "People are constantly reminding me that the U.S. government was made for white people, and not for black people. There's no doubt that this is true, and only a fool would try to deny it.
> "But some abolitionists seem to think that

while I wouldn't want a negro woman for a slave, that I might like to have her for a wife. I'm telling you once and for all that this is ridiculous! I believe that I shouldn't have a black woman as either my slave or my wife. Why?

"Because God made whites and blacks separate races. To me this means that we should leave each other alone. I think this is the right thing to do.

"Listen, white men should marry white women, and black men should marry black women, and in God's name I want to keep it that way!

"We whites are well aware of the terrible things that happen when you mix whites and blacks together: the inferior race, the blacks, bring down the quality of the superior race, the whites. This is why I say, don't let the two races mix together to begin with; here, or anywhere else in the United States. This is so obvious that I hope I never have to repeat it again!"

LINCOLN & BLACK COLONIZATION

Lincoln, of course, had a solution to the "problem of the races mixing together": ship all American blacks "back to Africa"!

They won't teach you this in school, but President Lincoln was not only a lifelong member of the American Colonization Society (or A.C.S.), he was a chapter leader of the organization in his home state of Illinois.

An 1833 A.C.S. penny.

We spoke about the American Colonization Society earlier in Chapter 3: you'll remember that its goal was to "make America white from coast to coast." And how did the Society plan on doing this?

By deporting all African-Americans to a foreign country, such as Liberia, an African colony that the organization had created especially for this purpose. Lincoln and other Yankees in the 1800s called this "colonization."

During a speech on October 16, 1854, at Peoria, Illinois, an audience member asked the future U.S. president what he was going to do about slavery and the "race problem." Here's how Lincoln replied:

> "If all earthly power were given me, I should not know what to do about the existing institution. My first impulse would be to free all the slaves, and then send them to Liberia [Africa]—to their own native land.
>
> "But if you think about it, in the long run any real hope of accomplishing this (and I believe there is hope!) would be impossible at the moment. Even if all our slaves were sent to Liberia, they probably wouldn't be able to take care of themselves, and so they'd all be dead within ten days.
>
> "Besides, there aren't enough ships and there's not enough money in the world to carry them there. What should we do with the blacks then? Free them all and keep them here among us whites as underlings? Do you really think this would help improve their condition?
>
> "I don't think I really want anyone to be a

slave. Yet I'm not really sure that it's so bad that I could tell a slave owner to give his slaves up.

"So what next? Free them, and make them the political and social equals of us whites? I say never! And if this is how I feel, then I know that the majority of other white people feel exactly the same as I do."

By July 17, 1858, four years later, Lincoln had become more convinced than ever that colonization (forcing blacks out of the U.S.) was the only reasonable solution to creating an all-white America. Here are the exact words he spoke on that day in a public speech at Springfield, Illinois:

> "What I would most desire would be the separation of the white and black races."

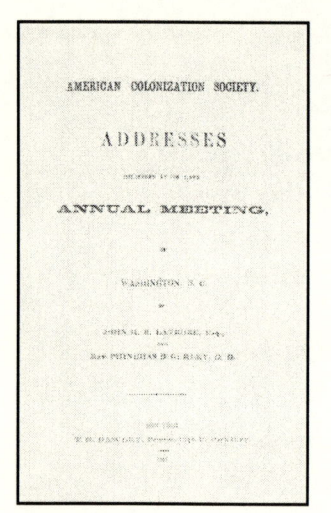

This booklet of speeches about deporting American blacks was printed by the American Colonization Society in New York in 1864. Lincoln was not only an outspoken supporter of this Northern organization, he was also a popular leader of an A.C.S. chapter in his home state of Illinois.

LINCOLN WAS A LIFELONG COLONIZATIONIST

Some Yankees and scallywags try to make excuses for Mr. Lincoln, saying that these racist ideas disappeared *before* he became president in 1860. Yet here is an example of what he said two years *after* he became president, during his Second Annual Message to Congress on December 1, 1862:

"I cannot make it better known than it already is, that I strongly favor colonization."

In fact, we have proof that Lincoln held this view until the day he died. Just a few days before Lincoln was assassinated on April 14, 1865, Union General Benjamin F. Butler says that the president called him to his office at the White House to get his opinion of his latest black colonization plans!

The Northern president who supported black deportation is the same man that Yankees call the "Great Emancipator"! But was he? Lincoln's own actions and words prove that his Emancipation Proclamation was both illegal and fake! What do you think? Now on to our next battle!

Photo of the U.S. Capitol Building in the Summer of 1863. While he was president, Lincoln used slave labor instead of free labor to finish constructing the Capitol. He also used slaves to complete, or build, many other government structures around Washington, D.C., including the White House and dozens of the District's main roads. Here in the South, it remains a mystery why Northerners and scallywags continue to call the man who freed no slaves and disliked blacks, the "Great Emancipator"!

CHAPTER 20

BATTLES 1863

THE BATTLE OF CHANCELLORSVILLE: 1863

The Battle of Chancellorsville was fought just four months after Lincoln issued his Final Emancipation Proclamation. The fighting took place from April 30 to May 6, 1863, at Spotsylvania County, Virginia.

The main Confederate commanders were General Robert E. Lee and Major General Stonewall Jackson, leading a combined force of about 60,000 men. The main Union commander was Major General Joseph Hooker, leading a force of about 100,000 men.

General Lee and General Jackson fought their troops hard, pushing the Yanks around the area of Chancellorsville with sporadic but violent fighting that lasted about a week. Finally, the Confederates were able to force the Union troops back across the Rappahannock River, ending in a major win for the South. In fact, the Battle of Chancellorsville is said to be General Lee's "greatest victory."

Confederate General Robert E. Lee achieved his greatest victory at the Battle of Chancellorsville.

But Lee's win came at an enormous cost. The beloved

Confederate officer Stonewall Jackson was mortally wounded here; not by Yankees, but by "friendly fire": on the night of May 2, Confederate soldiers from his own command mistook Jackson for the enemy and accidently shot him. The general tried to recover, but he died about a week later, on May 10, from pneumonia, which he got after doctors amputated his seriously injured left arm.

The total number of injured, missing, captured, and dead at the Battle of Chancellorsville was about 24,000: 10,000 Rebels and 14,000 Yanks. It was a major but extremely expensive victory for our people.

THE BATTLE OF GETTYSBURG: 1863

The Battle of Gettysburg was fought from July 1 to July 3, 1863, in Adams County, Pennsylvania.

The main Confederate commander was General Robert E. Lee, leading the Army of North Virginia—a force of about 75,000 men. The main Union commander was Major General George G. Meade, leading the Army of the Potomac—a force of about 83,000 men.

Though General Lee's officers made a number of serious mistakes at the Battle of Gettysburg, the great Confederate chieftain took full responsibility for his army's loss.

The battle began with Lee using the full strength of his army to push the Yankees back through the town of Gettysburg. Numerous smaller engagements followed, with continual reinforcements coming in on both sides. As the hours passed, Union soldiers began to take over more and more territory.

On the last day of the battle, July 3, one of Lee's officers, General George E. Pickett, led a fateful assault on the Union stronghold at Cemetery Ridge. In the famous attack, known as "Pickett's Charge," Pickett and his men were violently driven back, resulting in one of the most bloody defeats in the War.

The next day, July 4, General Lee withdrew his army toward Williamsport, Pennsylvania, ending what many believe to be the most famous and important of all the "Civil War" battles: the Battle of Gettysburg.

Gettysburg was truly the "turning point" of the War for Southern Independence.

Gettysburg will go down in the history books as one of the South's greatest and most serious losses. Confederate casualties numbered about 28,000, Union casualties about 23,000, totaling some 51,000. Lee's wagon train carrying his wounded soldiers was over fourteen miles long!

Just as importantly, our loss at Gettysburg ended any chance of Europe supporting the Confederacy (Europeans would only back us if we had consistent wins on the battlefield). The conflict also greatly deflated the morale of the Southern people, while greatly inflating the morale of the Northern people.

For the Confederacy, the Battle of Gettysburg was indeed the "turning point" of the War, *and* the "great lost opportunity." This is because this particular conflict occurred at a very crucial time.

Northerners were beginning to tire of the War, and

Lincoln was losing support. This means that if Lee and his fellow officers (James Longstreet, Richard S. Ewell, Jeb Stuart, and Ambrose P. Hill) had been able to defeat the Yanks here, especially in their own country (the U.S.A.), the entire War would have probably come to an end there and then, with the South ending up a truly free and sovereign country.

Instead, the Union win made the Yanks feel invincible, fueling Northern support for the War for another two years. It was during these two years that Lincoln was able to wear down the South, finally and illegally forcing us at gunpoint back into a Union we didn't want to be in.

THE BATTLE OF CHICKAMAUGA: 1863

The Battle of Chickamauga was fought from September 18 to September 20, 1863, in Catoosa and Walker Counties, Georgia.

The Battle of Chickamauga was a wonderful victory for the South, and helped maintain confidence in the Confederate Cause: personal freedom and self government.

The main Confederate commanders were General Braxton Bragg and Lieutenant General James Longstreet, leading the Army of Tennessee. The main Union commanders were Major General William S. Rosecrans and Major General George H. Thomas, leading the Army of the Cumberland.

The first day of the fight the Rebels held on, but were met with barrage after barrage from the Yankees' Spencer rifles, which could fire repeatedly at fast rates of speed. On the second day, our boys tried unsuccessfully to break the Union formation.

On the third day, however, the Confederates were able to pierce through a hole in the Yankee line, driving most of them from the battlefield.

Though the Rebels lost more men (19,000) than the Yanks (16,000) over that three day period, the Battle of Chickamauga was a decisive win for the South.

Confederate sharpshooters were always on the lookout for Yankees. These crack shot Rebel marksmen are about to take out an unsuspecting Union mortar boat chugging up the river.

CHAPTER 21

THE GETTYSBURG ADDRESS 1863

WHAT THE GETTYSBURG ADDRESS SAID

Like his Final Emancipation Proclamation, Lincoln's Gettysburg Address is so vital to understanding his War that we need to dedicate a whole chapter to it.

On November 19, 1863, just two months after Chickamauga, Lincoln delivered his now famous speech at the dedication of the cemetery at Gettysburg, Pennsylvania. Here are the president's exact words:

> "Fourscore and seven years ago our fathers brought forth on this continent a new nation, conceived in liberty, and dedicated to the proposition that all men are created equal.
>
> "Now we are engaged in a great civil war, testing whether that nation, or any nation so conceived and so dedicated, can long endure. We are met on a great battle-field of that war. We have come to dedicate a portion of that field as a final resting-place for those who here gave their lives that that nation might live. It is altogether fitting and proper that we should do this.
>
> "But, in a larger sense, we cannot

dedicate—we cannot consecrate—we cannot hallow—this ground. The brave men, living and dead, who struggled here, have consecrated it, far above our poor power to add or detract. The world will little note nor long remember what we say here, but it can never forget what they did here. It is for us, the living, rather, to be dedicated here to the unfinished work which they who fought here have thus far so nobly advanced. It is rather for us to be here dedicated to the great task remaining before us—that from these honored dead we take increased devotion to that cause for which they gave the last full measure of devotion—that we here highly resolve that these dead shall not have died in vain; that this nation, under God, shall have a new birth of freedom; and that government of the people, by the people, for the people, shall not perish from the earth."

While these words certainly are poetic, elegant, and stirring, what is Lincoln really saying here?

THE TRUTH ABOUT THE GETTYSBURG ADDRESS
Read his words carefully. He is saying that the South, by seceding, was threatening to destroy the U.S. government. Do you think this is true, or even possible? Of course not!

Not only did this never come close to occurring, but the Southern states never had any desire to injure let alone destroy the U.S. government. This was just a lie Lincoln made up to trick the Northern people into continuing to support his War! He thought that as long as he could make his people believe the

South wanted to hurt them, that they would stand by him long enough for him to beat us into submission.

The truth is that Southerners merely wanted to separate and form their own country, not do anything to damage the U.S. government. In fact, the secession of the Southern states didn't hurt the U.S. government at all. Quite the opposite: our leaving the U.S. could have helped strengthen it, if Lincoln had just let things be.

But this was not in his nature. He was a nosey liberal who wanted control over *all* of the states, not just the Northern ones. So he made up false words, like the Gettysburg Address, to make the people think he was fighting to preserve the Union, when really he was fighting to gain control over the South's people, money, and natural resources!

Pro-North writers like to pretend that Lincoln's Gettysburg Address was well received by a deeply moved and tearful crowd. However, Lincoln's own comments about its reception tell a very different story: "It fell on the audience like a wet blanket," the president later complained. "It was a flat failure and the people are disappointed." No wonder. It was a dishonest and inaccurate portrayal of the facts and, unlike today, the public back then knew it!

THE GETTYSBURG ADDRESS: A PACK OF LIES
There are some other things you should know about the Gettysburg Address, one of the most cruelly ironic speeches ever uttered.

In his speech Lincoln promises to uphold the

Constitution. But he actually did the opposite. He constantly violated the Constitution.

In his speech Lincoln blames the South for the War. Yet it was a conflict that he not only wanted, but that he also started.

In his speech Lincoln praises America's true political heritage: our original Confederate Republic, a constitutional government "of the people, by the people, for the people." Yet, his illegal and brutal four year War on the South and states' rights eventually destroyed this sacred institution, turning our country from a Confederate Republic into an evil empire ruled over by a big government, all-powerful dictator: Abraham Lincoln himself!

Lincoln's Gettysburg Address has misled generations of Americans into believing that the South wanted to destroy the U.S. Constitution and that the North wanted to preserve it. The opposite is true!

In other words, in the Gettysburg Address, Lincoln suggests that his armies are fighting for a free government, while the Southern Rebels are fighting against it. The reality is the reverse: it was Lincoln who was fighting *against* free government; it was the Southern Rebels who were fighting *for* it—for the right of the people to determine their own destinies.

Despite the fact that the Gettysburg Address was really just a "pack of lies" aimed at making the South look like the bad guy, uneducated pro-North authors have always loved the speech. In fact, they've written hundreds of books about it, unknowingly defending Lincoln's many false and absurd statements.

But we in the South know the truth about the Gettysburg Address. And to this day, this is one of the great differences between Southerners and Northerners.

Now we have more battles to cover!

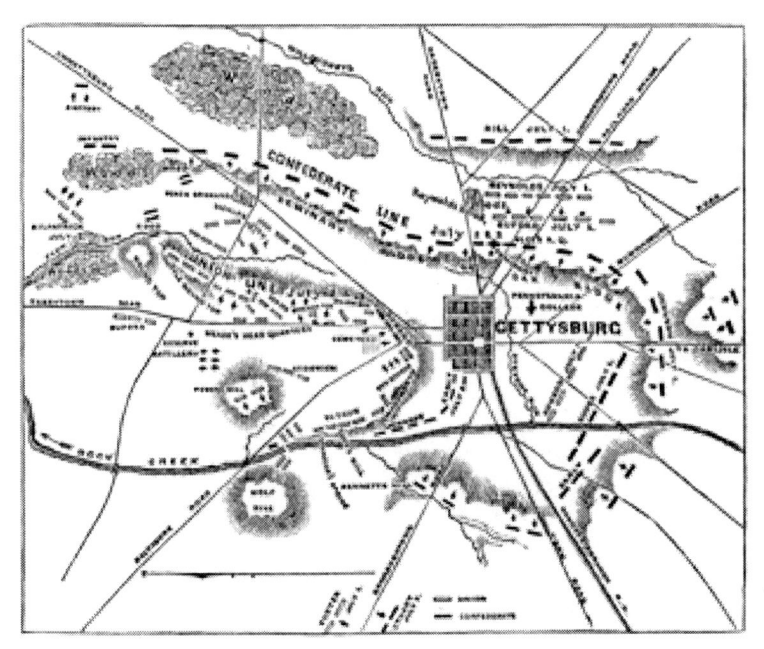

A map of the Battle of Gettysburg, fought from July 1 to July 3, 1863. Sadly for the Confederacy, it was here that the tide of the War began to turn in favor of the Union. Lincoln later filled his famous address at Gettysburg with devilish disinformation, meant to deceive the world into thinking that the North was in the right and the South was in the wrong.

CHAPTER 22

BATTLES
1864

THE BATTLE OF THE WILDERNESS: 1864

The Battle of the Wilderness was fought from May 5 to May 7, 1864, in Spotsylvania and Orange Counties, Virginia.

The main Confederate commander was General Robert E. Lee, leading some 62,000 men. The main Union commanders were Lieutenant General Ulysses S. Grant and Major General George G. Meade, leading about 100,000 men.

After numerous indecisive engagements spread out over three days, neither the Rebels or the Yanks were able to gain an advantage over the other, and the Battle of the Wilderness was considered a draw (no one won).

The Battle of the Wilderness dealt a devastating blow to the Confederacy.

Yet I list it here because of the sheer number of casualties and the impact these losses had on Lincoln's War: 11,000 Confederates were lost, 18,000 Yankees were lost, totaling about 30,000 men wounded, missing, captured, or dead.

The Battle of the Wilderness is also known as Combats at

Parker's Store, the Battle of Craig's Meeting House, the Battle of Todd's Tavern, the Battle of Brock Road, and the Battle of the Furnaces.

THE BATTLE OF SPOTSYLVANIA COURT HOUSE: 1864

The Battle of Spotsylvania Court House was actually a series of bloody engagements fought from May 8 to May 21, 1864, in Spotsylvania County, Virginia.

The separate battles each have their own names: Combats at Laurel Hill and Corbin's Bridge (May 8), Ni River (May 9), Laurel Hill, Po River, and Bloody Angle (May 10), Salient or Bloody Angle (May 12-13), Piney Branch Church (May 15), Harrison House (May 18), and Harris Farm (May 19).

General Lee and his men fought desperately at the Battle of Spotsylvania Court House, but neither side was able to score a victory.

The main Confederate commander was General Robert E. Lee, leading about 52,000 men. The main Union commanders were Lieutenant General Ulysses S. Grant and Major General George G. Meade, leading some 100,000 men combined.

During the two weeks this battle was fought, one of the engagements resulted in one of the most savage and prolonged fights of the entire War: a 20 hour nonstop struggle between the Rebs and the Yanks. Lee lost nearly an entire division and at one point his army was cut in two.

Despite the severity of the fight, the battle was a draw.

Casualties included 12,000 Confederates, and 18,000 Federals, making a total of 30,000 wounded, missing, captured, and killed.

THE BATTLE OF BRICE'S CROSS ROADS: 1864
The Battle of Brice's Cross Roads was fought June 10, 1864, in Prentiss and Union Counties, Mississippi.

The main Confederate commander was Major General Nathan Bedford Forrest, leading a cavalry corps of about 3,500 men. The main Union commander was Brigadier General Samuel D. Sturgis, leading a three brigade division of infantry and cavalry numbering about 8,100 men.

After being ferociously harassed by the brilliant Forrest and his men, after losing nearly two thirds of their soldiers, and after being severely pounded by Forrest's artillery for several hours, Sturgis and the remaining Yanks desperately fled for their lives across Tishomingo Creek. As they retreated, they cut loose some 2,000 of their horses in order to make a faster getaway.

After the Battle of Brice's Cross Roads, Union officers complained that Confederate General Nathan Bedford Forrest had handled their men "quite roughly." To add insult to injury, Forrest made off with millions of dollars of Federal supplies and captured 2,000 Yankee soldiers. This is just one of the many reasons Forrest will always be considered a hero here in the South!

Along with these 2,000 mounts, Forrest also captured nearly two dozen U.S. cannons, 250 wagons, 3,000 rifles and handguns, and 2,000 prisoners.

The Battle of Brice's Cross Roads is considered one of the most decisive, complete, and stunning victories of the War, on either side. The fight, in which Forrest fought and won against formidable odds, sealed for all time his well deserved reputation as an ingenious and fearless Confederate warlord.

Yankees call the Battle of Brice's Cross Roads the Battle of Tishomingo Creek.

LINCOLN IS REELECTED BY CHEATING & LYING
On November 8, 1864, in the midst of his War, U.S. President Abraham Lincoln, Dishonest Abe, was reelected to a second term in the White House. It's true that he won both the popular and the electoral vote in 1864. But just like his first win in 1860, his 1864 victory wasn't an authentic or an honorable one.

We know for a fact that bribery, lying, horse-trading, patronage, and cheating took place on Lincoln's behalf during both the 1860 and the 1864 elections, and that top government positions and other political favors were traded for votes.

Not only did Lincoln use countless tricks and crimes to make sure he'd be reelected in 1864, but none of the Southern states voted in the U.S. elections that year—for Lincoln a loss of eighty potential electoral votes. Why didn't the Southern states vote?

They were now part of a separate, sovereign, and foreign nation: the Confederate States of America, a country that Lincoln refused to recognize. Once when Confederate President Jefferson Davis correctly referred to the C.S.A. and the U.S.A. as "the two countries," Lincoln ignorantly corrected him, calling them "our one common country"!

Because the Southern states didn't participate in the U.S. elections in 1864, that year all of Lincoln's electoral votes came

Using underhanded tricks, fibs, scare tactics, backroom deals, and false promises, President Lincoln rigged the polls and managed to get himself reelected in 1864. And he "won," even though—just as in the 1860 election—he got less than 50 percent of the popular American vote: Lincoln banned the Southern states from voting in the U.S. election in 1864! But they wouldn't have wanted to vote anyway. They all belonged to a separate country at the time: The Confederate States of America.

from non-Southern states (except for West Virginia, which Lincoln had illegally created for this very purpose).

Yet, if only 38,111 people, a mere 1 percent of Northerners and Westerners, had changed their votes in specific regions, Lincoln would have lost even the electoral vote, and his opponent, George B. McClellan, would have won. If the South had also voted, Lincoln would have definitely lost in 1864, just as he would have in 1860.

Isn't it interesting that Lincoln lost the Illinois senate race to his conservative opponent Stephen A. Douglas in November 1858. Yet Yankees considered this same man, Lincoln, good enough to be president of the U.S. a mere two years later! How odd this is to us Southerners.

Again, this shows the enormous difference between the way Southerners and Northerners thought in the 1860s. And yes, we still think very differently than Yankees to this day!

THE BATTLE OF FRANKLIN II: 1864
The Battle of Franklin II was fought on November 30, 1864, in Williamson County, Tennessee.

The main Confederate commander was General John Bell Hood, leading the Army of Tennessee and some 25,000 men. The main Union commander was Major General John M. Schofield, leading the Army of the Ohio and the Cumberland with about 25,000 men.

Arriving in Franklin at dawn on November 30, the Yanks built up the defensive works that had been leftover from the Battle of Franklin I (April 10, 1863). At 4:00 that afternoon the Rebels arrived in town and, deploying from Winstead and Breezy Hills to the south, began their assault on the Union lines.

Numerous waves of brave Confederate soldiers charged across the Plain of Franklin, but were mowed down by the well-hidden Yanks and their powerful cannons and repeating rifles. The main battle ended around 9:00 that evening, with sporadic skirmishes continuing until after midnight.

Rebel sharpshooters knocked out dozens of Yankees at the Battle of Franklin II on November 30, 1864. But the Confederates still lost due to dirty fighting on the part of the Yanks and poor planning on the part of Confederate General John Bell Hood.

The next morning, December 1, the injured and the dead littered the fields for miles around in one of the bloodiest battles of Lincoln's War. Our Southern army lost about 7,000 men: 700 captured, 4,500 wounded, and about 1,750 killed. The

Union lost about 2,300 men.

The victorious Yanks marched onto Nashville with the Rebels in hot pursuit, resulting in the Battle of Nashville.

The Battle of Franklin II altered the course of the War. How? General Hood lost so many men, including 6 generals, and his remaining soldiers were so cold, tired, and hungry, that his army was no longer capable of defending the South properly. This made us weak and eventually unable to carry on the War.

Hood's Army of Tennessee was the last great Confederate army in the western theater of operations. Without it, the only large Rebel force left was the Army of Northern Virginia in the eastern theater, operating under General Robert E. Lee.

At the Battle of Franklin II the Yankees had successfully cut the Confederacy in two, and worn down both of our last two major forces. The end of the War was near.

THE BATTLE OF NASHVILLE: 1864
The Battle of Nashville was fought from December 15 to December 16, 1864, in Davidson County, Tennessee.

The main Confederate commander was General John Bell Hood. The main Union commander was General George H. Thomas.

After the Battle of Franklin II, the Confederate Army of Tennessee was exhausted and depressed, but still willing to fight the Yankees that had illegally invaded the state of Tennessee. So it chased after General Schofield's army, which had made a 15 mile dash north to Nashville on the night of November 30.

General Hood arrived in Nashville on December 2, but bad weather and combat preparations prevented an immediate attack on the U.S. troops.

By December 15, the Rebel earthworks were complete

and the snow and ice had cleared enough for the battle to begin. Hood and his men had set up their defenses on several hills surrounding Nashville, which turned out to be a big mistake!

Union soldiers battered the Confederate hill positions on December 15, and on December 16 they were able to overrun them completely. The Rebels, cold, hungry, and too worn out to fight anymore, were forced to run for their lives back south toward Franklin. This route, from Nashville south through Middle Tennessee, is called "Hood's Retreat."

Our boys gave it everything they had at the Battle of Nashville in December of 1864. But they were freezing, starving, and exhausted, and they were fighting an enemy that was not only well fed and well rested, but which had superior weapons. Afterward, the ragged remnants of the once mighty Army of Tennessee retreated south to Mississippi, where General Hood resigned and where Confederate power came to an end in the West.

The Yankees chased the Confederates all the way to the Mississippi border. Hood resigned and the tattered remains of the Army of Tennessee were turned over to Confederate General Richard Taylor (the son of U.S. President Zachary Taylor, and the brother of Sarah Knox Taylor, the first wife of Honest Jeff, C.S. President Jefferson Davis).

Middle Tennessee was now under Lincoln's complete control, and Confederate strength in the western theater was all but gone.

CHAPTER 23
THE FINAL BATTLE & SURRENDER 1865

THE BATTLE OF APPOMATTOX COURT HOUSE: 1865
The Battle of Appomattox Court House was fought on April 9, 1865, in Appomattox County, Virginia.
    The main Confederate commander was General Robert E. Lee. The main Union commander was General Ulysses S. Grant.
    Just four months after the Confederate disaster in Nashville, General Lee found himself in a situation not very different from General John Bell Hood's. Lee's troops were tired, starving, and mostly barefoot. His army was now surrounded on three sides by well fed, well rested, well shoed Yankees, who were slowly but surely advancing down on him.
    Lee, who loved his soldiers like they were his own sons, couldn't bear to see them suffer anymore. He knew the final day of the conflict had come. Though most of his men wanted to keep fighting, General Lee decided it would be best to put an end to the bloodshed.
    There and then he agreed to meet with General Grant to discuss the conditions of surrender.

LEE'S SURRENDER & THE END OF THE WAR

On April 9, 1865, a nearby house—belonging to Wilmer McLean who lived in the village of Appomattox Court House—was chosen for this very important meeting.

In one of the front parlors of the McLean house, Lee and Grant sat at a small marble topped table and talked about the terms of the South's capitulation. Grant wrote them out and handed the piece of paper to Lee, who signed it and handed it back to Grant.

Although General Grant had committed many crimes against the Southern people during the War, he acted like a gentleman at the meeting, and even allowed Lee and his men to keep their pistols, horses, and belongings.

Lee and Grant shook hands, after which the great Southern general got on his horse, politely raised his hat to the Yankee soldiers in the front yard, and rode off to tell his men the sad news of his surrender to the much larger and stronger Union forces.

The War was over. It was time to go home.

After signing the papers of surrender over to Grant, General Lee rode back through his tearful troops, waved his hat to them, and said goodbye for the last time. Since nearly all of the train tracks had been destroyed, most soldiers had to walk home, a journey that took several weeks.

Though the very last Confederates didn't turn in their weapons until later that Autumn, Lee's "surrender" to General Grant on April 9, 1865, marked the official final day of the so-called "Civil War."

Section 3

THE TRUTH ABOUT DISHONEST ABE

CHAPTER 24

THE MAN OUR SOUTHERN ANCESTORS CALLED "STINKIN' LINCOLN"

THE TRUTH OF HOW LINCOLN GOT HIS NICKNAMES
Your schoolbooks will tell you that our sixteenth president, Abraham Lincoln, was called "Honest Abe" because he was so truthful, plain-spoken, and modest. But this itself is a lie, one worthy of Old Abe himself!

The reason he was called Honest Abe is because he was so *dishonest*! This is called a "reverse nickname."

Have you ever known someone who was really tall, but they were nicknamed "Shorty"?

This is the same thing that happened to Lincoln. He was so dishonest that they gave him a reverse nickname: Honest Abe.

This image of Dishonest Abe was used on our 5 dollar bill from 1914 to 2007. This was wrong!

But here in the South, we know the truth about Lincoln, so I gave him the nickname he truly deserves: Dishonest Abe!

WHY I CALL LINCOLN DISHONEST ABE
Many Northerners and scallywags have a hard time understanding why we think so badly of Lincoln. They think we're being unfair to him, and that we've made up things to make him look like a terrible person on purpose. This is just

another Northern myth.

I'm a historian: I study and write about history for a living. I've been studying and writing about Lincoln for many years, and have written three books about him, one of them over 1,000 pages long.

What I've discovered is that during his lifetime Lincoln committed a truly stunning number of well-known constitutional, civil, political, ethical, social, and moral crimes. Let's look at some of these now.

- Lincoln completely undermined the Constitution.
- Lincoln ruled the American people by "arbitrary power."
- the Lincoln administration was a thugocracy: the rule of a country by thugs, criminals, and bullies.
- Lincoln arrested and deported Yankee antiwar advocates, like Ohio Congressman Clement L. Vallandigham, who, though a civilian, was illegally tried by a military court.
- Lincoln indiscriminately arrested and tried (by military commission) civilian draft resistors and others suspected of "disloyalty."
- Lincoln seized rail and telegraph lines leading to the capital.
- Lincoln suppressed and shut down over 300 hundred pro-peace Northern newspapers, then arrested their owners.
- Lincoln went against precedent by "packing" the Supreme Court with his own personal picks.
- Lincoln censored telegraph communications in the North.

Lincoln had nearly 50,000 Northerners illegally arrested and imprisoned for saying things he didn't like!

- Lincoln tortured both Northern soldiers (accused of desertion) and Northern citizens (accused of spreading antiwar sentiment, which Lincoln referred to as "treason"); his favorite methods of torture were "violent cold water torture" and being suspended for long periods of time by handcuffed wrists.

Lincoln delayed emancipation for as long as possible and actually prevented his cabinet members and military officers from freeing any slaves.

- Lincoln murdered unarmed Confederate prisoners, even in Southern states (like Kentucky) that had not fully joined the Confederacy.
- Lincoln prohibited former Confederates and supporters of the Confederacy from voting in the 1864 election, thereby helping to guarantee that he would be reelected.
- Lincoln used spies, gangs, detectives, "secret agents," fraud, and bribery to make sure he'd be reelected in 1864. This resulted in "the foulest corruptions," said to have been obvious at every level of his party.
- Lincoln forced foreigners (that is, citizens of the Confederate States of America) to take an oath of allegiance to the United States of America, or face arrest and imprisonment.
- Lincoln illegally banned the writ of *habeas corpus* across the entire U.S., and for the first time in U.S. history. (*Habeas corpus* is a Constitutional law promising that you get a fair trial if you're convicted of a crime.)
- Lincoln assumed the extraordinary right of "extraordinary

powers" (unconstitutional and therefore illegal).
- Lincoln prohibited the emancipation of slaves by his cabinet members and Union military officers, men such as General John. C. Frémont, General David Hunter, John W. Phelps, Jim Lane, and General Simon Cameron. This proves once and for all, if nothing else does, that Lincoln did not wage war against the South over slavery!
- Lincoln unlawfully ordered a naval blockade of Southern ports (unlawful because he never recognized the Confederacy as a separate nation and war had not yet been officially declared).
- Lincoln completely removed every inhabitant living in certain counties, "en masse," as Lincoln put it, in the Southern states.
- Lincoln engaged in "checking" (that is, arresting) clergymen who had "become dangerous to the public interest" (that is, who contradicted him).

Lincoln called Confederate privateers "pirates" and said he would hang them if caught. Yet, privateering was perfectly legal at the time—and still is today.

- Lincoln declared all medicines "contraband of war" (meaning he made them illegal), which helped kill countless thousands of Southerners, both soldiers and civilians, not to mention thousands of Yankee soldiers held in Confederate prisons.
- Lincoln threatened war on any nation, particularly England and France, if they in any way supported, aided, or recognized the Confederacy.
- Lincoln proclaimed Confederate privateersmen "insurgents"

and "pirates," subject to the death penalty (privateering, that is, working on an armed privately-owned vessel, was and still is a legal profession).
- Lincoln intimidated judges who disagreed with him.
- Lincoln closed the post office in an effort to prevent anti-Lincoln, antiwar mail from being sent or delivered.
- Lincoln forced all Federal employees to contribute 5 percent of their annual income to his 1864 reelection campaign.
- Lincoln refused to exchange military prisoners (which aided in the deaths of thousands of soldiers, both Confederate and Union).
- Lincoln defied the Supreme Court.
- Lincoln refused to officially acknowledge Jefferson Davis as the president of the Confederacy.
- Lincoln instituted the largest number of military drafts in U.S. history.
- Lincoln fabricated unknown types of political offices, such as "military governor," in conquered Southern states.
- Lincoln shut down the governments of entire Northern states and arrested members of their state legislatures (usually for suspicion of advocating peace with the South). One of the more notable of these was the state of Maryland, which originally had hoped to join the Confederacy.
- Lincoln established U.S. military rule in a foreign nation (the C.S.A.), and even within states still part of the Union

Lincoln wouldn't admit that the Confederacy was a real country and that Jefferson Davis (above) was our president. This was a great insult to the Southern people.

(such as Missouri).
- Lincoln inaugurated America's first federal monetary monopoly (meaning, he tried to control all of America's wealth by himself).
- Lincoln imprisoned some 38,000 to 50,000 Northern civilians (men, women, and children), without trial, many for as long as four years.
- Lincoln incarcerated civilians, like Rebel Vice President Alexander H. Stephens, in military prisons.
- Lincoln imposed the first personal income tax, launching what would later become the Internal Revenue Service (IRS).
- Lincoln wouldn't allow governmental debate over secession.
- When Lincoln had 38 Indians hanged on December 26, 1862, he became the first and only president in U.S. history to order a mass execution of his own citizens.

In 1862 Lincoln had 38 Indians put to death for complaining about the U.S. government's broken treaties. He had wanted to hang over 300 of them, but he was talked out of it at the last minute!

- Lincoln changed the meaning of the "United States" from plural to singular. (The original meaning was "States United," which has the opposite meaning of "United States.")
- Lincoln set up temporary courts in conquered Southern states (this was illegal because Dixie's own civilian courts remained open during the War).
- Lincoln illegally created the state of West Virginia from the

state of Virginia (Lincoln encouraged the western area of Virginia to secede while he was at war with the South because she had seceded).
- In the 1864 election, Lincoln stationed armed U.S. soldiers at polling places in order to intimidate voters into casting their votes for him.
- Lincoln rigged Northern elections to skew the outcome in his favor.
- Lincoln bribed, threatened, and paid voters, soldiers, and fellow politicians to vote for his party.

Lincoln put out an order to have his own chief justice, Roger B. Taney, arrested for telling him to stop committing crimes against the Constitution. The only reason Taney didn't go to prison was because the sheriff wisely defied Lincoln and refused to make the arrest!

Everything in this list was either deceptive, immoral, unethical, or downright illegal! It's obvious that our sixteenth U.S. president had nothing but contempt for the Constitution and the other laws of the land.

Liberal Lincoln even signed an order for the arrest of the U.S. Supreme Court's Chief Justice Roger B. Taney. Why? Because Taney had told him that suspending *habeas corpus* was unconstitutional and therefore unlawful!

Keep in mind that the things in the list above are only a few of Lincoln's crimes!

We'll never know them all, simply because he committed so many. In fact, legal scholars are still counting them and trying to figure them all out.

The Lincoln administration (1861 to 1865) was so corrupt that many historians, even from the North, believe that this was not only the worst period for civil liberties up until then, but that it also ranks as one of the worst in all of American history.

Even many Northerners recognized this fact. One of them, a Constitution-loving Yankee named Henry Clay Dean—who was arrested by the president for promoting peace—rightly called "Lincoln's reign" a government that operated "between lawlessness and a dictatorship."

Someday someone is going to ask you why you don't like Old Abe, and why we Southerners call him "Stinkin' Lincoln." All you have to do is show them this chapter!

Dishonest Abe committed so many crimes during the time he was president that no one has been able to count them all.

Section 4

LIFE IN THE CONFEDERATE ARMY

CHAPTER 25

THE WORLD OF THE CONFEDERATE SOLDIER

WHAT IT WOULD BE LIKE TO BE A REBEL SOLDIER

What was life like for the average Confederate soldier, a man given the nickname "Johnny Reb"? What did he wear, eat, and do for fun? What kinds of weapons did he use, and how did he protect himself from harsh weather? In this chapter we're going to answer these and lots of other questions as well.

If you've ever wondered what it would be like to be a soldier in President Jefferson Davis' army, you're about to find out!

CLOTHING

A full Confederate outfit was, out of necessity, extremely simple, and consisted of the following items, one of each per soldier: forage cap (called a kepi), shirt, jacket, overcoat, poncho, pants, underwear, a pair of shoes, and a pair of socks.

A Confederate forage cap, or kepi, as it was also known.

Due to a lack of state money, however, there were simply not enough regulation uniforms to demand that every soldier wear one. So, Confederate soldiers were given tremendous freedom as far as what they wore.

HOW SOUTHERN WOMEN HELPED OUR SOLDIERS
Southern women greatly aided the Southern Cause by forming huge sewing clubs, which produced enormous quantities of socks, shirts, pants, and jackets for their menfolk. This greatly helped the South's war effort and made our soldiers more comfortable.

Southern girls and women played a very important role in the Civil War: they sewed clothes and baked food for our Confederate soldiers, and raised money to help pay for military supplies for the armies.

UNUSUAL UNIFORMS
Many Rebel soldiers ended up dressing in every day clothing that they normally wore at home.

One of the more popular of these types of outfits was the "butternut" uniform: ordinary clothing that was dyed a tan or yellow-brown color using tree bark, walnut shells, and even rust. This "uniform" was so common that Yankee soldiers took to calling our Southern boys "Butternuts."

When their clothing wore out, Rebel soldiers would sometimes dress in the blue uniforms they "captured" from deceased Yankee soldiers. This could, and often did, lead to some confusion on the battlefield!

Whether Confederate or Union, however, government issue uniforms were usually made of *coarse* wool, flannel, and linen, which made them unpleasant to wear in both the Summer and the Winter months.

One of the more peculiar Confederate uniforms was the Zouave outfit, patterned on the clothing of the French light infantry regiments known as the "Zouaves." This uniform featured a short open front jacket, colorful shirt, a vest, baggy trousers, a sash, leggings, and an oriental tasseled cap (a "fez"), or even a turban!

A Louisiana Zouave.

JOHNNY REB DISLIKED REGULATION CLOTHING!
Stiff and heavy regulation military boots were soon discarded in favor of the far more comfortable brogan: large broad leather shoes. But like so many other things on the Confederate side, both boots and brogans were hard to come by. This means that many Rebel soldiers went barefoot, even in the Winter!

To try and keep their feet warm and protected, soldiers would sometimes tie rags or sew pieces of rawhide around their feet. Confederate General Robert E. Lee said that one of the reasons he surrendered the Confederacy to the Yankees in April 1865, was because so many of his men had no shoes. He simply couldn't bear to see them suffer anymore.

Like their painful regulation boots, most soldiers also found their regulation forage caps rigid and uncomfortable. These were usually replaced with "slouch hats," soft felt hats that were lightweight and comfy on the head.

JOHNNY REB WAS A STYLISH SOLDIER

While the Confederate "uniform" was actually a hodgepodge of wildly different styles, colors, and personal tastes, for sheer variety, creativeness, elegance, and flamboyance, the Yankees never came close to matching the Southern soldier's sense of style!

FOOD

The common meal of the Confederate soldier was supposed to be a well rounded table of meat, bread, fruits, vegetables, coffee, and sweets. And for the first few months of the War, he ate exactly that.

But as the War dragged on, money dried up, and so did the amount and variety of foods that were available. To make matters worse, this caused Confederate authorities to begin reducing the amount of rations a soldier could have on a daily basis.

This mounted rifleman from North Carolina fought bravely against Lincoln and his meddling bluecoats.

A BORING DIET

Soon Johnny Reb found himself eating an almost steady diet of monotonous food throughout the day, usually cornbread and beef—if he was lucky! More often he was forced to eat whatever he could get his hands on: apples from an orchard, raw corn from a farmer's field, or a watermelon from a stranger's garden along the roadside.

With the ongoing shortage of meat, Confederate soldiers soon took to eating rats, mules, and even their own horses—sometimes raw! Whenever possible, hunting and fishing filled in the gaps.

UNCLE SAM'S LARDER
When all else failed, there was what was called "Uncle Sam's Larder": captured Yankee chuck wagons and food kits. Naturally, "Billy Yank," our nickname for a Union soldier, didn't like this one bit. But this was a favorite method of eating among our men, for the Union armies always had more variety and fresher foods than the Confederate armies.

However they managed to get their food, from the reports, letters, and eyewitness testimony from this period, it's clear that many of our soldiers were hungry, or even starving, throughout most of Lincoln's War.

WHY OUR SOLDIERS DIDN'T HAVE ENOUGH FOOD

Confederate soldiers gather round a sutler's tent to pick up food and other provisions.

The terrible irony of all this was that there was actually a lot of food in the South at the time: millions of black servants, known as "slaves" to Yankees, stayed at home with their "white families" and planted and harvested tons of crops throughout the War. The problem was that the food couldn't be distributed to our soldiers. Why? Mainly because:

- the South's already small railroad system was being destroyed by the War.
- the Yankees had captured the Mississippi River, the South's

main transportation waterway.
- there was a lack of containers (like wooden boxes and tins) to store food for long distance transport.
- Lincoln's illegal naval blockade hindered the movement of goods.
- the Confederate Commissary Department—the official source of all Rebel military supplies, provisions, and food—was not always run as well as it should have been.

POPULAR FOODS AND DRINKS

When they were available, the most popular food ingredients were sugar, flour, and lard, probably because almost anything could be made with these three items quickly and easily. Coffee was the favored beverage.

When even these foods were scarce, Rebels ground up rice and mixed this "flour" with hot water to form a sort of horrid gruel. Another trick was to boil grass, and whatever else was growing nearby, creating an unpleasant drink that I'll call "weed tea"!

Confederate armies kept their food and cooking utensils in camp chests, which were loaded into large chuck wagons like this one.

Sometimes, between battles, Billy Yank got hungry too, and he would cross over the Confederate lines and barter items for food from our boys. A common swap among the two sides was a postal stamp for a cup of coffee, or a pocket knife for a strip of bacon.

COOKING, SERVING, & EATING UTENSILS

For preparing, serving, and eating food, a wide assortment of items were used, the more common being: the skillet, the frying pan, the kettle, the lard bucket, the coffee boiler, and of course forks, spoons, knives, plates, and tin cups.

When eating utensils weren't available, Johnny Reb ate with his fingers, or for the more particular, with sticks and pocket knives.

Some specific foods had their own containers, such as the coffee box, the meal box, the flour box, and the salt box. All of these items were kept in a camp chest, about ten which would fit into a regular army chuck wagon.

Camp wasn't always the most comfortable experience for our Rebel soldiers. These Confederates are sleeping out in the cold and rain without tents, or even blankets.

Meals were informal and were announced by beating a frying pan with a spoon. Since eating was Johnny Reb's favorite pastime, we can be sure this was a sound he loved to hear!

CAMP LIFE

In the warm months Confederate encampments were simple affairs, with the lower ranking soldiers living out in the open around their campfires, and the officers dwelling in either a tent, or sometimes the nearby house of an unfortunate citizen.

WINTER QUARTERS

During the winter months it became too cold to march and fight.

So Confederate troops went into what was called "Winter Quarters," a type of hibernation for soldiers.

Winter Quarters lasted from two to four months, or until the snow melted enough for armies to begin moving over the (usually muddy) roads again.

During Winter Quarters, instead of tents, the men built small crude log cabins, which were easier to heat and gave more protection from the biting winds.

Since the idea was to create something as much like home as possible, many of these structures were quite elaborate, and some even had well built temporary chimneys!

FLAGS

Confederate armies kept up morale and distinguished themselves from other units by carrying colorful and creatively designed flags.

Rebel flags were made from just about any material that was at hand, from expensive silk to a pair of old pants. Most were usually decorated with camp mottos, such as: "Long Live the South!", "Yankee Go Home!", "Don't Tread On Me!", or "We Will Never Surrender!"

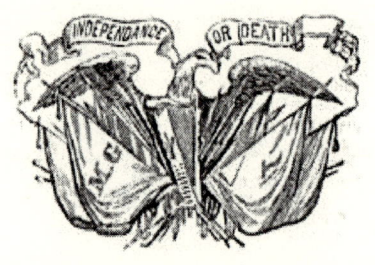

The slogan on this Confederate banner shows how strongly our Southern ancestors felt about their freedom.

CARRYING THE COLORS

Confederate soldiers viewed their flags as beloved symbols of both the Confederate States of America and their families and homes. As such, they bore these colorful pieces of cloth into battle with great pride and emotion. This was called "carrying the colors," and whoever was assigned this task approached it as a very solemn and important duty.

Sadly, the flag carrier was often the first man to be shot down. This is because the waving, brightly designed flag was so easy to see across the battlefield. If and when this happened, the closest soldier would pick up the flag and keep running forward, holding it proudly high above his head. Sometimes as many as four or five flag carriers would be killed before the battle ended.

This particular regimental flag was carried into battle by some of our brave boys from North Carolina. Notice the reference on the flag to the first Revolutionary War, May 20, 1775.

REBEL FLAGS STOLEN BY YANKEES

Yankees considered it a great prize if they could "capture" one of our flags, and many were. This is why, at one time, there were so many Confederate flags in Northern museums.

Since then, some of the nicer Yankees have returned our flags to us. These people knew how much these beautiful Southern symbols mean to Dixie, and we thank them for their kindness. One of these individuals was U.S. President Grover Cleveland, of Caldwell, New Jersey.

In 1887, President Cleveland kindly ordered all captured Confederate flags returned to the South. But there were some very mean Yankees who got upset over the ruling, so he had to cancel it! Because of this, it wasn't until 1905 that the last remaining flags were given back to the South, 40 years after Lincoln's War. Better late than never.

SLEEPING

Confederate soldiers usually slept on the cold hard ground, out in the open. The luckier ones had canvas tents, such as the Sibley Tent, which looked something like an Indian teepee, had wooden doors, and was raised up off the ground.

Some Confederate officers, like General Robert E. Lee, refused to follow the usual custom of high-ranking officials of staying in a house or a tent, and instead slept on the ground with their men. This is one of the many reasons Lee was so loved by his soldiers!

COMMUNICATION

During Lincoln's War, it was very rare that two officers would go to meet each other in person. The distances were too great and travel was slow and dangerous.

Instead, Confederate armies communicated mainly by way of couriers (who delivered letters from one officer to another on horseback), the telegraph (electronic taps transmitted over wires), and signal towers—whose signalmen used colored lights, disks, and flags to send messages from tower to tower over many miles.

This Confederate courier is getting ready to deliver a field dispatch to another Rebel camp several miles away.

Sometimes secret messages were sent in coded telegrams called "ciphers." This way, if the message got intercepted, the Yankees wouldn't know what it said.

MUSIC

Many Confederate armies had their own regimental bands, made up mainly of bugles, flutes, and drums. Regimental bands performed for special occasions, like ceremonies and funerals.

The other type of band was the field band. Infantry field bands were made up of fifers and drummers (known as a fife and drum corps), while cavalry field bands were mainly just buglers.

Field musicians played a vital role in the War, announcing everything from when to get out of bed ("Reveille"), when to assemble ("Fall In"), and when to go to sleep ("Taps").

During battle, when the voice of the lead commander couldn't be heard (and sometimes he couldn't be seen either due to the powder smoke from cannons), the field musicians played various sounds and rhythms to help maneuver the soldiers around the battlefield.

This drummer served with the Louisiana Tigers.

Many of the musicians in our Rebel bands were African-American soldiers. At night around the campfire, these talented musicians would pull out their fiddles and banjos and everyone would sing and dance.

On some occasions, Yankees would yell out requests from across the battlefield, and our boys would play the songs for them to distant whistles and applause!

Black Confederate soldiers were among our most talented musicians.

CHAPTER 26

CONFEDERATE IMPLEMENTS OF WAR

WEAPONRY: SMALL ARMS

What kind of weapons did our Confederate ancestors use? They employed so many different types that it would be impossible to list them all here. So we'll only review some of their principle small arms.

Among them were:

- The 1816 Flintlock Musket: this slow-firing, slow-loading gun, using technology left over from the first Revolutionary War (1775-1783), was so out-of-date when it was handed out to soldiers at the beginning of the "Civil War" that it was almost unusable.
- The 1835 U.S. Musket: this old fashioned .69 caliber muzzle loader was also already outdated when Lincoln's War began in 1861. It was difficult to load, didn't shoot very far, was very heavy to carry, and was not very accurate.
- The 1841 U.S. Percussion Rifle: this .54 caliber gun was the first officially made military percussion rifle in America and was extremely popular.
- The 1842 Musket: this .69 caliber smoothbore was made at the Harpers Ferry Arsenal in Virginia. This out-of-date gun was the only rifle that many Southern soldiers had for the entire war.
- The 1855 Enfield Percussion Infantry Rifle: this reliable .577 caliber gun was made in Great Britain, and was quite

popular with the Rebel armies because it was lightweight and could hit its target at a great distance.

- The 1861 U.S. Springfield Rifle: because it was light, powerful, and accurate, this muzzle loading .58 caliber was one of the War's most commonly used rifles. Unfortunately for our Southern soldiers, most Springfields had to be taken from captured Yankee soldiers, for the Confederate government never had enough money to purchase large quantities.

ONE OF JOHNNY REB'S FAVORITE RIFLES

This Virginia volunteer infantryman is ready for battle with his 1842 musket and attached bayonet.

The guns the Confederate soldiers really wanted and needed were never available to them in great supply, due both to lack of money in the Confederate Treasury and Lincoln's illegal naval blockade—which greatly interfered with the shipment and delivery of goods in the South.

One of the most favored of the hard-to-get guns was the 1860 Spencer Carbine, a lightweight, long range, .52 caliber, repeating rifle that held seven bullets at once. This meant that it could be fired rapidly seven times in a row, all without stopping each time to reload.

The Yankees owned most of the Spencers that were made. Possessing these amazing longarms gave them a huge advantage over our Southern troops, most who had to use old fashioned muzzle loading rifles.

The muzzle loaders could only fire one shot at a time. After each shot, a soldier had to reload the rifle using a time-consuming process that took at least one to two minutes (usually more). During these precious 120 seconds, Confederate soldiers were left virtually defenseless, and many a brave Rebel died while trying to reload his father's old Revolutionary War musket.

Confederate soldiers were able to capture quite a few Spencer Carbines, but they could only use them until the ammunition ran out: Confederate bullet makers weren't able to make the cartridges these guns needed.

This Tennessee sharpshooter is carrying an 1855 Enfield rifle, capable of shooting accurately at long distances.

ONE OF JOHNNY REB'S FAVORITE HANDGUNS

One of the favorite handguns among Confederate soldiers was the Colt Model 1851 Navy Revolver. Though it only fired one bullet at a time, this .36 caliber weapon was easy to shoot and clean. Confederate General Nathan Bedford Forrest was well-known for his love of this particular gun.

Other handguns that were used by Rebel soldiers were the 1854 Lefaucheux Pinfire Revolver, the English Kerr Revolver, and the LeMat Revolver.

WEAPONRY: ARTILLERY

Artillery, that is, moveable guns, were heavily relied on by the Confederate armies, and for good reason: they could be the deciding factor in winning or losing a battle.

ONE OF JOHNNY REB'S FAVORITE FIELD GUNS
Among the preferred weapons from this class was the 1857 12-Pounder Field Gun, which could shoot a 12 pound ball an astonishing distance of nearly a mile (very far for that time period).

This gun was given the nickname the "Napoleon" because it was developed by the 19th-Century French Emperor Louis Napoleon Bonaparte. The Napoleon was the most commonly used artillery weapon throughout the War, and was responsible for helping the Southern armies win many battles against the Yankees.

Other Confederate artillery included the 1841 6-Pounder Field Gun, the 1841 32-Pounder (which swivelled on a hinge), the 1841 Coehorn Mortar, the lightweight 1841 Mountain Howitzer, the Whitworth Rifle, the Armstrong Rifle, and the massive and highly destructive Parrott Rifle—which could accurately fire 20 and 30 pound shells up to a distance of almost a mile and a half!

The Whitworth was one of the most common breech loading field cannons used by the Confederate armies.

These guns were incredibly destructive and, for four years, they helped Honest Jeff keep Dishonest Abe from taking over our homeland, the South.

DEFENSIVE FORTIFICATIONS

To protect *themselves* against such dangerous weapons, Confederate soldiers dug trenches (holes below ground) and earthworks (walls of dirt above ground).

For further protection, Rebels would often surround their defensive shelters with landmines, fallen trees, and abatis: tree branches that were carved into long sharp deadly points (the forerunner of barbed wire).

OTHER CONFEDERATE WEAPONS

Many other weapons were used by both sides during the "Civil War." Among these were:

- The Saber, Cutlass, and the Sword: these long edged weapons were used for close-quarter combat. But they went out of style among many Confederate regiments because they were so heavy and cumbersome.
- The Bayonet: used, like the saber, for hand-to-hand combat, the 18 inch bayonet was attached to the front of a rifle. Soldiers didn't like the bayonet any more than the sword, and found many other uses for it besides fighting, such as sticking a piece of meat on the tip for roasting over a campfire.
- Knives: Confederate soldiers carried a bewildering number of different types of knives, from the famous Bowie knife to homemade 16 inch blades created from used metal scraps.

This dangerous array of knives and daggers is an example of some of the many weapons used by our Confederate troops.

When it came to actual

combat though, soldiers found little use for their knives, and usually ended up throwing the heavy weapons away.
- The Mounted Railroad Cannon: as the name suggests, these were guns placed on trains so they could be moved quickly from one location to another. The most popular cannon in this group was the powerful 13 inch seacoast mortar known as the *Dictator*. When it was fired, the blast was so intense that the train car it was attached to would move as much as 12 feet down the railroad track!
- The Landmine: this devious weapon was invented by a Southerner named Brigadier General Gabriel J. Rains, and was used for the first time in Lincoln's War. Hidden under the surface of the ground, it was triggered by someone stepping on it. The landmine was never put to great use because both the Rebels and the Yankees rightly regarded it as a cowardly weapon.

These marine contact mines were made to explode if a ship touched them.

- The Hand Grenade: these small but deadly devices were made to explode after being thrown at an object.
- The Machine Gun: almost a half dozen different types of these "modern" weapons were employed during the "Civil War," but the Confederates preferred the William Rapid-Fire Gun, which was able to mow down the enemy with astonishing speed.
- The Observation Balloon: like the Union, the Confederacy used these large balloons to go high up into the sky, where they could keep an eye on the enemy.

Confederate soldiers used them early on in the War: Yankees spotted the first one near Big Bethel, Virginia, in the Summer of 1861.

CONFEDERATE ACCESSORIES
With all of this weaponry, Confederate soldiers had to have equipment to carry it and maintain it all. Here are some of the more common of these types of items, known as military "accouterments":

- The Tent: one of the Rebel soldier's most important accessories, the tent was intended to help keep the men warm in the winter and cool in the summer—though it often worked out the other way around! The smaller and lighter the tents were, the easier they were to carry, but the more uncomfortable they were to sleep in. The more common tents were the wedge tent, the wall tent, the umbrella tent, and the Sibley tent. However, the most popular was the pup tent: a simple piece of canvas thrown over a center pole, it held two men tightly crammed together. The Confederate armies never had enough tents to go around, and so they often created their own primitive shelters. Known as "shebangs," these were made from tree limbs, sticks, leaves, sod, blankets,

Tents were a staple of Civil War life. Unfortunately, the Confederate government never had enough to supply all of its soldiers.

and anything else that might keep out the sun, wind, and rain.
- The Haversack: made of canvas, the haversack had a large flap and a shoulder strap, and was carried like a modern day mailman's bag. Confederate soldiers used the haversack to carry all of their personal items, from food to letters.
- The Canteen: made from tin, the canteen was one of the Rebel soldier's most vital items. It was usually covered with wool (to keep the contents cool) and had a sling strap for carrying over the shoulder. The spout was often made of pewter, which was sealed with a cork stopper. Some rare canteens were made of wood. Most Rebel soldiers eventually ditched their canteens and replaced them with a tin cup, which was easier to carry and had more uses than a canteen.

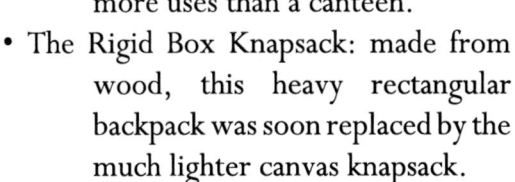

A Confederate haversack, with a wool blanket and a tin canteen.

- The Rigid Box Knapsack: made from wood, this heavy rectangular backpack was soon replaced by the much lighter canvas knapsack.
- The Knapsack: like modern knapsacks and backpacks, the Confederate's knapsack was worn on the back. In it he carried essentials, such as extra clothing, overcoat, blanket, rubber ground cloth, leftover food, pen, ink, paper, photographs, a Bible, and playing cards. Weighing as much as 25 pounds, most soldiers got rid of their canvas knapsacks early on in the War.
- The Holster: the common leather holster, which came in many different sizes and designs, was used to hold a soldier's

firearm.
- The Scabbard: those soldiers who carried swords and daggers (not many did) used this sheath to hold and protect them.
- The Sword Belt: the scabbard attached to the sword belt, which was worn around the waist.
- The Waist Belt: this simple leather belt, made to hold up the pants, was actually used for many different functions.
- The Cap Box: a leather pouch worn on the waist belt, it was used to carry copper percussion caps, a type of ammunition for old fashioned firearms.
- The Havelock: a small curtain attached to a soldier's hat to protect his neck.
- The Shoulder Belt and Cartridge Box: a small leather pouch attached to a shoulder strap, the "box" was used to carry rifle cartridges. Inside were pockets for carrying gun tools.

The havelock.

- The Wool Blanket: a vital necessity, no Rebel soldier wanted to be without one—though many were. Some rolled theirs up and tied them to the tops of their knapsacks.
- The Bullet Mold: a small metal item that looked something like a nutcracker, the bullet mold was used for making bullets—a common pastime in Confederate camps.
- The Caisson: a wooden chest used to hold ammunition.
- The Limber: cannons and caissons were attached to this two-wheeled vehicle for transportation.
- The Rubber Cloth: this waterproof "blanket" was used for a variety of purposes, such as spreading on the ground to keep from getting wet during the night, or making temporary shelters when tents weren't available.
- Spurs: made of brass, cavalrymen strapped spurs to the heels of their boots, and used them to urge on their horses.

This Confederate unit is transporting a large cannon on an ox-drawn limber to the site of their next battle.

PERSONNEL ORGANIZATION OF THE REBEL ARMY
If you've ever wondered about how the Confederate army was organized, here's a list of all the categories and their names:

- Squad or platoon: less than 100 soldiers.
- Company: 100 soldiers, commanded by a captain.
- Regiment: ten companies (equaling about 1,000 men), commanded by a colonel.
- Battalion: a military unit; also a regiment or a near regimental size unit (equaling about 1,000 men).
- Brigade: four regiments (equaling about 4,000 men), commanded by a brigadier general.
- Division: two to four brigades (equaling from 8,000 to 16,000 men), commanded by a major general.
- Corps: two to four divisions (equaling from 32,000 to 64,000 men), commanded by a lieutenant general.
- Army: two to four corps (equaling from 128,000 to 256,000 men), commanded by a full general.

COMMAND STRUCTURE OF THE REBEL ARMY

There were many different officer ranks in the Confederate military. To better understand them, here's a list, from highest to lowest rank:

General
Lieutenant General
Major General
Brigadier General
Colonel
Lieutenant Colonel
Major
Captain
First Lieutenant
Second Lieutenant

This, the first Confederate White House, was located at Montgomery, Alabama.

ENLISTED RANK STRUCTURE

Enlisted Confederate officers had a different ranking system. Here it is, from highest to lowest rank:

Sergeant Major
Quartermaster Sergeant
Ordnance Sergeant
First Sergeant
Sergeant
Corporal
Musician
Private

Section 5

FORBIDDEN FACTS THEY DON'T TEACH YOU IN SCHOOL

CHAPTER 27

THE HIDDEN TRUTH ABOUT THE CIVIL WAR

WHY YOUR TEACHERS WON'T TELL YOU THE TRUTH

In this chapter we're going to look at some "Civil War" facts that you'll never learn about in school. Why don't they teach these things? There are three possible answers to this question:

1. Some teachers may honestly not be aware of these facts: they've been hidden for so long that many teachers don't know anything about them.
2. Some teachers know about these facts, and want to teach them, but the school authorities won't allow them to.
3. By far the most common reason is that many teachers *do* know these hidden facts about the "Civil War." But they and the school authorities have decided that they don't want you to know about them. Why?

THE LIBERAL WAR AGAINST FREE SPEECH

As we discussed earlier, most of these types of people are liberals, people who only want their views heard. They only believe in freedom of speech for themselves, not for you and me!

However, it's illegal to prevent others from speaking and sharing their opinions, thoughts, and views, because the First Amendment of the Constitution promises each one of us "freedom of speech." Because this is a violation of the Constitution, what they're doing is wrong.

WHY YOU'RE NOT SUPPOSED TO KNOW THE TRUTH

But why would liberals want to keep you from knowing the truth about the "Civil War"?

It's because the South (C.S.A.) was actually the "good guy" in the War, while the North (U.S.A.) was actually the "bad guy." But the North won the War, so it has to pretend that it was in the right and that the South was in the wrong.

You see, the South fought for personal freedom, self-determination, self-government, and the Constitution. But the North fought *against* personal freedom, self-determination, self-government, and the Constitution. Who do *you* think was the good guy and the bad guy? Isn't it obvious?

The South fought for the Constitution, not slavery. General Stonewall Jackson, for example, was just one of millions of Southern non-slave owners who wanted to abolish slavery and allow blacks to fight in the Confederate army.

And it's obvious to your liberal school teachers too! But most liberals, scallywags, Yankees, and Northerners can't bring themselves to admit that the U.S. fought for all the wrong reasons. So they've had to make up all kinds of lies so that the South looks like the bad guy.

But the truth is something completely different dear reader. As Southern defender John Anderson Richardson wrote in 1914: "The South was right and the North was wrong!"

CIVIL WAR LIES CREATED BY THE NORTH

Here are the three main lies about the War that pro-North people thought up to make the South look bad:

Lie 1: The Civil War was fought over slavery: the South fought to preserve it; the North fought to destroy it.

Lie 2: The Civil War was fought over the Union: the South fought to destroy it; the North fought to preserve it.

Lie 3: The Civil War was fought over race: Southerners back then were racists, which is why they loved slavery and wanted to preserve it. Northerners back then were not racists, which is why they hated slavery and wanted to destroy it.

THE TRUE CAUSES OF THE CIVIL WAR
If these are all lies, then what's the truth? Actually, it's the opposite!

The Civil War wasn't fought over slavery, the Union, or race. In early 1861, Confederate Colonel John Brown Baldwin visited Lincoln at the White House and asked him why he wouldn't let the Southern states secede peacefully. Here's how Lincoln replied:

> "If I let the South go, what will become of the taxes the Southern states once paid the U.S. government?"

What is Lincoln saying here? He's saying that for him at least, the Civil War was about money! He didn't want to lose the millions of dollars in taxes that Southerners gave to the government each year.

But, some will ask, I thought the Civil War was fought over slavery? Not according to President Lincoln. Here, on August 15, 1864, is what Dishonest Abe had to say about this:

> "My enemies pretend I am now carrying on this

war for the sole purpose of abolition. So long as I am President, it shall be carried on for the sole purpose of restoring the Union."

Like Lincoln, Confederate President Jefferson Davis, Honest Jeff, was also clear about the real cause of the War—and it wasn't slavery:

"The truth remains intact and impossible to deny: the existence of African servitude in the South was in no way the cause of the conflict; it was only a side incident. In the later arguments that arose, however, people got so emotional over the topic that the historical facts were lost. I repeat: slavery was *not* the cause of the Civil War!"

What then did the South fight for?

THE SOUTH FOUGHT FOR FREEDOM

Southerners fought to defend their constitutional freedoms, and one of these freedoms was the right to decide what to do about slavery.

Even though nearly everyone in Dixie hated slavery and knew it was coming to an end, each of the Southern states simply wanted to decide how and when to end it themselves, one of the states' rights silently guaranteed in the Constitution (Tenth Amendment). Our people didn't want the North

Edmund Ruffin of Virginia was a farmer, author, and proud Confederate soldier who loved freedom so much that he refused to live in a nation ruled by Yankees.

telling them how and when to do it.

NOSEY NORTHERNERS
But Northerners at the time were very nosey. They wouldn't mind their own business. They didn't care about states' rights and they didn't like the Constitution. They thought they knew what was best for the South, and so they pushed and pushed us to end slavery before we were ready.

Have you ever seen what happens when someone tries to push a mule too hard? It kicks! And this is what the South did in 1861. When the North pushed too hard, the South kicked back. Lincoln called this the "Civil War." We call it the "War for the Southern Independence"!

Yankees wouldn't leave the South alone. They meddled in our business, preached to us, and tried to tell us what to do and how to live. When we refused to listen to them, they sent soldiers into Dixie to try and force us to do what they wanted. We had to defend ourselves. The result was the "Civil War"!

Though he died in 1850, some 11 years before the start of the Civil War, John C. Calhoun of South Carolina was one of the South's most important figures. Calhoun served in numerous important political positions, from senator and secretary of war, to secretary of state and vice president of the United States. He was also a strong supporter of some of our most cherished Southern principles: states' rights, free trade, small government, and nullification (the right of a state to throw out a Federal government law it believes is unconstitutional). Calhoun had a significant influence on the Southern secession movement, and was a great inspiration to our people when it came time for them to leave the Union beginning in December 1860.

CHAPTER 28

CABINETS, SOLDIERS, AND AN UNFAIR FIGHT

Now we're going to look at some everyday facts as well as some hidden facts about the "Civil War." Since this book is about the Southern view of the conflict, we're going to focus mainly on the Confederacy.

FULL CABINET OF THE DAVIS ADMINISTRATION

Although we mentioned the original men in President Jefferson Davis' cabinet earlier, some of these positions had more than one occupant during Lincoln's War. Here is a complete list in the order of their service:

Alexander Hamilton Stephens, vice president of the Confederate States of America under President Davis.

- President: Jefferson Davis (Honest Jeff)
- Vice President: Alexander H. Stephens
- Secretary of State: Robert A. Toombs, Robert M. T. Hunter, Judah P. Benjamin
- Secretary of the Treasury: Christopher G. Memminger, George A. Trenholm
- Secretary of War: LeRoy Pope Walker, Judah P. Benjamin,

George W. Randolph, Gustavus W. Smith, James A. Seddon, John C. Breckinridge
- Secretary of the Navy: Stephen R. Mallory
- Attorney General: Judah P. Benjamin, Thomas Bragg, Thomas H. Watts, George Davis
- Postmaster General: John H. Reagan
- General-in-Chief of Confederate Forces: Robert E. Lee

FULL CABINET OF THE LINCOLN ADMINISTRATION

Though our main interest is in our Confederate history, if you truly want to understand the "Civil War," you should familiarize yourself with the names of the men who served under Lincoln as well.

Along with Lincoln, many of these men were directly responsible for the terrible suffering our people went through between 1861 and 1865. Here are their names in the order of their service:

Hannibal Hamlin, vice president of the United States of America under President Lincoln.

- President: Abraham Lincoln (Dishonest Abe)
- Vice President: Hannibal Hamlin, Andrew Johnson
- Secretary of State: William H. Seward
- Secretary of the Treasury: Salmon P. Chase, William P. Fessenden, Hugh McCulloch
- Secretary of War: Simon Cameron, Edwin M. Stanton
- Secretary of the Navy: Gideon Welles
- Secretary of the Interior: Caleb B. Smith, John P. Usher
- Attorney General: Edward Bates, James Speed

- Postmaster General: Horatio King, Montgomery Blair, William Dennison
- General-in-Chief of Union Forces: Ulysses S. Grant

WHITE SOLDIERS FROM ALL THE STATES
Which states provided the most men to the "Civil War"? The following list shows the top ten states according to the total number of white soldiers that were recruited from each one:

1. New York: 450,000 Union soldiers
2. Pennsylvania: 340,000 Union soldiers
3. Ohio: 315,000 Union soldiers
4. Illinois: 260,000 Union soldiers
5. Indiana: 200,000 Union soldiers
6. Virginia: 193,000 Confederate soldiers
7. Tennessee: 167,000 Confederate soldiers
8. Missouri: 150,000 Confederate soldiers
9. Massachusetts: 147,000 Union soldiers
10. North Carolina: 135,000 Confederate soldiers

If you're a sharp reader, you'll notice that there are only four Southern states listed in the top ten. This is one of the many reasons that the South lost the "Civil War": we didn't have nearly as many soldiers as the North did.

THE YANKEES WERE THREE TIMES MORE POWERFUL
Here are the facts:

- The United States had about 3 million white soldiers.
- The Confederate States had about 1 million white soldiers.

This means that the Yankees had three times as many soldiers as we did in the South.

The North also had three times the amount of money we did, three times as many factories as we did, three times as much food, guns, and clothing for their soldiers, and three times the number of railroad tracks. These things gave the Yankees a huge advantage over us. Does this sound like a fair fight to you? Of course not.

But our soldiers were so courageous that they fought the Yanks anyway—and nearly won!

Confederate General Nathan Bedford Forrest had the perfect plan for beating the Yanks and winning the War, but none of the top Confederate authorities seriously considered his idea until it was too late.

HOW THE SOUTH COULD HAVE WON THE WAR

Keep this in mind: even though we were greatly outnumbered in almost every area, our brave soldiers kept the Yankees from illegally taking over the South for four long years.

But we *would* have won:

- if only Lincoln hadn't threatened war on Europe to keep her from supporting us.
- if only the Border states (Maryland, Delaware, West Virginia, Kentucky, and Missouri) had *fully* joined the Confederacy.
- if only we had stayed in the fight just one more year.
- if only General Nathan Bedford Forrest had been allowed to carry out his brilliant plan of keeping the War going long enough to wear out the North.

If any one of these things had occurred, you and I would be living in a free and independent country called the Confederate States of America today! There's proof that this is true.

In his 1885 *Memoirs*, here's what Union General Ulysses S. Grant said would have happened if the South had prolonged the War just 12 months past April 9, 1865, the day General Lee surrendered:

> "I think that this idea was the best one that could have been pursued by the South: keep the war going for as long as possible. This was all that was necessary to enable the Confederacy to gain recognition and independence in the end. We Yankees in the North were already growing weary. Anything that could have prolonged the war *one year* beyond the time that it finally ended, would have exhausted the North to such an extent that it might then have abandoned the contest and agreed to separation."

WHITE SOLDIERS FROM SOUTHERN STATES

Now let's look at the Southern states alone, and see how many white men actually served in the Confederate military from each one. Keep in mind that because there are very few exact records for the Confederacy, these are all rough estimates:

Union General Ulysses S. Grant said that the South could have won the War if she had only kept fighting for one more year.

1. Virginia: 155,000 soldiers
2. Georgia: 130,000 soldiers
3. North Carolina: 127,000 soldiers
4. Tennessee: 115,000 soldiers
5. Alabama: 100,000 soldiers
6. Mississippi: 85,000 soldiers
7. South Carolina: 60,000 soldiers
8. Texas: 58,000 soldiers
9. Louisiana: 53,000 soldiers
10. Arkansas: 45,000 soldiers
11. Missouri: 40,000 soldiers
12. Kentucky: 25,000 soldiers
13. Maryland: 20,000 soldiers
14. Florida: 15,000 soldiers
15. Indian Territory: 5,000 soldiers

This well dressed Frenchman served with the Confederacy in the Virginia cavalry.

Total: about 1 million white soldiers. This list doesn't include the 1 million black soldiers who served with the Confederacy.

Yes, I said black Confederate soldiers. Never heard of them? Since your school won't teach you the true facts of the "Civil War," that's not surprising. Read on!

This 13 inch Blakely gun was made specifically for the Confederacy by Alexander Blakely, an Irish cannon maker who supported the Southern Cause.

CHAPTER 29

OUR MULTI-COLORED CONFEDERATE ARMIES

A CONFEDERACY OF MANY COLORS

Though your history books at school tell you that the Confederate military was an all-white European-American force, this is a lie meant to keep you from knowing the truth. And what is the truth?

The Southern armies were a mixture of nearly every race, creed, nationality, religion, and color, encompassing people from around the globe, from Europe and Asia to South America and Australia! Let's look at some of these.

The Confederate army was composed of the following nationalities (listed in alphabetical order):

African	Italian
Asian	Jewish
Australian	Latino
British	Mexican
Canadian	Mixed
Danish	Polish
English	Scottish
French	Spanish
German	Swedish
Greek	Swiss
Hungarian	Welsh
Irish	West Indian

There were many other nationalities in the Confederate army than these, of course. This is only a partial list. The South's First Louisiana regiment alone had almost forty different nationalities in it.

BLACK CONFEDERATE SOLDIERS

One of the most common statements you'll read in your school history books is this: "No African-Americans (blacks) fought on the Confederate side." Northerners, liberals, and scallywags love to repeat this supposed "fact" over and over again. There's only one problem with it: it's completely false!

Actually, so many black men fought for the Confederacy that no one has ever been able to count them all! The lowest estimate is 300,000 while the highest estimate is 1 million. Using the Yankee's definition of a "soldier," it was probably the higher of the two: "A soldier is any man employed in military service who receives pay, whether officially or unofficially."

Hundreds of thousands of black men worked for pay for the Confederate armies in such occupations as

As many as 1 million African-Americans served with the Confederacy. The black soldier above was attending a Confederate Reunion in 1913 when this photo was taken.

Nelson W. Winbush, a friend of the author, is the living grandson of Private Louis Napoleon Nelson, a black Confederate soldier who served in the Civil War under Rebel General Nathan Bedford Forrest. Mr. Winbush is holding his grandfather's Confederate uniform. On his lapel is a General Forrest button. Like the author, Mr. Winbush is a member of the Sons of Confederate Veterans, an organization devoted to preserving the truth about our Confederate heritage. (Photo © N. W. Winbush.)

laborers, teamsters, sutlers, chaplains, cooks, miners, nurses, musicians, sappers (soldiers who specialize in mines), spies, cattle drovers, pioneers, and construction workers alone. Hundreds of thousands more actually put on Confederate gray uniforms, drilled and trained, and fought right next to their white brothers on the battlefield.

Here's something you won't ever learn about in school: the first Yankee to be killed in the "Civil War," Major Theodore Winthrop of the Seventh New York Regiment, was shot down by a highly skilled black Confederate sharpshooter at the Battle of Bethel Church, June 10, 1861.

Confederate General John H. Morgan enlisted blacks from Mississippi for his fearsome partisan rangers, while Louisiana Governor Thomas O. Moore enrolled hundreds of blacks in the state's militia. General Stonewall Jackson's army alone had some 3,000 black soldiers. This was more than the population of most Southern towns!

Yankee soldiers who witnessed Jackson's African-American troops were paralyzed with fear and shock: they had never seen anything like it before. This is because, at the time, Lincoln wouldn't allow black men to serve in the U.S. armies.

So white Yankee troops weren't used to seeing blacks on the battlefield.

One Union soldier who saw them described Jackson's black soldiers like this:

"They were wearing all kinds of uniforms, and were armed with rifles, muskets, swords, Bowie knives, and Scottish daggers. They were obviously a real and integral part of the Confederate army."

One of the South's favorite officers, General Nathan Bedford Forrest, had sixty-five blacks fighting with him throughout the War. A half dozen of these proudly served as his personal armed guards.

A friend of mine, African-American educator Nelson W. Winbush, is the living grandson of one of the black soldiers who rode with General Forrest. His name was Private Louis Napoleon Nelson, the only known black Confederate chaplain.

Confederate Private Louis Napoleon Nelson, one of the hundreds of thousands of African-American who served with the Rebel army and navy during the Civil War. Private Nelson is the grandfather of Nelson W. Winbush. (Photo © N. W. Winbush.)

The black Confederate soldier was real, so don't let anyone try to tell you he wasn't! Here is more proof.

LINCOLN REFUSED TO ENLIST BLACKS

All through the first few years of his War, Lincoln banned people of color from serving in the U.S. armies. This included not only blacks, but Indians and other "colored people" as well, or "mongrels," as Lincoln called *all* people with light brown skin.

In particular, Lincoln didn't like the "inferior race," his term for black people. He often said that he wished they could all be put in their own all-black state; or better yet, be sent out of the U.S. to another country altogether. You'll remember that Lincoln was a black colonizationist who wanted to deport all African-Americans to a foreign country, like Liberia in Africa.

Lincoln was so against the idea of arming blacks that in October 1861 he "strongly warned" his cabinet against introducing any bills that called for giving guns to "negroes." When his secretary of war, Edwin M. Stanton, ignored the warning and issued a statement favoring the idea, Lincoln fired him!

During the first year of the Civil War, black abolition leader Frederick Douglass grew very angry with President Lincoln for refusing to allow African-Americans to serve in the U.S. army.

American black leaders were furious at Lincoln's obvious racism. One of these was a former Northern slave named Frederick Douglass.

Douglass was a brilliant speaker, writer, and abolitionist who wanted to fight in the Union army. But Lincoln wouldn't let him because of the color of his skin.

Finally, in late 1861, Douglass got so mad he decided to write the racist president a letter. He wanted to try and convince Lincoln to allow blacks to fight in the U.S. armies. He did this by telling Lincoln about all of the blacks that were already serving in the Confederate army. Here's what Douglass wrote:

> "Dear Mr. President: There are at the present moment, many colored men in the Confederate Army doing duty not only as cooks, servants and laborers, but as real soldiers, having muskets on their shoulders and bullets in their pockets, ready to shoot down loyal Yankee troops, and do all that soldiers may do to destroy the Federal government and build up that of the traitors and rebels. There were such soldiers at Manassas, and they are probably there still. There is a negro in the Confederate army as well as in the fence, and our Government is likely to find it out before the war comes to an end. That the negroes are numerous in the Rebel army, and do for that army it heaviest work, is beyond question."

Despite Douglass' letter, Lincoln waited nearly another two years before he allowed blacks to fight in his military, only allowing them to join after he issued his Final Emancipation Proclamation on January 1, 1863! Even then, Dishonest Abe kept them segregated in their own all-black units, wouldn't let them wear proper Yankee uniforms or carry guns, and gave them less money than he gave his white soldiers!

DAVIS TREATED BLACK SOLDIERS FAIRLY
This was quite the opposite of how Confederate President Jefferson Davis, Honest Jeff, handled the South's black troops. Our black soldiers were integrated right alongside our white soldiers; they wore proper Confederate uniforms and carried guns; and they were paid the same as our white soldiers, and in some cases, were paid much more!

This black Union soldier guarding a Whitworth field gun didn't have it easy serving in Lincoln's army: the racist Yankee president segregated his African-American soldiers into black-only units, wouldn't let them become commissioned officers, paid them half as much as white soldiers, and refused them their military pensions. Lincoln even ordered that injured white soldiers were to be given medical treatment before injured black soldiers. As a result, thousands of black Yankee soldiers deserted the Union and joined forces with the Confederacy, where they were treated as equals!

CHAPTER 30

BLACK, INDIAN, JEWISH, & LATINO CONFEDERATE SOLDIERS

MORE ABOUT AFRICAN-AMERICAN CONFEDERATES

Let's look at one more piece of evidence showing that hundreds of thousands of Southern blacks fought for the Confederacy.

The following article appeared in the *Charleston Evening News*, May 1, 1861:

> "Quite a novel spectacle was witnessed recently in Petersburg, Virginia, as we are informed by a gentleman who just arrived from that city. One hundred and twenty free negroes, uniformed with red shirts and dark pants, and bearing a flag of the Southern Confederacy, which had been presented to them by the ladies, marched through the city and got on the trains for Norfolk, Virginia. They proceeded upon this excursion of their own free will, in response to the request made by Confederate General Gwynn for the services of six hundred negroes from any portion of the State, to work upon the fortifications around Norfolk harbor. They were all in the finest spirits, and seemed anxious to 'catch Old Linkum one time'— a desire which appeared to be foremost in their thoughts. They certainly deserve great credit for their selflessness, and will

find that it is appreciated by all Southern people."

Many more examples of this sort of thing could be given.

The truth is that not only did blacks serve with the Confederacy, but many more blacks fought for the Confederacy than fought for the Union!

Here are some statistics you need to know:

- Of the North's 3 million soldiers, only 200,000 were black, just 6 percent of the total.
- To the South's 1 million white soldiers we must add an additional 300,000 black soldiers (never officially counted), who made up 23 percent of the total. If we go with the higher estimate of 1 million black Confederate soldiers, then 50 percent of the Southern army and navy were African-Americans!

Judah P. Benjamin, known as the "brains of the Confederacy," served in numerous important positions under President Davis. Benjamin was just one of tens of thousands of Jews who sided with the Confederacy.

OTHER GROUPS WHO FOUGHT FOR THE SOUTH

There were tens of thousands from other races and ethnic groups that fought for the Confederacy as well, such as Native-Americans and Jews.

Here is the closest thing we have to a complete list. The men who wore Confederate gray and sided with the South included soldiers from the following backgrounds:

- 1 million European-Americans (whites)
- 300,000 to 1 million African-Americans (blacks)
- 70,000 Native-Americans (reds)
- 60,000 Latin-Americans (browns)
- 50,000 foreigners (all colors)
- 12,000 Jewish-Americans (whites)
- 10,000 Asian-Americans (yellows)

NATIVE-AMERICAN CONFEDERATES
Native-Americans in particular battled courageously against Lincoln and his illegal invaders.

For example, thousands from the "Five Civilized Tribes"—the Cherokee, the Creek, the Choctaw, the Chickasaw, and the Seminoles—served under Rebel officers like General Earl Van Dorn and Colonel Douglas H. Cooper. The Choctaw were so supportive of the South that they officially sided with the Confederacy in February 1861, two months *before* the start of the "Civil War."

Thousands of Native-Americans fought bravely with the Confederacy against Lincoln and Northern tyranny.

And let's not forget the amazing and loyal Indian officer, General Stand Watie (Chief Degataga), the last Confederate general of the entire War to surrender.

To all of these fearless men the South owes its eternal gratitude!

While most of your school teachers may want to ignore the truth about the Confederacy and our multi-colored soldiers, we Southerners are proud of our multiracial history and armies!

THE OCCUPATIONS OF CIVIL WAR SOLDIERS

Have you ever wondered what Rebel and Yankee soldiers did for a living before they fought in the "Civil War"? Here's the answer:

- Most Confederate private soldiers were farmers.
- Most Union private soldiers were businessmen.
- Most Confederate officers were lawyers.
- Most Union officers were professional military men.
- About 42 percent of Confederate officers were farmers.
- Only 23 percent of Union officers were farmers.
- About 3 percent of Confederate officers were clergymen.
- Only 1 percent of Union officers were clergymen.

EUROPEAN ROYALS IN THE CONFEDERACY

Did you know that a number of European knights fought in the Confederate armies? Here are the names of some of them:

- George St. Leger
- Justus Scheibert
- Prince de Polignac
- Charles Cavenish
- Augustus Buchel
- Adolphus H. Adler
- Heros von Borcke
- Arthus Fremantle
- Karl Friedrich Henningson
- Bela Estran
- George Gordon
- Morton Stanley

Many Europeans knights served with the South.

A section of the Confederate Memorial at Arlington National Cemetery. Look closely at the man in the middle: he's an armed black Confederate soldier, marching off to war, side by side with his white brothers—more proof of the African-American Confederate!

CHAPTER 31

WOMEN, HORSES, BEARDS, & MUSIC

WHITE FEMALE CONFEDERATE SOLDIERS

Although only males were allowed to join the Confederate military, many girls and women wanted to fight for Dixie so badly that they snuck in, usually by disguising themselves as boys and men!

We don't know how many female Confederate soldiers there were, but they probably numbered in the hundreds, or perhaps even the thousands.

Here are the names of some of our white female soldiers:

- Laura J. Williams
- Amy Clarke
- Mary Wright
- Molly Bell
- Loreta J. Velasquez
- Malinda Blalock
- Mary Bell
- Margaret Henry

A number of our most important Confederate spies were women. Among the most famous were Rose O'Neal Greenhow and Belle Boyd. Both were caught and served time in prison, after which they were sent back to Dixie. Before their arrest, however, they each managed to obtain very valuable information from the Yankees that helped the Confederacy.

CAPTAIN SALLY TOMPKINS

Though she didn't fight on the battlefield, Sally Tompkins of Virginia was given a Confederate officer's commission for operating the South's best, cleanest, and most efficient civilian military hospital.

"Captain Sally," as she was affectionately known, treated 1,300 wounded Rebel soldiers at Robertson Hospital (the home of Judge John Robertson) in Richmond, and had the lowest death rate of all the private Rebel hospitals. For her dedication and hard work she was called the "Angel of the Confederacy."

Confederate spy Rose O'Neal Greenhow is still considered a heroine here in Dixie for risking her life for the Southern Cause.

FEMALE CONFEDERATE CIVILIANS

There were also Southern women who did duty in the Confederacy but were not soldiers, such as the vivandières: civilian females who were connected to the Confederate armies and who were assigned a variety of camp and hospital chores.

BLACK FEMALE CONFEDERATE SOLDIERS

There were plenty of Southern black girls and women who snuck into the Confederate armies too. We don't know their names, but we do know that many of them served as spies, cooks, and couriers.

Black girls and women also picked up guns and went out onto the battlefield. Of the estimated 1 million black males who fought on the side of the Confederacy, we can be quite sure that some of them were brave black women disguised as men!

A CONFEDERATE BOY SOLDIER

One of the most famous Confederates was a boy named "Little Irish." He joined Kentucky's celebrated "Orphan Brigade" when he was only ten years old, serving as a drummer boy at such fights as the Battle of Shiloh and the Battle of Murfreesboro.

Southern men were extremely grateful for the enormous aid Southern women provided the Confederacy during the Civil War. Years later, President Davis, Honest Jeff, wrote: "Our women's zealous faith in our cause shone like a guiding star undimmed by the darkest clouds of war."

HORSES

All of the important Confederate figures had their prize horses. Here are the names of some of the more famous ones:

- Robert E. Lee's favorite horse: Traveller.
- Stonewall Jackson's favorite horse: Old Sorrel.
- Nathan Bedford Forrest's favorite horse: Roderick.
- M. Jeff Thompson's favorite horse: Sardanapalus.
- William B. Bate's favorite horse: Black Hawk.
- Jeb Stuart's favorite horse: Virginia.

- Belle Boyd's favorite horse: Fleeter.
- Patrick R. Cleburne's favorite horse: Dixie.
- Albert S. Johnston's favorite horse: Fire-Eater.
- William I. Rasin's favorite horse: Beauregard.
- Adam R. Johnson's favorite horse: Joe Smith.
- Richard S. Ewell's favorite horse: Rifle.
- Fitzhugh Lee's favorite horse: Nellie Gray.

Confederate General Robert E. Lee astride his favorite warhorse Traveller.

Most generals in the War had at least one horse shot out from under them. Confederate General Nathan Bedford Forrest had the most: 29 mounts were killed while he was riding them! Yankee war criminal General William T. Sherman had only 5 horses shot while he was riding them. In one battle alone, Confederate General Patrick R. Cleburne had two horses killed—one which he was in the process of mounting!

BEARDS & MUSTACHES

Facial hair was more popular in the mid 1800s than it is today. And so most Civil War officers on both sides had beards and mustaches: almost 90 percent, or almost three-quarters. Only about 10 percent were clean shaven.

Like most Confederate officers, General Wade Hampton sported a beard and mustache.

JOHNNY REB'S FAVORITE CIVIL WAR SONGS

Just like today, during Lincoln's War Southerners had their favorite songs. The following is a list of some of them (a few of these were favorites of Yankee soldiers too—marked with an asterisk):

- The Bonnie Blue Flag
- Just Before the Battle, Mother*
- Dixie's Land
- Yellow Rose of Texas
- When This Cruel War is Over*
- The Rebel Soldier
- God Save the South
- All Quiet Along the Potomac Tonight*
- I'm a Good Ole' Rebel
- Lorena*
- Stonewall Jackson's Way
- Tenting On the Old Camp Ground*

CONFEDERATE GENERALS WHO DIED IN THE WAR

Here's a sad statistic: The South had 425 generals. Of these, 77 were killed while fighting Lincoln and his illegal invaders. That's a little over 18 percent of the total number of Rebel generals.

The cover sheet of a popular 19th-Century piece of Confederate music known as The Conquered Banner.

THE LONGEST SURVIVING REBEL GENERAL

The Confederate general who lived the longest after the "Civil War" was Felix Huston Robertson of Washington, Texas. General Robertson was born March 9, 1839, and died April 20, 1928. This means that the 89 year old officer lived another 63 years after the War ended.

THE LAST SOLDIERS

The last Confederate Reunion was held in 1951. Only three (very old) Confederate veterans were there.

Although no one will ever know for sure who the last surviving Confederate soldier was, it was almost certainly Walter Washington Williams from Mississippi. Williams was born in 1842 and died in 1959. He was 117 years old at the time of his death!

The last surviving Union soldier seems to have been Albert Woolson of Minnesota. He died in 1956 at age 106.

Section 6

IMPORTANT FACTS YOU NEED TO KNOW

CHAPTER 32

IMPORTANT FACTS ABOUT THE CIVIL WAR

YOU SHOULD KNOW THAT . . .
- The total cost of the War to the North was the equivalent of $9 trillion in today's money.
- It would have only cost the modern equivalent of $900 billion to free America's slaves, ten times *less* than it cost to go to war. (Obviously, the War was *not* over slavery!)
- Lincoln and his Yankee soldiers were directly responsible for the deaths of about 1 million Southern whites and 1 million Southern blacks. (These deaths were never recorded, and the truth about them has been suppressed by pro-North historians for the past 150 years.)
- It's estimated that there were about 10,455 military engagements during the "Civil War," but there were probably far more than that.
- Yankee General Winfield Scott proposed the "Anaconda Plan," meant to strangle and eventually cut the Confederacy in two.

Yankee General Winfield Scott came up with the idea that won the War for the North: the Anaconda Plan.

- The state that had the most Civil War battles fought in it was Virginia.
- As early as 1864, Northerners planned on murdering President Jefferson Davis and his entire cabinet.
- The South was blamed for the murder of President Abraham Lincoln, yet his killer was actually a Northerner named John Wilkes Booth.
- The American abolition movement started in the South, not in the North.
- Both American slavery and the American slave trade began in the North, not in the South.
- Cotton was once so important to the American economy that it was called "white gold."
- Confederate cavalrymen sometimes spent as much as 24 hours, an entire day and night, in the saddle without stopping.
- The famous American outlaw Jesse James was a Confederate soldier.
- The United States Constitution doesn't mention God.
- The Confederate Constitution not only mentions God, it calls him "Almighty God."
- The Battle of Cold Harbor was so ferocious that during one particular engagement nearly 2 Yankee soldiers were killed per second.
- Africans were enslaving one another thousands of years before the arrival of Yankee slave traders in the 1600s.
- There were white slaves in America before there were black slaves.

King Cotton ruled both the South and the North for over 100 years.

- White slavery in early America laid the groundwork for the introduction of black slavery.
- From the beginning of Lincoln's War, numerous important Confederate leaders, from Patrick R. Cleburne to Robert E. Lee, were pushing for both emancipation and black enlistment.
- As many as 1,000,000 blacks fought for the Confederacy, 80 percent more than fought for Lincoln and the North.
- While only 6 percent of the Union military was black, up to 50 percent of the Confederate military was black.
- Of the South's 3,500,000 black servants, only 500,000 (just 14 percent) were imported by Yankees from Africa between 1607 (the settling of Jamestown, Virginia) and 1861. (The other 3,000,000, that is, the remaining 86 percent, were all American-born, the result of natural reproduction.)
- Most black Union soldiers didn't voluntarily join Lincoln's armies, as you've been taught. They were forced to "enlist" at gunpoint, and blacks who resisted were often whipped or even shot on the spot by white Yankee officers!
- There were tens of thousands of black and Native-American slave owners in the North and in the South before and up to the "Civil War."

Union General William T. Sherman was directly responsible for the deaths of thousands of Southerners and the destruction of millions of dollars of Southern property. This Yankee war criminal's name is still spoken with distaste here in the South.

- Percentage wise, there were far more black slave owners than white, and on average Indian slave owners owned more slaves than white slave owners.
- Southern whites and blacks had friendly relationships before and during the Civil War.
- Northern whites and blacks had unfriendly relationships before and during the Civil War.
- In 1884, Southern writer Mark Twain wrote a children's book called *Adventures of Huckleberry Finn*, about the wonderful friendship between a white boy and a black boy in the 1830s South.
- White Southerners didn't whip or keep their slaves in chains. Instead, they treated them with great respect, and even love, and considered them "members of the family."
- The "Civil War Amendments" are the Thirteenth, Fourteenth, and Fifteenth Amendments of the U.S. Constitution.
- The Fourteenth Amendment was an anti-South document, written by Yankees to purposefully hurt Southerners.
- The Fourteenth Amendment was never officially or correctly formalized, and is therefore not legal.
- The "Civil War" produced hundreds of Yankee war criminals, such as Abraham Lincoln, Ulysses S. Grant, William T. Sherman, Benjamin "the Beast" Butler, Philip Sheridan,

Native-Americans were practicing slavery on each other for millennia before Europeans arrived. After African slaves were brought to America by Yankee slave traders in the 1600s, Indians also became avid owners of black slaves, and owned more, on average, than white slave owners did.

John Pope, David Hunter, Robert H. Milroy, and Edward Hatch, just to name a few.
- Yankee General William T. Sherman's 26 day "March to the Sea" (November 15 to December 10, 1864) destroyed the equivalent of $150 billion of property in Georgia.
- Southerners usually named Civil War battles after the nearest town, while Northerners named them after the nearest river or lake.
- The last Confederate ship to fly the Rebel flag was the CSS *Shenandoah*, which lowered our sacred banner for the last time on November 6, 1865.
- Despite the fact that Lincoln was a racist, an immoral man, and a war criminal, every year uneducated Americans continue to vote him "America's best president"!
- Lincoln did so much damage to the South during his War that we still haven't fully recovered.

Lincoln and his soldiers did their best to destroy as many of our beautiful Southern cities as possible. Here is how one of them, Richmond, Virginia, looked shortly after the Civil War ended in April 1865. Richmond has since been rebuilt and we long ago forgave the North. But we will never forget.

CHAPTER 33

IMPORTANT FACTS ABOUT JEFFERSON DAVIS

YOU SHOULD KNOW THAT...
- Confederate President Jefferson Davis and U.S. President Abraham Lincoln were both from Kentucky.
- Davis and Lincoln were born only 100 miles from each other, and some people think they were secret brothers.
- Northern writers try to portray President Davis as a cold and inhumane man, even nicknaming him the "Sphinx." The truth is that all who knew him personally said he was warm, friendly, and generous.
- Davis served faithfully in the U.S. army before the "Civil War."
- Davis served as secretary of war under U.S. President Franklin Pierce.
- While serving as U.S. secretary of war, Davis introduced a new type of gun to the U.S. army, the rifle, which—tragically—later helped the Yankees beat the Rebels during the "Civil War."
- At first Davis didn't want the South to secede from the Union.
- Davis didn't ask to be or want to be president of the Confederacy. He was elected against his wishes by other

Honest Jeff was the first and only president of the Southern Confederacy—so far. We're hoping to elect a second C.S. president someday!

Southerners, who believed the brilliant but humble statesman would make the best leader.
- I call Davis "Honest Jeff" because, unlike "Dishonest Abe," he didn't repeatedly violate the Constitution, arrest, imprison, torture, and murder his own people, rig his own election, start an unnecessary and illegal war against the North, or lie to the America public.
- Davis was the Confederacy's first and only president. When the South rises again, and we hope this happens soon, we'll elect our second president!

President Davis' library at his home "Beauvoir" in Biloxi, Mississippi.

- During the War, Davis and his wife Varina adopted an orphaned black boy named Jim Limber and raised him at the Confederate White House in Richmond, Virginia.
- Davis and his wife always treated their black servants fairly and with the greatest respect, as part of their family in fact.
- In November 1864, Davis began promoting the idea of enlisting and drilling blacks for military service.
- In March 1865, Davis officially allowed blacks to enlist in the Confederate armies. (Remember: Southern blacks had been serving *unofficially* in the Confederate army and navy from the very beginning of the War.)
- Unlike Lincoln, Davis integrated his black Confederate soldiers in with his white Confederate soldiers, gave them equal pay, and provided them with military pensions.

- Like all other Southerners, Davis knew that slavery was coming to an end, and he was happy to see it finally abolished.
- After General Lee's surrender, during the Davis family's escape to the south, their coachman was a "faithful" free black man.
- After the War, President Davis sold his plantation, "Brierfield," to a former slave.
- Davis once led a group of armed "negroes against a lawless body of armed white men . . ." (This is something we can be sure Mr. Lincoln never did!)
- After the War, Davis was illegally arrested and jailed for "treason," and almost died in prison.
- Davis asked to be tried in a court of law but the U.S. government refused him because they knew that a trial would expose the illegalities of Lincoln's War on the South!

A Confederate reunion, about 1890. This one is for the men of General Nathan Bedford Forrest's Escort. Three of Forrest's black soldiers are in attendance. One is holding a Confederate flag (far right, back row).

CHAPTER 34

IMPORTANT FACTS ABOUT ABRAHAM LINCOLN

YOU SHOULD KNOW THAT . . .
- U.S. President Abraham Lincoln was mentally ill, and also had a medical condition called "Marfan Syndrome."
- Lincoln called himself "dumb," and didn't think he was worthy of being president.
- Lincoln was elected with less than half the popular vote in 1860.
- Lincoln only won the 1864 election because he bribed government officials, threatened voters, promised gifts to his supporters, pressured his soldiers to vote for him, censored the newspapers (so they couldn't write bad things about him), and imprisoned all those who didn't like him (so they couldn't speak out against him).
- Lincoln didn't "preserve the union," he destroyed it. (Our Union was meant to be *voluntary*. Lincoln made it *involuntary*.)
- Lincoln's Emancipation Proclamation freed no slaves.
- Lincoln funded the "Civil War" and his two presidential campaigns using profits from Northern slavery.

Lincoln suffered from a host of physical and psychological ailments, from mental illness and depression, to terrifying premonitions and Marfan Syndrome.

- One of Lincoln's best friends and his business partner, William H. Herndon, called the president "a tricky, cunning, dangerous, shrewd man, who must be watched closely and never trusted."
- Secession is legal, therefore the South had every right to secede, making the "Civil War" illegal and Lincoln a war criminal.
- It was not the South, but Lincoln who started the Civil War.
- Lincoln did not fight the South over slavery. It was about money (the tariff), as he stated clearly in his First Inaugural Address.
- Ignoring the oath he took at swearing in, Lincoln undermined the U.S. Constitution, eventually drastically altering it from the original version created by the Founding Fathers.
- Lincoln's goal was always to stop the spread of slavery across the U.S., not end slavery completely.

As Lincoln himself declared in his First Inaugural Address on March 4, 1861, he never had any intention of ending slavery. What he really wanted, as he clearly stated in an October 16, 1854, speech at Peoria, Illinois, was merely to restrict it to the South. The reason? So that he and other Northerners wouldn't have to live around blacks, or compete with them for jobs and housing.

- Lincoln wanted to restrict the spread of slavery because he didn't want whites to have to compete with blacks for jobs and homes.
- Lincoln said that if there was ever a race war between whites and blacks, he would be "for the whites."

- Lincoln said whites are intellectually and physically superior to blacks, just one reason abolitionists didn't like him.
- Lincoln once declared that he wished that all African-Americans could be put in their own all-black state.
- Throughout 1861 and 1862, Lincoln barred both blacks and Indians from serving in the U.S. military (even though many, like black leader Frederick Douglass, begged to be allowed to enlist).
- Lincoln's ban on enlisting blacks in the Union army was supported by most of his cabinet members and military officers, among them: William T. Sherman, George H. Thomas, and Henry W. Halleck.
- After Lincoln finally reluctantly allowed blacks to enlist in the U.S. army in 1863, his white soldiers harassed and abused them so badly that military laws had to be passed to protect black Union soldiers.

Lincoln's general-in-chief at the time, Henry W. Halleck, backed the president's racist policy to prohibit blacks from serving in the U.S. army.

- Unlike President Davis, Lincoln segregated black Union soldiers into their own all-black units, paid them half as much as white soldiers, and refused to give them pensions or proper medical care.
- Lincoln wouldn't allow black Union soldiers to become commissioned officers.
- Lincoln's Preliminary Emancipation Proclamation, issued on September 22, 1862, asked Congress to fund black

deportation, and contained his promise to continue efforts to have all American blacks shipped "back to Africa."
- Lincoln had to be pushed, cajoled, and pressured for years by abolitionists to issue the Final Emancipation Proclamation on January 1, 1863.
- Lincoln cared so little about ending slavery and black civil rights that if he had not become president, slavery would have been abolished sooner.
- During his presidency, most African-Americans deplored and condemned Lincoln because of his many anti-black policies.
- Modern educated blacks dislike Lincoln for the same reasons.
- Lincoln actually proposed a proslavery amendment to the Constitution in 1861, one that would have allowed the Southern states to continue practicing slavery indefinitely.
- Early in the War, Lincoln prohibited his cabinet members and military officers from freeing Southern slaves.
- Lincoln committed thousands of unlawful acts, not only against the South, but against the North as well.
- Lincoln ordered or allowed the illegal arrest, imprisonment, torture, and murder of hundreds of thousands of Southerners and Northerners, soldiers and civilians,

Lincoln referred to all light brown skinned people, like Mexicans, as "mongrels," the name for an unwanted or undesirable animal.

whites, blacks, coloreds, and Native-Americans.
- Lincoln referred to blacks, Hispanics, and Native-Americans as "inferior races."
- Lincoln referred to light brown skinned people, like Mexicans, as "mongrels."
- Lincoln was a white racist, a white supremacist, and a white separatist who campaigned throughout his entire political career for American apartheid, and who helped create and pass laws designed to restrict the advancement of black people.
- Many modern racist groups, like the KKK, actually admire Lincoln because of his racist views.
- As a lawyer Lincoln defended not slaves, but slave owners.
- Lincoln used slaves to finish building the White House, the U.S. Capitol, and many other government buildings around Washington, D.C.
- Lincoln hated abolitionists and believed that abolition caused more problems than slavery.
- Lincoln was a leader in the American Colonization Society, an organization whose stated mission was to ship all blacks back to Africa in order to make America "white from

As a lifelong member of the Yankees' American Colonization Society, Lincoln supported the idea of shipping all African-Americans "back to their native land," as he put it. Very few blacks wanted to leave the U.S. and the plan was completely unworkable. But this didn't stop the colonizationist president from promoting his racist plan at every opportunity—both in private and in public—until the day he died.

coast to coast."
- Lincoln's Emancipation Proclamation was unlawful, as he himself admitted.
- Lincoln never intended his Emancipation Proclamation to be permanent; it was meant to be only a temporary "war measure."
- Lincoln issued the Emancipation Proclamation primarily because his armies were dwindling and he needed more men.
- Though a Republican, Lincoln was an ultra left-wing liberal who was obsessed with big government, big business, big spending, and Big Brother politics, the complete opposite of the Confederacy's conservative, Democratic President Jefferson Davis.
- Lincoln had no interest at all in true civil rights for blacks, women, children, or any other minority.
- Lincoln was wholly against interracial marriage, black citizenship, and black suffrage.
- One of Lincoln's closest black "friends," Frederick Douglass, said that the president's policies regarding American blacks were "missing the genuine spark of humanity."
- Polls in his day show that Lincoln was voted the worst president in U.S. history by the American people.
- During the Mexican-American War, Lincoln repeatedly put

Lincoln was an anti-Christian atheist who once wrote a "little book" calling the Bible an "uninspired" work of fairy tales, Jesus an ordinary man, and God a childish myth. This is quite unlike here in the South where the Bible is our favorite book, where we worship Jesus as our divine Savior, and where all reasonable people believe in God.

U.S. troops at risk by issuing antiwar statements.
- Lincoln was an atheist who wrote a "little book" denying the divinity of Christ and declaring the Bible to be false.
- One of Lincoln's lifelong goals was to rid the U.S. of all "persons of African descent," as he phrased it.
- Lincoln once said the following during a public speech: "What I would most desire would be the separation of the white and black races."
- Blacks weren't allowed to attend Lincoln's funeral.
- Lincoln was not called "Honest Abe" because he was honest. It was because he was dishonest!
- Lincoln altered the original and intended meaning of the term United States from plural to singular. Before the Civil War, one said "The United States are . . ." After the War, one said "The United States is . . ."
- Lincoln was hated in the South for being a Northerner and hated in the North for being a Southerner.

Lincoln allowed his Yankee soldiers to bomb the lovely Southern city of Charleston, South Carolina, into rubble, seen here in April 1865. He called this type of mindless violence on innocent civilians "preserving the Union"!

CHAPTER 35

IMPORTANT FACTS ABOUT ROBERT E. LEE

YOU SHOULD KNOW THAT . . .
- Confederate General Robert E. Lee descended from European royalty, and that he was related to hundreds of kings and queens.
- In 1816 Yankee soldiers stole Lee's beautiful home, "Arlington House," then kicked his wife and children out into the street, ruined their furniture, and robbed the family of their valuables.
- "Arlington House" is now a part of our country's most famous graveyard: Arlington National Cemetery, in Virginia.
- In 1829, Lee graduated second in his class at West Point Military Academy with no demerits.
- Lee's wife, Mary Anne Custis, was the step great-granddaughter of U.S. President George Washington.
- Even though Lee was a full four-star general, the highest rank

General Lee was a lifelong devout Christian, whose favorite song was "How Firm a Foundation."

in the Confederacy, the always modest officer refused to wear anything but his lower ranked colonel's uniform, which had only three stars on the collar.

- Lee slept on the ground or in a tent with his soldiers, going completely against military tradition. (Most generals slept in houses during the War.)
- Lee once risked his life by walking out onto a live battlefield to save a baby bird that had fallen from its nest.
- Lee often gave his meals to his soldiers, or even went without food altogether, so his men could eat.
- Lee was the highest ranked officer (a full general and also commander-in-chief of the entire military) in the Confederacy.

Robert E. Lee (left) with his son William Henry Fitzhugh Lee in 1845.

- After the War, General Lee sometimes rode his favorite horse Traveller off into the mountains of Virginia by himself, not returning until after dark.
- Traveller outlived his owner by several months and was buried by the General's grave at Lee Chapel (Lexington, Virginia) so the two could be near each other in death.
- After the War, Lee turned down hundreds of offers of wealth, fame, mansions, titles, and high paid jobs because he preferred being at home with his family.

- After the War, Lee became the president of Washington College, in Lexington, Virginia.
- Washington College was later renamed Washington and Lee University in honor of General Lee.
- Two of General Lee's cousins, Francis Lightfoot Lee and Richard Henry Lee, both signed the Declaration of Independence.
- General Lee's father, Henry "Light Horse Harry" Lee, was a celebrated Revolutionary War hero.

Arlington House, the Lee family home in Arlington, Virginia, was stolen by Union troops in the Summer of 1861. Yankee soldiers were then purposefully buried in the front yard so that General Lee and his family could never return and live there.

- General Lee had nearly one dozen relatives who also fought in Lincoln's War (some on the Yankees' side). They were: George Washington Lee (his son); William Henry Fitzhugh Lee (his son); Fitzhugh Lee (his nephew); Samuel P. Lee (his cousin); James Terrill (his cousin); William R. Terrill (his cousin); Richard L. Page (his cousin); Samuel Cooper (related by marriage); and Frank Wheaton (related by marriage).
- General Lee, like nearly all white Southerners, couldn't stand slavery and was an enthusiastic abolitionist.
- General Lee freed his wife's family's slaves *before* Lincoln issued his fake and illegal Final Emancipation Proclamation.

CHAPTER 36

IMPORTANT FACTS ABOUT NATHAN BEDFORD FORREST

YOU SHOULD KNOW THAT . . .
- Confederate General Nathan Bedford Forrest was born in poverty, but was a multimillionaire by the time he was 40 years old.
- Forrest stood six feet, two inches, had blazing fiery eyes, a "cavalier" style haircut, and didn't drink alcohol or smoke cigarettes.
- Forrest freed his slaves two years before the War.
- Forrest was the only man on either side to rise from private to lieutenant general.
- Forrest trained his horse King Philip to attack anybody wearing blue.
- Forrest had a reputation among Yankee troops for being a ferocious warrior who would die rather than surrender.
- Forrest was an excellent fighter who killed 30 Yanks with his

General Forrest could outride, out shoot, outmaneuver, and out fight any Yankee any time!

bare hands.
- Forrest was known as the "Wizard of the Saddle" due to his amazing horsemanship.
- Forrest had 39 horses shot out from under him during the War.
- Forrest's cavalry was known as the "Critter Company."
- Forrest won *all* of the battles he led except one.
- Yankee soldiers were so afraid of General Forrest that they would often surrender just at the mere mention of his name.
- Forrest didn't care about the time of day or the weather. He was ready to fight at any time, and he expected his men to be the same!
- Forrest would sometimes arrange his little army in several revolving circles to make it appear to Yankees that he had many more men than he actually did.

General Forrest often pulled his cannons up to the front line and used them like riflemen. This went completely against accepted military rules. But it worked!

- Forrest received four official "Thanks" from the Confederate Congress for his bravery and military achievements.
- Forrest's wife, Mary Ann Montgomery, was a cousin of Texas Governor Sam Houston, after whom the city of Houston, Texas, is named.
- Forrest could quietly hide his entire cavalry in the brush alongside a road without being detected by Yankee soldiers, who were passing by only a few feet away!

- There are more statues of General Forrest in Tennessee than there are of Abraham Lincoln in Illinois.
- Forrest only had six months of proper schooling, but many Confederate leaders, like General Robert E. Lee, considered him the greatest officer on either side of the War.
- The South would have won the "Civil War" if Forrest had been promoted to full general and placed in command of the Army of Tennessee.
- After the War, Forrest fought for black civil rights.
- After the War, Forrest worked with former Yankee officers, rented them his land, and had them over for dinner on Sundays.
- Thousands of blacks attended General Forrest's funeral in Memphis, Tennessee, in October 1877.

General Forrest, with sword drawn, leads an attack on a Yankee battery.

Confederate General Nathan Bedford Forrest was widely adored in the South and greatly feared in the North. In this illustration he's preparing to launch another one of his many successful assaults on the Yanks.

CHAPTER 37

THE SOUTH & THE CONFEDERACY TODAY

THE SOUTH LIVES ON

The South did not give up, and the Confederacy did not die at Appomattox Court House on April 9, 1865, the day General Lee "surrendered." The South is still very much alive!

Our people still love to be free and independent; they still love God and the Constitution; they still love their families, the great outdoors, their horses, their farms, and the beautiful countryside of Dixie!

You see, the South and the Confederacy are not things that can be destroyed. The South is a 400 year old society of 150 million people, and the Confederacy is an idea that burns in the heart of every true Southerner. This means that no one can ever take these things away from us.

As this photo of a Confederate Reunion Parade in 1917 in Washington, D.C., clearly shows, our Confederate heritage was once widely accepted: that's the White House in the background!

Now think about this: if someone bigger than you beats

you up, it doesn't mean anything, other than that he or she is physically larger and stronger than you are. That's all. Bullies never win a fight. Their abuse of others only proves how foolish, weak, and immature they are!

This is what happened in the "Civil War." Lincoln and the Yankees think they "won." But they really didn't. The War was just an example of a bully (the Union) picking on someone smaller and younger (the Confederacy)!

All Lincoln proved was that he had a bigger army, and more money to feed and clothe his soldiers, than we did. But beating us up didn't make the North right and the South wrong. Not at all!

The South has always respected the Constitution. But many Northerners, like Lincoln, have tried to destroy it!

We know that the South was in the right because we fought for the Constitution, and for the values and principles of the Southern Founding Fathers; men like George Washington, Thomas Jefferson, James Madison, Patrick Henry, and George Mason.

And what did the North fight for? It fought to destroy the Constitution and the values and principles of the Southern Founding Fathers! How could this ever be right?

SOUTHERN VALUES AND PRINCIPLES

Yes, despite what they try to teach you in school, the truth is that our Confederate ancestors fought for their own Southern values, *not* to keep slavery going or to destroy the United States.

Let's go over these principles now, so that you'll never forget them. Our Southern values are:

- God: your Heavenly Father, Creator, and Savior.
- Family: your mother, father, sisters, brothers, grandmothers, grandfathers, aunts, uncles, cousins, nieces, and nephews.
- Home: the place where you live with your family and spend most of your time.
- Ancestors: from your parents all the way back to your earliest known ascendant. You have thousands of ancestors. Without them you wouldn't be here, so it's only right to honor them.
- Tradition: the morals and customs you inherited from your parents and ancestors.
- The Constitution: our most sacred document, written by Southerners!
- The Confederacy: the United States was a Confederacy from 1781 to 1789, and of course we created our own second Confederacy in 1861 in an attempt to continue the first one. We love them both for what they stood for: a voluntary union made up of a small weak government and powerful independent states!
- Individualism: the right to be yourself, whoever that might be.
- Personal freedom: the liberty to make yourself happy.
- States' rights: the power of each state to do as it pleases.

Dixie is a land of freedom loving people, tradition, family values, good manners, and great Southern cooking!

- Self-determination: the right to decide your own life.
- Hard work: Southerners believe in working hard for what they get out of life.
- Self-reliance: we're independent minded people, and we want to keep it that way. We don't want the government taking care of us and turning us into babies!
- Racial harmony: Southerners love all colors of people, not just their own. Remember, God made each and every one of us. Whatever our skin color, we are all children of God—sisters and brothers in spirit!
- The land: Indians call the earth beneath our feet the "Great Mother." This is because Mother Earth keeps us strong and healthy by providing us with foods that come from our farms. True Southerners always respect the land.
- The great outdoors: out of the millions of other planets that exist out in space, ours is the only one known to have wild forests, mountains, valleys, deserts, meadows, rivers, lakes, and oceans. This makes our great outdoors unique in the entire Universe! We hunt and fish in nature, enjoy her natural splendor, and relax in her peacefulness. So that

The South has always been a place of rural peace and incredible natural beauty. Many Northerners would prefer that we become like Massachusetts or New York. But we'd rather stay the way we've always been. It's a Southern thing!

your children can experience the wonders of the great outdoors too, try to be a good steward of the land, and always do your best to preserve and honor it.
- Animals: God made animals so that we could enjoy their companionship, majesty, mysteries, and beauty. From the smallest insect to the largest whale, each one is an important part of the Web of Life. Whether you like to hunt and fish, or you just enjoy looking at animals, all of them deserve your respect, admiration, and protection.

These are the primary values and principles that we live by here in the South. Other people in the world share some of them. But I promise you, only in Dixie will you find all of them in one place!

BE PROUD THAT YOU'RE A SOUTHERNER!

You're a Southerner, either by being born here, or by moving here and accepting and loving Dixie. So always show pride in the South; in our history, our culture, our customs, our traditions, our architecture, our foods, our clothing, and our music.

There's nowhere else on earth anything like the American South. It's a unique and special place to live. And you're blessed to be here.

Cover sheet of a Victorian song called The Confederate Flag, *written by a proud Southerner!*

Share your love of the South, and the new knowledge you've learned from this book, with your family and friends. And tell your parents to read my books (listed in the front of this book), so they'll know the truth about the War too.

Don't forget to celebrate "Confederate Memorial Day" and "Confederate Flag Day," both which fall on different days in different states. Display a Confederate flag outside your home and show the world your Confederate pride. For our beautiful banner represents *all* Southerners, no matter what their race, color, religion, or nationality.

Keep the ideas of the Confederacy alive by teaching others the truth about the "Civil War," the fight that we rightly call the War for Southern Independence!

FINAL WORDS

In the end, let's remember the words of the great Southern hero and Confederate General Robert E. Lee. He understood the bad feelings left over after the "Civil War," and the anger that so many Southerners felt towards the North.

Yes, it's true that Yankees did a lot of terrible things to our Southern ancestors. So it's easy to dislike them, even today, 150 years later! But, as General Lee liked to remind us:

General Robert E. Lee.

"Don't grow up being bitter about the War. We must learn to get along together. Remember, we are all Americans."

Someday the South *will* rise again! Until then, let's hope that our neighbors to the North will remember his words as well. In the meantime, you can never go wrong if you follow the example of Robert E. Lee!

In this photo, two of the last living Confederate soldiers attend a Confederate Reunion in Washington, D.C. in 1917. Our ancestors were proud of their heritage 100 years ago, not ashamed, and we should be proud of it today!

APPENDIX A
For Children

OTHER NAMES FOR THE "CIVIL WAR"

Brothers' War, the*
Confederate War, the
Great Rebellion, the
Late Ruction, the
Late Friction, the
Late Unpleasantness, the
Lincoln's War*
Lost Cause, the
Mr. Lincoln's War*
Northern War Against the Constitution, the*
Schism, the
Second American Revolution, the*
Second War for Independence, the*
Southern Rebellion, the
Uncivil War, the*
War Against Northern Aggression, the*
War Against Slavery, the
War Between the States, the
War for Abolition, the
War for Constitutional Liberty, the*
War for Nationality, the*
War for Separation, the*
War for Southern Freedom, the*

War for Southern Independence, the*
War for Southern Nationality, the*
War for Southern Rights, the*
War for States' Rights, the*
War for Union, the
War of North and South, the
War of Rebellion, the
War of Secession, the
War of Sixties, the
War of Southern Planters, the
War of Southrons, the
War, the*
War to Suppress Yankee Arrogance, the*
Yankee Invasion, the*

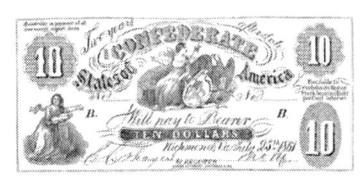

A Confederate ten-dollar bill.

Note: only names marked with an asterisk should be used by Southerners!

APPENDIX B

For Parents

AN EARLY ATTEMPT TO PREVENT THE NORTHERNIZATION OF OUR SCHOOLS

> The following was taken from *Confederate Veteran* magazine, and will be of great interest, and hopefully great inspiration, to all Southern parents. — L. Seabrook

"The report of the History Committee, Gen. C. I. Walker, of South Carolina, Chairman, set out the work that had been accomplished in eliminating from schools such histories as were found to be unfair to the South. A part of this report was the commendation of the pamphlet by Col. H. W. Johnstone, of Curryville, Ga., which brings out some heretofore unknown history of events just preceding the War between the States. The report is here given in full:

"To the United Confederate Veterans, Richmond, Va.:

"Comrades: Your Rutherford Committee, appointed to endeavor to have the truth of Confederate history presented to the world, and especially to the young of the South, has the honor to submit its annual report.

"For reasons heretofore given, your committee has been obliged to restrict its scope of work, almost exclusively, to watching and influencing State school book adoptions, in order to secure the adoption of textbooks for use in the Southern schools, teaching our youths the great historic truths of the Confederate struggle, thus enabling them to justify, approve, and commend the actions of their forbears in the sixties. As previously reported, Mississippi and Texas had made selections of histories fair to the South, and we are glad now to report that during the past year the States of North Carolina, Louisiana, and South Carolina have made adoptions of books fair to the South. In every case your committee has presented the importance of this matter to the adopting boards. It is gratifying that this sentiment is sweeping over the South, and the various adopting boards seem determined to allow in their schools only such histories which fairly teach the magnificent history of the Southern States of our Union.

"It is with the utmost pleasure that we invite attention to the splendid work done in the State adoptions by the textbook committees of the respective State divisions of the United Daughters of the Confederacy. These committees have worked most earnestly and efficiently and have largely contributed to the glorious achievements of securing in the States histories true and loyal to the Confederacy.

"To show how fully this sentiment has been aroused, we cite North Carolina's action in particular. This State had on its list of adopted books for high schools, from a previous adoption, a history which taught the young that the Confederate cause was 'an unworthy one.' The contract had some time to run. But when the false teachings of this history was called to the attention of the State Board of Education it broke the contract, assuming whatever pecuniary damage may arise, and eliminated the book from its schools.

"Your committee would, especially commend a pamphlet by Colonel Huger W. Johnstone, of Curryville, Ga., on the 'Truth of the War Conspiracy of 1861,' and published by that great-hearted Southern historian, Miss Mildred Rutherford. This presents the official evidence gathered principally from the United States government archives, which proves the Confederate war was deliberately and personally conceived and its inauguration made by Abraham Lincoln, and that he was personally responsible for forcing the war upon the South.

"To instill further into the young of the South the truths of the Confederacy's magnificent struggle for constitutional liberty, the chairman of our committee has prepared a lecture teaching these truths, which should be impressed upon the young of the South. This lecture has been delivered in the colleges and high schools and much good has been thereby accomplished. Your members can aid in this good work by suggesting to any institutions of learning in their respective neighborhoods that they arrange to have this lecture delivered. It will be history told by one who helped to make it.

"Your committee, unless you direct otherwise, will continue its work. We believe that the constant agitation of the great Confederate organizations, the Veterans, Daughters, and Sons, is producing fruit; that the sentiment has been so aroused that perverted Yankee histories will no longer be used to instruct our children; that the young will now be taught that the South was right, yea, eternally and everlastingly right, in fighting for these principles upon which our glorious country was founded.

"Respectfully submitted for the Rutherford committee.

"C. I. Walker, Chairman."

Source: *Confederate Veteran*, January 1922, Vol. 30, No. 1, page 244.

GLOSSARY

Civil War Words & Terms

ABATIS: A defensive structure made from sharpened tree branches, and laid facing forward toward the enemy.

ANTEBELLUM: A Latin word meaning "before the [Civil] war."

BILLY YANK: A nickname for a Union soldier.

BLUE COAT: A Southern nickname for Union soldiers due to their blue uniforms.

BREASTWORK: A temporary fortification, like a trench or a mound of dirt.

BUMMERS: The name for often vicious gangs of stragglers, thugs, and homeless people who followed Yankee General William T. Sherman during his infamous "March to the Sea."

BUTTERNUTS: A nickname for Confederate soldiers who wore yellowish tan clothing known by its color: butternut. The color was created from tree bark, rust, or walnut shells.

CARPETBAGGER: A crafty Yankee who came to the South and tried to take advantage of Southerners after the War.

CHEVAUX-DE-FRISE: Logs fitted with large sharpened stakes that face outward for protection against the enemy.

Confederate chevaux-de-frise on a battlefield at Atlanta, Georgia, in 1864.

COPPERHEAD: A nickname given to Northerners who side with the South and the Confederacy. Lincoln created the term from the deadly copperhead snake: he saw these types of Yankees as "dangerous" to the Union. It was actually Lincoln who was dangerous to the Union!

ENFILADE: Gunfire directed from the side, along the length of the enemy's battle line.

FEINT: The feint was a fake attack used by Civil War soldiers to lure the enemy away from the main army.

GALVANIZED SOLDIER: A turncoat or a traitor; or more usually a captive in a military prison who changed sides in order to spare himself the terrifying ordeal of prison life. This type of person was called "galvanized" because, like metal coated with zinc (galvanization)—which changes the color of the surface but remains the same color underneath—the soldier was still loyal to his original country beneath his new uniform. There were both galvanized Yankees and galvanized Rebels.

GRAYBACKS: A Yankee nickname for Confederate soldiers due to their gray uniforms.

HOMEMADE YANKEE: A Southerner who sided with or fought for the North. He was greatly disliked in the South!

JAYHAWKER: An anti-South guerilla, usually from Kansas or Missouri, who raided and plundered the homes of slave owners.

JOHNNY REB: A nickname for a Confederate soldier.

NEW SOUTH: A term for those Southern states that have become Northernized since the Civil War.

NORTHERNER: Someone from one of the Northern states, or someone who has moved to one of the Northern states, and who respects their people, their ways, their customs, and their history.

NORTHERNIZATION: The villainous process of trying to make the Southern states just like the Northern states.

OLD NORTH: The Northern states before Lincoln's War.

OLD SOUTH: The Southern states before Lincoln's War.

PARTISAN RANGERS: Groups of official (and sometimes unofficial) Rebel guerillas who fought secretly behind enemy lines.

POSTBELLUM: A Latin word meaning "after the [Civil] war."

PRIVATEER: A privately owned ship hired by the Confederate government to protect the southern coastline from Yankee vessels. Lincoln put out an order that all privateers were to be considered "pirates" and hanged on the spot. But this was just another one of Lincoln's many war crimes: privateering is perfectly legal!

QUAKER GUNS: Our Southern armies were so poor that they sometimes resorted to painting logs black to make them look like cannons. These were called "Quaker guns" because they didn't hurt anyone. Quaker guns were a favorite ploy of General Nathan Bedford Forrest, and he tricked many a Yankee officer using them!

REBEL: A nickname for a Confederate soldier. It was originally made up by Yankees like Lincoln, Dishonest Abe, who wanted the South to feel bad about "rebelling" against the United States and leaving the Union. So at first Southerners didn't like the name. But later, when they realized it meant they were standing up for God, the Constitution, and Southern honor, they adopted the name with pride!

This realistic looking Confederate "cannon" is actually a Quaker gun: a log carved to look like a cannon, with the visible end painted black.

REBEL YELL: Confederate soldiers inherited this terrifying banshee-like scream from their Celtic ancestors. The eerie high pitched battle cry made every Yankee tremble with fear, it's very purpose.

RECONSTRUCTION: A 12 year period—that lasted from right after the Civil War ended in 1865 to 1877—in which Yankees violently and illegally tried to Northernize the South. It was a terrible time for our people, and was almost as bad as the Civil War itself. Southern men, women, and children were forced to adopt Northern ways, beliefs, and ideas. Those who refused were arrested, beaten up, and put in prison. Southern school textbooks were replaced with Northern textbooks, in an effort to cover up the illegalities of the War and make Southern children think like Northern children! The Reconstruction period actually added 12 more years to the Civil War, making the entire conflict 16 years long. When Reconstruction ended in 1877, Southerners celebrated by kicking the last Yankee soldier out and taking back control of Dixie.

SCALLYWAG: A Southerner who has become Northernized, who believes in Northern myths about the "Civil War," and who, in general, has turned against his or her own homeland: Dixie. Obviously, scallywags are not well liked in the South! (This word is also spelled scalawag.)

SOUTHERNER: Someone from one of the Southern states, or someone who has moved to one of the Southern states, and who respects our people, our culture, our ways, our customs, and our history.

SUTLER: A person who provides food, drink, and other types of provisions to soldiers.

TRADITIONAL SOUTHERNER: A Southerner who embraces traditional Southern values: God, country, family, faith, conservatism, states' rights, racial harmony, capitalism, self determination, individualism, and limited government.

UNRECONSTRUCTED: A Southerner who has not allowed himself or herself to become "reconstructed," that is, Northernized.

VICTORIAN: A person living between about 1835 and 1900 during an era called the "Victorian Period," was known as a Victorian. This means that all the soldiers on both sides of the Civil War were Victorians. The Victorian Period was named after England's Queen Victoria, who lived from 1837 to 1901. The Victorian Period was known for its emphasis on religion, refinement, manners, and the arts.

VIDETTE: A guard on horseback who protects military outposts.

VIVANDIÈRE: A female sutler.

WHITE-WASHED SOLDIER: Same as a galvanized soldier.

YANKEE: This nickname used to mean someone from one of the New England states specifically: Massachusetts, Vermont, New Hampshire, Maine, Rhode Island, and Connecticut. But today, here in the South, we use it for a person from any one of the Northern states.

A Confederate railway battery.

BIBLIOGRAPHY

Abbott, John Stevens Cabot. *The Life of General Ulysses S. Grant.* Boston, MA: B. B. Russell, 1868.

Adams, Charles. *When in the Course of Human Events: Arguing the Case for Southern Secession.* Lanham, MD: Rowman and Littlefield, 2000.

Adams, Francis D., and Barry Sanders. *Alienable Rights: The Exclusion of African Americans in a White Man's Land, 1619-2000.* 2003. New York, NY: Perennial, 2004 ed.

Adams, Henry (ed.). *Documents Relating to New-England Federalism, 1800-1815.* Boston, MA: Little, Brown, and Co., 1877.

Adams, Nehemiah, Rev. *A South-side View of Slavery: Three Months at the South, in 1854.* Boston, MA: T. R. Marvin, 1855.

Alexander, William T. *History of the Colored Race in America.* Kansas City, MO: Palmetto Publishing, 1887.

Alotta, Robert I. *Civil War Justice: Union Army Executions Under Lincoln.* Shippensburg, PA: White Mane, 1989.

An Appeal From the Colored Men of Philadelphia to the President of the United States. Philadelphia, PA, 1862.

Anastaplo, George. *Abraham Lincoln: A Constitutional Biography.* Lanham, MD: Rowman and Littlefield, 1999.

Anderson, John Q. (ed.). *Brokenburn: The Journal of Kate Stone, 1861-1868.* 1955. Baton Rouge, LA: Louisiana State University Press, 1995 ed.

Anderson, John Richardson. *Richardson's Defense of the South.* Atlanta, GA: A. B. Caldwell, 1914.

Andrews, Elisha Benjamin. *The United States in Our Own Time: A History From Reconstruction to Expansion.* 1895. New York, NY: Charles Scribner's Sons, 1903 ed.

Andrews, Sidney. *The South Since the War: As Shown by Fourteen Weeks of Travel and Observation.* Boston, MA: Ticknor and Fields, 1866.

Angle, Paul M. (ed.). *The Complete Lincoln-Douglas Debates of 1858.* Chicago, IL: University of Chicago Press, 1991.

Annunzio, Frank (chairman). *The Capitol: A Pictorial History of the Capitol and of the Congress.* Washington, D.C.: U.S. Joint Committee on Printing, 1983.

Anonymous. *Life of John C. Calhoun: Presenting a Condensed History of Political Events, From 1811 to 1843.* New York, NY: Harper and Brothers, 1843.

Appleman, Roy Edgar (ed.). *Abraham Lincoln: From His Own Words and Contemporary*

Accounts. Washington, D.C.: U.S. Department of the Interior, National Park Service, 1942.
Arnett, Benjamin William (ed.). *Duplicate Copy of the Souvenir From the Afro-American League of Tennessee to Honorable James M. Ashley of Ohio*. Philadelphia, PA: A. M. E. Church, 1894.
Arnold, Isaac Newton. *The History of Abraham Lincoln, and the Overthrow of Slavery*. Chicago, IL: Clarke and Co., 1866.
Aron, Stephen. *American Confluence: The Missouri Frontier from Borderland to Border State*. Bloomington, IN: Indiana University Press, 2009.
Ashdown Paul, and Edward Caudill. *The Myth of Nathan Bedford Forrest*. 2005. Lanham, MD: Rowman and Littlefield, 2006 ed.
Ashe, Captain Samuel A'Court. *A Southern View of the Invasion of the Southern States and War of 1861-1865*. 1935. Crawfordville, GA: Ruffin Flag Co., 1938 ed.
Ashworth, John. *Slavery, Capitalism, and Politics in the Antebellum Republic*. 2 vols. New York, NY: Cambridge University Press, 2007.
Astor, Gerald. *The Right to Fight: A History of African Americans in the Military*. Cambridge, MA: Da Capo, 2001.
Baepler, Paul (ed.). *White Slaves, African Masters: An Anthology of American Barbary Captivity Narratives*. Chicago, IL: University of Chicago Press, 1999.
Bailey, Anne C. *African Voices of the Atlantic Slave Trade: Beyond the Silence and the Shame*. Boston, MA: Beacon Press, 2005.
Bailey, Hugh C. *Hinton Rowan Helper: Abolitionist-Racist*. Tuscaloosa, AL: University of Alabama Press, 1965.
Bailyn, Bernard, Robert Dallek, David Brion Davis, David Herbert Donald, John L. Thomas, and Gordon S. Wood. *The Great Republic: A History of the American People*. 1977. Lexington, MA: D. C. Heath and Co., 1992 ed.
Baker, George E. (ed.). *The Works of William H. Seward*. 5 vols. 1861. Boston, MA: Houghton, Mifflin and Co., 1888 ed.
Baker, Jean H. *Mary Todd Lincoln: A Biography*. New York, NY: W. W. Norton and Co., 1989.
Ballagh, James Curtis. *White Servitude in the Colony of Virginia: A Study of the System of Indentured Servitude in the American Colonies*. Whitefish, MT: Kessinger Publishing, 2004.
Bancroft, Frederic. *The Life of William H. Seward*. 2 vols. New York, NY: Harper and Brothers, 1900.
———. *Slave-Trading in the Old South*. Baltimore, MD: J. H. Furst, 1931.
Bancroft, Frederic, and William A. Dunning (eds.). *The Reminiscences of Carl Schurz*. 3 vols. New York, NY: McClure Co., 1909.
Barnes, Gilbert H., and Dwight L. Dumond (eds.). *Letters of Theodore Dwight Weld, Angelina Grimké Weld and Sarah Grimké, 1822-1844*. 2 vols. New York, NY: D. Appleton-Century Co., 1934.
Barney, William L. *Flawed Victory: A New Perspective on the Civil War*. New York, NY: Praeger Publishers, 1975.
Barrow, Charles Kelly, J. H. Segars, and R. B. Rosenburg (eds.). *Black Confederates*.

1995. Gretna, LA: Pelican Publishing Co., 2001 ed.

———. *Forgotten Confederates: An Anthology About Black Southerners.* Saint Petersburg, FL: Southern Heritage Press, 1997.

Bartlett, Irving H. *John C. Calhoun: A Biography.* New York, NY: W. W. Norton, 1994.

———. *Wendell Phillips: Brahmin Radical.* Boston, MA: Beacon Press, 1961.

Barton, William E. *The Soul of Abraham Lincoln.* New York, NY: George H. Doran, 1920.

Basler, Roy Prentice (ed.). *Abraham Lincoln: His Speeches and Writings.* 1946. New York, NY: Da Capo Press, 2001 ed.

——— (ed.). *The Collected Works of Abraham Lincoln.* 9 vols. New Brunswick, NJ: Rutgers University Press, 1953.

Bateman, William O. *Political and Constitutional Law of the United States of America.* St. Louis, MO: G. I. Jones and Co., 1876.

Baxter, Maurice G. *Henry Clay and the American System.* Lexington, KY: University Press of Kentucky, 2004.

Beard, Charles A., and Birl E. Schultz. *Documents on the State-Wide Initiative, Referendum and Recall.* New York, NY: Macmillan, 1912.

Beard, Charles A., and Mary R. Beard. *The Rise of American Civilization.* 1927. New York, NY: MacMillan, 1930 ed.

Beck, Glenn. *Glenn Beck's Common Sense: The Case Against an Out-of-Control Government, Inspired by Thomas Paine.* New York, NY: Threshold, 2009.

Belz, Herman. *Abraham Lincoln, Constitutionalism, and Equal Rights in the Civil War Era.* Bronx, NY: Fordham University Press, 1997.

Bennett, Lerone. *Forced into Glory: Abraham Lincoln's White Dream.* Chicago, IL: Johnson Publishing Co., 2000.

Benson, Al, Jr., and Walter Donald Kennedy. *Lincoln's Marxists.* Gretna, LA: Pelican Publishing Co., 2011.

Benton, Thomas Hart. *Thirty Years View; or A History of the Working of the American Government for Thirty Years, From 1820 to 1850.* 2 vols. New York, NY: D. Appleton and Co., 1854.

Bergh, Albert Ellery (ed.). *The Writings of Thomas Jefferson.* 20 vols. Washington, D.C.: Thomas Jefferson Memorial Association of the U.S., 1905.

Bernhard, Winfred E. A. (ed.). *Political Parties in American History* (Vol. 1, 1789-1828). New York, NY: G. P. Putnams' Sons, 1973.

Berry, Stephen William. *House of Abraham: Lincoln and the Todds, A Family Divided by War.* New York, NY: Houghton Mifflin, 2007.

Berry, Wendell. *The Unsettling of America: Culture and Agriculture.* San Francisco, CA: Sierra Club Books, 1996.

Berwanger, Eugene H. *The Frontier Against Slavery: Western Anti-Negro Prejudice and the Slavery Extension Controversy.* 1967. Urbana, IL: University of Illinois Press, 1971 ed.

Beschloss, Michael R. *Presidential Courage: Brave Leaders and How They Changed America, 1789-1989.* New York, NY: Simon and Schuster, 2007.

Beveridge, Albert Jeremiah. *Abraham Lincoln: 1809-1858.* 2 vols. Boston, MA: Houghton Mifflin, 1928.
Black, Chauncey F. *Essays and Speeches of Jeremiah S. Black.* New York, NY: D. Appleton and Co., 1886.
Black, Robert W., Col. *Cavalry Raids of the Civil War.* Mechanicsburg, PA: Stackpole, 2004.
Blackerby, Hubert R. *Blacks in Blue and Gray.* New Orleans, LA: Portals Press, 1979.
Blair, William A., and Karen Fisher Younger (eds.). *Lincoln's Proclamation: Emancipation Reconsidered.* Chapel Hill, NC: University of North Carolina Press, 2009.
Blassingame, John W. *The Slave Community: Plantation Life in the Antebellum South.* 1972. New York, NY: Oxford University Press, 1974 ed.
Bledsoe, Albert Taylor. *An Essay on Liberty and Slavery.* Philadelphia, PA: J. B. Lippincott and Co., 1856.
——. *A Theodicy; or a Vindication of the Divine Glory, as Manifested in the Constitution and Government of the Moral World.* New York, NY: Carlton and Porter, 1856.
——. *Is Davis a Traitor; or Was Secession a Constitutional Right Previous to the War of 1861?* Richmond, VA: Hermitage Press, 1907.
Blee, Kathleen M. *Women of the Klan: Racism and Gender in the 1920s.* 1991. Berkeley, CA: University of California Press, 1992 ed.
Blight, David W. *Frederick Douglass' Civil War: Keeping Faith in Jubilee.* 1989. Baton Rouge, LA: Louisiana State University Press, 1991 ed.
Bliss, William Dwight Porter (ed.). *The Encyclopedia of Social Reform.* New York, NY: Funk and Wagnalls, 1897.
Boatner, Mark Mayo. *The Civil War Dictionary.* 1959. New York, NY: David McKay Co., 1988 ed.
Bode, Carl, and Malcolm Cowley (eds.). *The Portable Emerson.* 1941. Harmondsworth, UK: Penguin, 1981 ed.
Boorstin, Daniel J. *The Discoverers: A History of Man's Search to Know His World and Himself.* 1983. New York, NY: Vintage, 1985 ed.
Boritt, Gabor S. *Lincoln and the Economics of the America Dream.* Urbana, IL: University of Illinois Press, 1994.
——. (ed.) *Lincoln's Generals.* New York, NY: Oxford University Press, 1995.
——. *The Gettysburg Gospel: The Lincoln Speech That Nobody Knows.* New York, NY: Simon and Schuster, 2006.
Bowen, Catherine Drinker. *John Adams and the American Revolution.* 1949. New York, NY: Grosset and Dunlap, 1977 ed.
Bowers, John. *Chickamauga and Chattanooga: The Battles that Doomed the Confederacy.* New York, NY: HarperCollins, 1994.
Bowman, John S. (ed.). *The Civil War Day by Day: An Illustrated Almanac of America's Bloodiest War.* 1989. New York, NY: Dorset Press, 1990 ed.
——. *Encyclopedia of the Civil War* (ed.). 1992. North Dighton, MA: JG Press, 2001 ed.
Bowman, Virginia McDaniel. *Historic Williamson County: Old Homes and Sites.* 1971. Franklin, TN: Territorial Press, 1989 ed.
Bradford, James C. (ed.). *Atlas of American Military History.* New York, NY: Oxford

University Press, 2003.
Bradford, Ned (ed.). *Battles and Leaders of the Civil War*. 1-vol. ed. New York, NY: Appleton-Century-Crofts, 1956.
Bradley, Michael R. *Nathan Bedford Forrest's Escort and Staff*. Gretna, LA: Pelican Publishing Co., 2006.
Brady, Cyrus Townsend. *Three Daughters of the Confederacy*. New York, NY: G. W. Dillingham, 1905.
Brady, James S. (ed.). *Ronald Reagan: A Man True to His Word - A Portrait of the 40th President of the United States In His Own Words*. Washington D.C.: National Federation of Republican Women, 1984.
Brent, Linda. *The Deeper Wrong; or Incidents in the Life of a Slave Girl, Written by Herself*. London, UK: W. Tweedie, 1862.
Brinkley, Alan. *The Unfinished Nation: A Concise History of the American People*. 1993. Boston, MA: McGraw-Hill, 2000 ed.
Brockett, Linus Pierpont. *The Life and Times of Abraham Lincoln, Sixteenth President of the United States*. Philadelphia, PA: Bradley and Co., 1865.
Brooks, Gertrude Zeth. *First Ladies of the White House*. Chicago, IL: Charles Hallberg and Co., 1969.
Brooksher, William R., and David K. Snider. *Glory at a Gallop: Tales of the Confederate Cavalry*. 1993. Gretna, LA: Pelican Publishing Co., 2002 ed.
Brown, Dee. *Bury My Heart at Wounded Knee: An Indian History of the American West*. 1970. New York, NY: Owl Books, 1991 ed.
Brown, Rita Mae. *High Hearts*. New York, NY: Bantam, 1987.
Brown, William Wells. *The Black Man: His Antecedents, His Genius, and His Achievements*. New York, NY: Thomas Hamilton, 1863.
Browne, Ray B., and Lawrence A. Kreiser, Jr. *The Civil War and Reconstruction*. Westport, CT: Greenwood Publishing, 2003.
Bruce, Philip Alexander. *The Plantation Negro As a Freeman*. New York, NY: G. P. Putnam's Sons, 1889.
Brunner, Borgna (ed.). *The Time Almanac* (1999 ed.). Boston, MA: Information Please, 1998.
Bryan, William Jennings. *The Commoner Condensed*. New York, NY: Abbey Press, 1902.
Buchanan, James. *The Works of James Buchanan*. 12 vols. Philadelphia, PA: J. B. Lippincott Co., 1911.
Buchanan, Patrick J. *A Republic, Not an Empire: Reclaiming America's Destiny*. Washington, D.C.: Regenry, 1999.
Buckingham, James Silk. *The Slave States of America*. 2 vols. London, UK: Fisher, Son, and Co., 1842.
Buckley, Gail. *American Patriots: The Story of Blacks in the Military From the Revolution to Desert Storm*. New York, NY: Random House, 2001.
Bultman, Bethany. *Redneck Heaven: Portrait of a Vanishing Culture*. New York, NY: Bantam, 1996.
Burkhimer, Michael. *Lincoln's Christianity*. Yardley, PA: Westholme, 2007.
Burlingame, Michael. *The Inner World of Abraham Lincoln*. Champaign, IL: University of

Illinois Press, 1997.
Burns, James MacGregor, and Jack Walter Peltason. *Government by the People: The Dynamics of American National, State, and Local Government.* 1952. Englewood Cliffs, NJ: Prentice-Hall, 1964 ed.
Burns, James MacGregor, Jack Walter Peltason, Thomas E. Cronin, David B. Magleby, and David M. O'Brien. *Government by the People* (National Version). 1952. Upper Saddle River, NJ: Prentice Hall, 2001-2002 ed.
Burton, Orville Vernon. *The Age of Lincoln.* New York, NY: Hill and Wang, 2007.
Burton, Robert. *The Anatomy of Melancholy.* 3 vols. 1621. London, UK: George Bell and Sons, 1896 ed.
Bushnell, Horace. *The Census and Slavery, Thanksgiving Discourse, Delivered in the Chapel at Clifton Springs, New York, November 29, 1860.* Hartford, CT: L. E. Hunt, 1860.
Butler, Benjamin Franklin. *Butler's Book (Autobiography and Personal Reminiscences of Major-General Benjamin F. Butler: A Review of His Legal, Political, and Military Career).* Boston, MA: A. M. Thayer and Co., 1892.
Butler, Lindley S., and Alan D. Watson (eds.). *The North Carolina Experience: An Interpretive and Documentary History.* Chapel Hill, NC: University of North Carolina Press, 1984.
Butler, Trent C. (ed.). *Holman Bible Dictionary.* Nashville, TN: Holman Bible Publishers, 1991.
Calvert, Thomas H. *The Federal Statutes Annotated.* 10 vols. Northport, NY: Edward Thompson, 1905.
Cannon, Devereaux D., Jr. *The Flags of the Confederacy: An Illustrated History.* Memphis, TN: St. Luke's Press, 1988.
Carey, Matthew, Jr. (ed.). *The Democratic Speaker's Hand-Book.* Cincinnati, OH: Miami Print and Publishing Co., 1868.
Carlton, Frank Tracy. *Organized Labor in America.* New York, NY: D. Appleton and Co., 1920.
Carnahan, Burrus M. *Lincoln on Trial: Southern Civilians and the Law of War.* Lexington, KY: University Press of Kentucky, 2010.
Carpenter, Stephen D. *Logic of History: Five Hundred Political Texts, Being Concentrated Extracts of Abolitionism.* Madison, WI: published by author, 1864.
Cartmell, Donald. *Civil War 101.* New York, NY: Gramercy, 2001.
Carwardine, Richard. *Lincoln: A Life of Purpose and Power.* New York, NY: Vintage, 2006.
Cash, W. J. *The Mind of the South.* 1941. New York, NY: Vintage, 1969 ed.
Catton, Bruce. *The Coming Fury* (Vol. 1). 1961. New York, NY: Washington Square Press, 1967 ed.
——. *Terrible Swift Sword* (Vol. 2). 1963. New York, NY: Pocket Books, 1967 ed.
——. *A Stillness at Appomattox* (Vol. 3). 1953. New York, NY: Pocket Books, 1966 ed.
Celeste, Sister Mary. *The Old World's Gifts to the New.* 1932. Long Prairie, MN: Neumann Press, 1999 ed.
Chadwick, Bruce. *The Two American Presidents: A Dual Biography of Abraham Lincoln and*

Jefferson Davis. New York, NY: Citadel, 1999.
Chambers, Robert (ed.). *The Book of Days: A Miscellany of Popular Antiquities in Connection with the Calender*. 2 vols. London, UK: W. & R. Chambers, 1883.
Channing, Steven A. *Confederate Ordeal: The Southern Home Front*. 1984. Morristown, NJ: Time-Life Books, 1989 ed.
Chernow, Ron. *Alexander Hamilton*. New York, NY: Penguin, 2004.
Chesnut, Mary. *A Diary From Dixie: As Written by Mary Boykin Chesnut, Wife of James Chesnut, Jr., United States Senator from South Carolina, 1859-1861, and afterward an Aide to Jefferson Davis and a Brigadier-General in the Confederate Army*. (Isabella D. Martin and Myrta Lockett Avary, eds.). New York, NY: D. Appleton and Co., 1905 ed.
———. *Mary Chesnut's Civil War*. 1860-1865 (Woodward, Comer Vann, ed.). New Haven, CT: Yale University Press, 1981 ed.
Chodes, John. *Destroying the Republic: Jabez Curry and the Re-Education of the Old South*. New York, NY: Algora, 2005.
Christian, George L. *Abraham Lincoln: An Address Delivered Before R. E. Lee Camp, No. 1 Confederate Veterans at Richmond, VA, October 29, 1909*. Richmond, VA: L. H. Jenkins, 1909.
Cimprich, John. *Fort Pillow, a Civil War Massacre, and Public Memory*. Baton Rouge, LA: Louisiana State University Press, 2005.
Cisco, Walter Brian. *War Crimes Against Southern Civilians*. Gretna, LA: Pelican Publishing Co., 2007.
Civil War Book of Lists. 1993. Edison, NJ: Castle Books, 2004 ed.
Civil War Society, The. *Civil War Battles: An Illustrated Encyclopedia*. 1997. New York, NY: Gramercy, 1999 ed.
———. *The Civil War Society's Encyclopedia of the Civil War*. New York, NY: Wings Books, 1997.
Clark, L. Pierce. *Lincoln: A Psycho-Biography*. New York, NY: Charles Scribner's Sons, 1933.
Clarke, James W. *The Lineaments of Wrath: Race, Violent Crime, and American Culture*. 1998. New Brunswick, NJ: Transaction, 2001 ed.
Cluskey, Michael W. (ed.). *The Political Text-Book, or Encyclopedia*. Philadelphia, PA: Jas. B. Smith, 1859 ed.
Cmiel, Kenneth. *Democratic Eloquence: The Fight Over Popular Speech in Nineteenth-Century America*. Berkeley, CA: University of California Press, 1990.
Coe, Joseph. *The True American*. Concord, NH: I. S. Boyd, 1840.
Coffin, Charles Carleton. *Abraham Lincoln*. New York, NY: Harper and Brothers, 1893.
Coit, Margaret L. *John C. Calhoun: American Portrait*. Boston, MA: Sentry, 1950.
Collier, Christopher, and James Lincoln Collier. *Decision in Philadelphia: The Constitutional Convention of 1787*. 1986. New York, NY: Ballantine, 1987 ed.
Collins, Elizabeth. *Memories of the Southern States*. Taunton, UK: J. Barnicott, 1865.
Collins, John A. (ed.). *The Anti-Slavery Picknick: A Collection of Speeches, Poems, Dialogues and Songs Intended for Use in Schools and Anti-Slavery Meetings*. Boston, MA: H.

W. Williams, 1842.
Commager, Henry Steele, and Erik Bruun (eds.). *The Civil War Archive: The History of the Civil War in Documents.* 1950. New York, NY: Black Dog and Leventhal, 1973 ed.
Conner, Frank. *The South Under Siege, 1830-2000: A History of the Relations Between the North and the South.* Newnan, GA: Collards Publishing Co., 2002.
Conway, Moncure Daniel. *Testimonies Concerning Slavery.* London, UK: Chapman and Hall, 1865.
Cooke, Alistair. *Alistair Cooke's America.* 1973. New York, NY: Alfred A. Knopf, 1984 ed.
Cooke, John Esten. *A Life of General Robert E. Lee.* New York, NY: D. Appleton and Co., 1871.
Cooley, Henry S. *A Study of Slavery in New Jersey.* Baltimore, MD: Johns Hopkins University Press, 1896.
Cooper, William J., Jr. *Jefferson Davis, American.* New York, NY: Vintage, 2000.
———. (ed.). *Jefferson Davis: The Essential Writings.* New York, NY: Random House, 2003.
Cornish, Dudley Taylor. *The Sable Arm: Black Troops in the Union Army, 1861-1865.* 1956. Lawrence, KS: University Press of Kansas, 1987 ed.
Coulter, Ann. *Guilty: Liberal "Victims" and Their Assault on America.* New York, NY: Three Rivers Press, 2009.
Cox, Hank H. *Lincoln and the Sioux Uprising of 1862.* Nashville, TN: Cumberland House, 2005.
Cox, LaWanda. *Lincoln and Black Freedom: A Study in Presidential Leadership.* Columbia, SC: University of South Carolina Press, 1994.
Crallé, Richard Kenner. (ed.). *The Works of John C. Calhoun.* 6 vols. New York: NY: D. Appleton and Co., 1853-1888.
Craven, John J. *Prison Life of Jefferson Davis.* New York: NY: Carelton, 1866.
Crawford, Samuel Wylie. *The Genesis of the Civil War: The Story of Sumter, 1860-1861.* New York, NY: Charles L. Webster and Co., 1887.
Crocker, H. W., III. *The Politically Incorrect Guide to the Civil War.* Washington, D.C.: Regnery, 2008.
Cromie, Alice Hamilton. *A Tour Guide to the Civil War: The Complete State-by-State Guide to Battlegrounds, Landmarks, Museums, Relics, and Sites.* 1964. Nashville, TN: Rutledge Hill Press, 1990 ed.
Cromwell, John Wesley. *The Negro in American History: Men and Women Eminent in the Evolution of the American of African Descent.* Washington, D.C.: American Negro Academy, 1914.
Cross, F. L., and F. A. Livingston (eds.). *The Oxford Dictionary of the Christian Church.* 1957. London, UK: Oxford University Press, 1974 ed.
Crutchfield, James A. *Franklin: A Photographic Recollection.* 2 vols. Franklin, TN: Canaday Enterprises, 1996.
Crutchfield, James A., and Robert Holladay. *Franklin: Tennessee's Handsomest Town.* Franklin, TN: Hillsboro Press, 1999.

Cummins, Joseph. *Anything For a Vote: Dirty Tricks, Cheap Shots, and October Surprises in U.S. Presidential Campaigns*. Philadelphia, PA: Quirk, 2007.

Current, Richard N. *The Lincoln Nobody Knows*. 1958. New York, NY: Hill and Wang, 1963 ed.

——. (ed.) *The Confederacy (Information Now Encyclopedia)*. 1993. New York, NY: Macmillan, 1998 ed.

Curry, Leonard P. *Blueprint for Modern America: Nonmilitary Legislation of the First Civil War Congress*. Nashville, TN: Vanderbilt University Press, 1968.

Curti, Merle, Willard Thorpe, and Carlos Baker (eds.). *American Issues: The Social Record*. 1941. Chicago, IL: J. B. Lippincott, 1960 ed.

Curtin, Philip D. *The Atlantic Slave Trade: A Census*. Madison, WI: The University of Wisconsin Press, 1969.

——. *The Rise and Fall of the Plantation Complex: Essays in Atlantic History*. 1990. Cambridge, UK: Cambridge University Press, 1999 ed.

Curtis, George Ticknor. *Life of James Buchanan: Fifteenth President of the United States*. 2 vols. New York, NY: Harper and Brothers, 1883.

Curtis, William Eleroy. *Abraham Lincoln*. Philadelphia, PA: J. B. Lippincott Co., 1902.

Cushman, Horatio Bardwell. *History of the Choctaw, Chickasaw and Natchez Indians*. Greenville, TX: Headlight Printing House, 1899.

Custer, George Armstrong. *Wild Life on the Plains and Horrors of Indian Warfare*. St. Louis, MO: Excelsior Publishing, 1891.

Dabney, Robert Lewis. *A Defense of Virginia and the South*. Dahlonega, GA: Confederate Reprint Co., 1999.

Daniel, John M. *The Richmond Examiner During the War*. New York, NY: John M. Daniel, 1868.

Daniel, John W. *Life and Reminiscences of Jefferson Davis by Distinguished Men of His Time*. Baltimore, MD: R. H. Woodward, and Co., 1890.

Darwin, Charles. *On the Origin of Species By Means of Natural Selection*. London, UK: John Murray, 1866.

Daugherty, James. *Abraham Lincoln*. 1943. New York, NY: Scholastic Book Services, 1966 ed.

Davidson, Basil. *The African Slave Trade*. 1961. Boston, MA: Back Bay Books, 1980 ed.

Davis, Jefferson. *The Rise and Fall of the Confederate Government*. 2 vols. New York, NY: D. Appleton and Co., 1881.

——. *A Short History of the Confederate States of America*. New York, NY: Belford, 1890.

Davis, Kenneth C. *Don't Know Much About the Civil War: Everything You Need to Know About America's Greatest Conflict But Never Learned*. 1996. New York, NY: HarperCollins, 1997 ed.

Davis, Michael. *The Image of Lincoln in the South*. Knoxville, TN: University of Tennessee Press, 1971.

Davis, Varina. *Jefferson Davis: Ex-President of the Confederate States of America - A Memoir by His Wife*. 2 vols. New York, NY: Belford Co., 1890.

Davis, William C. *Jefferson Davis: The Man and His Hour*. New York, NY: HarperCollins, 1991.

———. *An Honorable Defeat: The Last Days of the Confederate Government.* New York, NY: Harcourt, 2001.

———. *Look Away: A History of the Confederate States of America.* 2002. New York, NY: Free Press, 2003 ed.

Davenport, Robert R. *Roots of the Rich and Famous: Real Cases of Unlikely Lineage.* Dallas, TX: Taylor Publishing Co., 1998.

Dawson, Sarah Morgan. *A Confederate Girl's Diary.* London, UK: William Heinemann, 1913.

Dean, Henry Clay. *Crimes of the Civil War, and Curse of the Funding System.* Baltimore, MD: William T. Smithson, 1869.

De Angelis, Gina. *It Happened in Washington, D.C.* Guilford, CT: Globe Pequot Press, 2004.

DeCaro, Louis A., Jr. *Fire From the Midst of You: A Religious Life of John Brown.* New York, NY: New York University Press, 2002.

Deems, Edward Mark. *Holy-Days and Holidays: A Treasury of Historical Material, Sermons in Full and Brief, Suggestive Thoughts, and Poetry.* New York, NY: Funk and Wagnalls, 1902.

De Forest, John William. *A Volunteer's Adventures: A Union Captain's Record of the Civil War.* 1946. North Haven, CT: Archon, 1970 ed.

DeGregorio, William A. *The Complete Book of U.S. Presidents.* 1984. New York, NY: Barricade, 1993 ed.

Delbanco, Andrew. *The Portable Abraham Lincoln.* New York, NY: Penguin, 1992.

Deloria, Vine, Jr. *Custer Died for Your Sins: An Indian Manifesto.* 1969. New York, NY: Avon, 1973 ed.

Denney, Robert E. *The Civil War Years: A Day-by-Day Chronicle of the Life of a Nation.* 1992. New York, NY: Sterling Publishing, 1994 ed.

Denson, John V. (ed.). *Reassessing the Presidency: The Rise of the Executive State and the Decline of Freedom.* Auburn, AL: Mises Institute, 2001.

Derosa, Marshall L. *The Confederate Constitution of 1861: An Inquiry into American Constitutionalism.* Columbia, MO: University of Missouri Press, 1991.

Desty, Robert. *The Constitution of the United States.* San Francisco, CA: Sumner Whitney and Co., 1881.

Diamond, Jared. *Guns, Germs, and Steel: The Fate of Human Societies.* 1997. New York, NY: W. W. Norton, 1999 ed.

Dicey, Edward. *Six Months in the Federal States.* 2 vols. London, UK: Macmillan and Co., 1863.

DiLorenzo, Thomas J. "The Great Centralizer: Abraham Lincoln and the War Between the States." *The Independent Review,* Vol. 3, No. 2, Fall 1998, pp. 243-271.

———. *The Real Lincoln: A New Look at Abraham Lincoln, His Agenda, and an Unnecessary War.* Three Rivers, MI: Three Rivers Press, 2003.

———. *Lincoln Unmasked: What You're Not Supposed to Know About Dishonest Abe.* New York, NY: Crown Forum, 2006.

———. *Hamilton's Curse: How Jefferson's Archenemy Betrayed the American Revolution—and What It Means for America Today.* New York, NY: Crown Forum, 2008.

DiLorenzo, Thomas J., and Joseph A. Morris. *Abraham Lincoln: Friend or Foe of Freedom?* Chicago, IL: Heartland Institute, 2008.

Dinkins, James. *1861 to 1865: Personal Recollections and Experiences in the Confederate Army, by an "Old Johnnie".* Cincinnati, OH: Robert Clarke, 1897.

Doddridge, Joseph. *Notes on the Settlement and Indian Wars of the Western Parts of Virginia and Pennsylvania, From 1763 to 1783, Inclusive.* Albany, NY: Joel Munsell, 1876.

Dodge, Daniel Kilham. *Abraham Lincoln: Master of Words.* New York, NY: D. Appleton and Co., 1924.

Donald, David Herbert. *Lincoln Reconsidered: Essays on the Civil War Era.* 1947. New York, NY: Vintage Press, 1989 ed.

———. (ed.). *Why the North Won the Civil War.* 1960. New York, NY: Collier, 1962 ed.

———. *Lincoln.* New York, NY: Simon and Schuster, 1995.

Douglas, Henry Kyd. *I Rode With Stonewall: The War Experiences of the Youngest Member of Jackson's Staff.* 1940. Chapel Hill, NC: University of North Carolina Press, 1968 ed.

Douglass, Frederick. *Narrative of the Life of Frederick Douglass: An American Slave.* 1845. New York, NY: Signet, 1997 ed.

———. *The Life and Times of Frederick Douglass, From 1817 to 1882.* London, UK: Christian Age Office, 1882.

Drescher, Seymour, and Stanley L. Engerman (eds.). *A Historical Guide to World Slavery.* New York, NY: Oxford University Press, 1998.

Du Bois, William Edward Burghardt. *Darkwater: Voices From Within the Veil.* New York, NY: Harcourt, Brace and Howe, 1920.

DuBose, John Witherspoon. *General Joseph Wheeler and the Army of Tennessee.* New York, NY: Neale Publishing Co., 1912.

Duff, Mountstuart E. Grant. *Notes From a Diary, 1851-1872.* 2 vols. London, UK: John Murray, 1897.

Duke, Basil W. *Reminiscences of General Basil W. Duke, C.S.A.* New York, NY: Doubleday, Page and Co., 1911.

Dunbar, Rowland (ed.). *Jefferson Davis, Constitutionalist: His Letters, Papers, and Speeches.* 10 vols. Jackson, MS: Mississippi Department of Archives and History, 1923.

Durden, Robert F. *The Gray and the Black: The Confederate Debate on Emancipation.* Baton Rouge, LA: Louisiana State University Press, 1972.

Early, Jubal A. *A Memoir of the Last Year of the War for Independence in the Confederate States of America.* Lynchburg, VA: Charles W. Button, 1867.

Eaton, Clement. *A History of the Southern Confederacy.* 1945. New York, NY: Free Press, 1966 ed.

———. *Jefferson Davis.* New York, NY: Free Press, 1977.

Eaton, John, and Ethel Osgood Mason. *Grant, Lincoln and the Freedmen: Reminiscences of the Civil War, With Special Reference to the Work of the Contrabands and Freedmen of the Mississippi Valley.* New York, NY: Longmans, Green, and Co., 1907.

Edmonds, Franklin Spencer. *Ulysses S. Grant.* Philadelphia, PA: George W. Jacobs and Co., 1915.

Egerton, Douglas R. *Year of Meteors: Stephen Douglas, Abraham Lincoln, and the Election that Brought on the Civil War.* New York, NY: Bloomsbury Press, 2010.

Elliot, Jonathan. *The Debates in the Several State Conventions on the Adoption of the Federal Constitution, As Recommended by the General Convention at Philadelphia in 1787.* 5 vols. Philadelphia, PA: J. B. Lippincott, 1891.

Elliott, E. N. *Cotton is King, and Pro-Slavery Arguments: Comprising the Writings of Hammond, Harper, Christy, Stringfellow, Hodge, Bledsoe, and Cartwright, on this Important Subject.* Augusta, GA: Pritchard, Abbott and Loomis, 1860.

Ellis, Joseph J. *American Sphinx: The Character of Thomas Jefferson.* 1996. New York, NY: Vintage, 1998 ed.

———. *Founding Brothers: The Revolutionary Generation.* 2000. New York, NY: Vintage, 2002 ed.

Eltis, David. *The Rise of African Slavery in the Americas.* Cambridge, UK: Cambridge University Press, 2000.

Emerson, Bettie Alder Calhoun. *Historic Southern Monuments: Representative Memorials of the Heroic Dead of the Southern Confederacy.* New York, NY: Neale Publishing Co., 1911.

Emerson, Ralph Waldo. *The Complete Works of Ralph Waldo Emerson.* 12 vols. 1878. Boston, MA: Houghton, Mifflin and Co., 1904 ed.

———. *Journals of Ralph Waldo Emerson.* 10 vols. Edward Waldo Emerson and Waldo Emerson Forbes, eds. Boston, MA: Houghton, Mifflin and Co., 1910.

———. *The Journals and Miscellaneous Notebooks of Ralph Waldo Emerson.* 16 vols. Cambridge, MA: Belknap Press, 1975.

Emison, John Avery. *Lincoln Über Alles: Dictatorship Comes to America.* Gretna, LA: Pelican Publishing Co., 2009.

Encyclopedia Britannica: A New Survey of Universal Knowledge. 1768. Chicago, IL/London, UK: Encyclopedia Britannica, 1955 ed.

Epstein, Daniel Mark. *The Lincolns: Portrait of a Marriage.* New York, NY: Ballantine, 2008.

———. *Lincoln's Men: The President and His Private Secretaries.* New York, NY: HarperCollins, 2009.

Escott, Paul D. (ed.). *North Carolinians in the Era of the Civil War and Reconstruction.* Chapel Hill, NC: University of North Carolina Press, 2008.

———. *"What Shall We Do with the Negro?": Lincoln, White Racism, and Civil War America.* Charlottesville, VA: University of Virginia Press, 2009.

Essah, Patience. *A House Divided: Slavery and Emancipation in Delaware, 1638-1865.* Charlottesville, VA: University Press of Virginia, 1996.

Etulain, Richard W. (Ed.). *Lincoln Looks West: From the Mississippi to the Pacific.* Carbondale, IL: Southern Illinois University Press, 2010.

Evans, Clement Anselm (ed.). *Confederate Military History: A Library of Confederate States History, in Twelve Volumes, Written By Distinguished Men of the South.* 12 vols. Atlanta, GA: Confederate Publishing Co., 1899.

Evans, Eli N. *Judah P. Benjamin: The Jewish Confederate.* 1988. New York, NY: Free Press, 1989 ed.

Evans, Lawrence B. (ed.). *Writings of George Washington.* New York, NY: G. P. Putnam's Sons, 1908.

Faragher, John Mack. *Sugar Creek: Life on the Illinois Prairie.* New Haven, CT: Yale University Press, 1986.

Farrar, Victor John. *The Annexation of Russian America to the United States.* Washington D.C.: W. F. Roberts, 1937.

Farrow, Anne, Joel Lang, and Jennifer Frank. *Complicity: How the North Promoted, Prolonged, and Profited From Slavery.* New York, NY: Ballantine, 2005.

Faulkner, William. *The Unvanquished.* 1934. New York, NY: Vintage, 1966 ed.

Faust, Patricia L. (ed.). *Historical Times Illustrated Encyclopedia of the Civil War.* New York, NY: Harper and Row, 1986.

Fay, Edwin Hedge. *This Infernal War: The Confederate Letters of Edwin H. Fay.* Austin, TX: University of Texas Press, 1958.

Fehrenbacher, Don E. (ed.). *Abraham Lincoln: A Documentary Portrait Through His Speeches and Writings.* New York, NY: Signet, 1964.

———. *Lincoln in Text and Context: Collected Essays.* Stanford, CA: Stanford University press, 1987.

———. (ed.) *Abraham Lincoln: Speeches and Writings, 1859-1865.* New York, NY: Library of America, 1989.

———. *The Slaveholding Republic: An Account of the United States Government's Relations to Slavery.* New York, NY: Oxford University Press, 2002.

Fehrenbacher, Don E., and Virginia Fehrenbacher (eds). *Recollected Works of Abraham Lincoln.* Stanford, CA: Stanford University Press, 1996.

Ferris, Marcie Cohen, and Mark I. Greenberg (eds.). *Jewish Roots in Southern Soil: A New History.* Waltham, MA: Brandeis University Press, 2006.

Fields, Annie (ed.) *Life and Letters of Harriet Beecher Stowe.* Cambridge, MA: Riverside Press, 1897.

Findlay, Bruce, and Esther Findlay. *Your Rugged Constitution: How America's House of Freedom is Planned and Built.* 1950. Stanford, CA: Stanford University Press, 1951 ed.

Finkelman, Paul. *Dred Scott v. Sanford: A Brief History With Documents.* Boston, MA: Bedford Books, 1997.

Fite, Emerson David. *Social and Industrial Conditions in the North During the Civil War.* New York, NY: Macmillan, 1910.

———. *The Presidential Election of 1860.* New York, NY: MacMillan, 1911.

Fleming, Walter Lynwood. *Civil War and Reconstruction in Alabama.* New York, NY: Macmillan, 1905.

Flood, Charles Bracelen. *1864: Lincoln At the Gates of History.* New York, NY: Simon and Schuster, 2009.

Fogel, Robert William. *Without Consent or Contract: The Rise and Fall of American Slavery.* New York, NY: W. W. Norton, 1989.

Fogel, Robert William, and Stanley L. Engerman. *Time On the Cross: The Economics of American Negro Slavery.* Boston, MA: Little, Brown, and Co., 1974.

Foley, John P. (ed.). *The Jeffersonian Cyclopedia.* New York, NY: Funk and Wagnalls,

1900.

Foner, Eric. *Free Soil, Free Labor, Free Men: The Ideology of the Republican Party Before the Civil War*. New York, NY: Oxford University Press, 1970.

———. *Reconstruction: America's Unfinished Revolution, 1863-1877*. 1988. New York, NY: Harper and Row, 1989 ed.

Foote, Shelby. *The Civil War: A Narrative, Fort Sumter to Perryville, Vol. 1*. 1958. New York, NY: Vintage, 1986 ed.

———. *The Civil War: A Narrative, Fredericksburg to Meridian, Vol. 2*. 1963. New York, NY: Vintage, 1986 ed.

———. *The Civil War: A Narrative, Red River to Appomattox, Vol. 3*. 1974. New York, NY: Vintage, 1986 ed.

Ford, Paul Leicester (ed.). *The Works of Thomas Jefferson*. 12 vols. New York, NY: G. P. Putnam's Sons, 1904.

Ford, Worthington Chauncey (ed.). *A Cycle of Adams Letters*. 2 vols. Boston, MA: Houghton Mifflin, 1920.

Forman, S. E. *The Life and Writings of Thomas Jefferson*. Indianapolis, IN: Bowen-Merrill, 1900.

Fornieri, Joseph (ed.). *The Language of Liberty: The Political Speeches and Writings of Abraham Lincoln*. Washington, D.C.: Regnery, 2009.

Förster, Stig, and Jörg Nagler (eds.). *On the Road to Total War: The American Civil War and the German Wars of Unification, 1861-1871*. 1997. Cambridge, UK: Cambridge University Press, 2002 ed.

Foster, John W. *A Century of American Diplomacy*. Boston, MA: Houghton, Mifflin and Co., 1901.

Fowler, John D. *The Confederate Experience Reader: Selected Documents and Essays*. New York, NY: Routledge, 2007.

Fowler, William Chauncey. *The Sectional Controversy; or Passages in the Political History of the United States, Including the Causes of the War Between the Sections*. New York, NY: Charles Scribner, 1864.

Fox, Gustavus Vasa. *Confidential Correspondence of Gustavus Vasa Fox, Assistant Secretary of the Navy, 1861-1865*. 2 vols. 1918. New York, NY: Naval History Society, 1920 ed.

Fox-Genovese, Elizabeth. *Within the Plantation Household: Black and White Women of the Old South (Gender and American Culture)*. Chapel Hill, NC: University of North Carolina Press, 1988.

Franklin, Benjamin. *The Complete Works of Benjamin Franklin*. 10 vols. New York, NY: G. P. Putnam's Sons, 1887.

Franklin, John Hope. *Reconstruction After the Civil War*. Chicago, IL: University of Chicago Press, 1961.

Fredrickson, George M. *The Black Image in the White Mind: The Debate on Afro-American Character and Destiny, 1817-1914*. New York, NY: Harper and Row, 1971.

———. *Big Enough to Be Inconsistent: Abraham Lincoln Confronts Slavery and Race*. Cambridge, MA: Harvard University Press, 2008.

Freiling, Thomas. *Walking With Lincoln: Spiritual Strength From America's Favorite*

President. Grand Rapids, MI: Revell, 2009.
Fremantle, Arthur James. *Three Months in the Southern States, April-June, 1863*. New York, NY: John Bradburn, 1864.
Friedman, Saul S. *Jews and the American Slave Trade*. New Brunswick, NJ: Transaction, 2000.
Furguson, Ernest B. *Freedom Rising: Washington in the Civil War*. 2004. New York, NY: Vintage, 2005 ed.
Furnas, J. C. *The Americans: A Social History of the United States, 1587-1914*. New York, NY: G. P. Putnam's Sons, 1969.
Galenson, David W. *White Servitude in Colonial America*. New York, NY: Cambridge University Press, 1981.
Garland, Hugh A. *The Life of John Randolph of Roanoke*. New York, NY: D. Appleton and Co., 1874.
Garraty, John A. (ed.). *Historical Viewpoints: Notable Articles From American Heritage, Vol. One to 1877*. 1970. New York, NY: Harper and Row, 1979 ed.
Garraty, John A., and Robert A. McCaughey. *A Short History of the American Nation*. 1966. New York, NY: HarperCollins, 1989 ed.
Garrison, Webb B. *Civil War Trivia and Fact Book*. Nashville, TN: Rutledge Hill Press, 1992.
——. *The Lincoln No One Knows: The Mysterious Man Who Ran the Civil War*. Nashville, TN: Rutledge Hill Press, 1993.
——. *Civil War Curiosities: Strange Stories, Oddities, Events, and Coincidences*. Nashville, TN: Rutledge Hill Press, 1994.
——. *The Amazing Civil War*. Nashville, TN: Rutledge Hill Press, 1998.
Garrison, Wendell Phillips, and Francis Jackson Garrison. *William Lloyd Garrison, 1805-1879*. 4 vols. New York, NY: Century Co., 1889.
Garrison, William Lloyd. *Thoughts on African Colonization*. Boston, MA: Garrison and Knapp, 1832.
Gates, Henry Louis, Jr. (ed.) *The Classic Slave Narratives*. New York, NY: Mentor, 1987.
Gates, Henry Louis, Jr., and Donald Yacovone (eds). *Lincoln on Race and Slavery*. Princeton, NJ: Princeton University Press, 2009.
Genovese, Eugene D. *Roll, Jordan, Roll: The World the Slaves Made*. New York, NY: Pantheon, 1974.
Gerster, Patrick, and Nicholas Cords (eds.). *Myth and Southern History*. 2 vols. 1974. Champaign, IL: University of Illinois Press, 1989 ed.
Gienapp, William E. *Abraham Lincoln and Civil War America: A Biography*. Oxford, UK: Oxford University Press, 2002.
Gilmore, James Roberts. *Personal Recollections of Abraham Lincoln and the Civil War*. Boston, MA: L. C. Page and Co., 1898.
Golay, Michael. *A Ruined Land: The End of the Civil War*. New York, NY: John Wiley and Sons, 1999.
Gordon, Armistead Churchill. *Figures From American History: Jefferson Davis*. New York, NY: Charles Scribner's Sons, 1918.

Gower, Herschel, and Jack Allen (eds.). *Pen and Sword: The Life and Journals of Randal W. McGavock*. Nashville, TN: Tennessee Historical Commission, 1959.

Gragg, Rod. *The Illustrated Confederate Reader: Extraordinary Eyewitness Accounts by the Civil War's Southern Soldiers and Civilians*. New York, NY: Gramercy Books, 1989.

Graham, John Remington. *A Constitutional History of Secession*. Gretna, LA: Pelican Publishing Co., 2003.

———. *Blood Money: The Civil War and the Federal Reserve*. Gretna, LA: Pelican Publishing Co., 2006.

Grant, Arthur James. *Greece in the Age of Pericles*. London, UK: John Murray, 1893.

Grant, Ulysses Simpson. *Personal Memoirs of U. S. Grant*. 2 vols. 1885-1886. New York, NY: Charles L. Webster and Co., 1886.

Gray, Robert, Rev. (compiler). *The McGavock Family: A Genealogical History of James McGavock and His Descendants, from 1760 to 1903*. Richmond, VA: W. E. Jones, 1903.

Gray, Thomas R. *The Confessions of Nat Turner: The Leader of the Late Insurrection in Southampton, Virginia*. Richmond, VA: Thomas R. Gray, 1831.

Greeley, Horace (ed.). *The Writings of Cassius Marcellus Clay*. New York, NY: Harper and Brothers, 1848.

———. *A History of the Struggle for Slavery Extension or Restriction in the United States From the Declaration of Independence to the Present Day*. New York, NY: Dix, Edwards and Co., 1856.

———. *The American Conflict: A History of the Great Rebellion in the United States, 1861-1865*. 2 vols. Hartford, CT: O. D. Case and Co., 1867.

Green, Constance McLaughlin. *Eli Whitney and the Birth of American Technology*. Boston, MA: Little, Brown, and Co., 1956.

———. *Washington: A History of the Capital, 1800-1950*. 1962. Princeton, NJ: Princeton University Press, 1976 ed.

Greenberg, Martin H., and Charles G. Waugh (eds.). *The Price of Freedom: Slavery and the Civil War—Vol. 1, The Demise of Slavery*. Nashville, TN: Cumberland House, 2000.

Greene, Lorenzo Johnston. *The Negro in Colonial New England, 1620-1776*. New York, NY: Columbia University Press, 1942.

Greenhow, Rose O'Neal. *My Imprisonment and the First Year of Abolition Rule at Washington*. London, UK: Richard Bentley, 1863.

Grimsley, Mark. *The Hard Hand of War: Union Military Policy Toward Southern Civilians, 1861-1865*. 1995. Cambridge, UK: Cambridge University Press, 1997 ed.

Grissom, Michael Andrew. *Southern By the Grace of God*. 1988. Gretna, LA: Pelican Publishing Co., 1995 ed.

Groom, Winston. *Shrouds of Glory - From Atlanta to Nashville: The Last Great Campaign of the Civil War*. New York, NY: Grove Press, 1995.

Guelzo, Allen C. *Abraham Lincoln: Redeemer President*. Cambridge, UK: William B. Eerdmans, 1999.

———. *Abraham Lincoln As a Man of Ideas*. Carbondale, IL: Southern Illinois University Press, 2009.

Gwatkin, H. M., and J. P. Whitney (eds.). *The Cambridge Medieval History, Vol. 2: The Rise of the Saracens and the Foundation of the Western Empire.* New York, NY: Macmillan, 1913.

Hacker, Louis Morton. *The Shaping of the American Tradition.* New York, NY: Columbia University Press, 1947.

Haggard, Dixie Ray (ed.). *African Americans in the Nineteenth Century: People and Perspectives.* Santa Barbara, CA: ABC-Clio, 2010.

Hall, B. C., and C. T. Wood. *The South: A Two-step Odyssey on the Backroads of the Enchanted Land.* New York, NY: Touchstone, 1996.

Hall, Kermit L. (ed). *The Oxford Companion to the Supreme Court of the United States.* New York, NY: Oxford University Press, 1992.

Hamblin, Ken. *Pick a Better Country: An Unassuming Colored Guy Speaks His Mind About America.* New York, NY: Touchstone, 1997.

Hamilton, Alexander, James Madison, and John Jay. *The Federalist Papers.* New York, NY: Signet Classics, 2003.

Hamilton, Neil A. *Rebels and Renegades: A Chronology of Social and Political Dissent in the United States.* New York, NY: Routledge, 2002.

Hanchett, William. *Out of the Wilderness: The Life of Abraham Lincoln.* Urbana, IL: University of Illinois Press, 1994.

Hannity, Sean. *Let Freedom Ring: Winning the War of Liberty Over Liberalism.* New York, NY: HarperCollins, 2002.

Hansen, Harry. *The Civil War: A History.* 1961. Harmondsworth, UK: Mentor, 1991 ed.

Harding, Samuel Bannister. *The Contest Over the Ratification of the Federal Constitution in the State of Massachusetts.* New York, NY: Longmans, Green, and Co., 1896.

Harper, William, James Henry Hammond, William Gilmore Simms, and Thomas Roderick Dew. *The Pro-Slavery Argument, As Maintained by the Most Distinguished Writers of the Southern States.* Charleston, SC: Walker, Richards and Co., 1852.

Harrell, David Edwin, Jr., Edwin S. Gaustad, John B. Boles, Sally Foreman Griffith, Randall M. Miller, and Randall B. Woods. *Unto a Good Land: A History of the American People.* Grand Rapids, MI: William B. Eerdmans, 2005.

Harris, Joel Chandler. *Stories of Georgia.* New York, NY: American Book Co., 1896.

Harris, Norman Dwight. *The History of Negro Servitude in Illinois.* Chicago, IL: A. C. McClurg and Co., 1904.

Harris, William C. *Lincoln's Rise to the Presidency.* Lawrence, KS: University Press of Kansas, 2007.

Harrison, Peleg D. *The Stars and Stripes and Other American Flags.* 1906. Boston, MA: Little, Brown, and Co., 1908 ed.

Hartzell, Josiah. *The Genesis of the Republican Party.* Canton, OH: n.p., 1890.

Harwell, Richard B. (ed.). *The Confederate Reader: How the South Saw the War.* 1957. Mineola, NY: Dover, 1989 ed.

Hattaway, Herman, and Archer Jones. *How the North Won: A Military History of the Civil War.* 1983. Champaign, IL: University of Illinois Press, 1991 ed.

Hawthorne, Julian (ed.). *Orations of American Orators*. 2 vols. New York, NY: Colonial Press, 1900.

Hawthorne, Julian, James Schouler, and Elisha Benjamin Andrews. *United States, From the Discovery of the North American Continent Up to the Present Time*. 9 vols. New York, NY: Co-operative Publication Society, 1894.

Hayden, Horace Edwin. *Virginia Genealogies: A Genealogy of the Glassell Family of Scotland and Virginia*. 1885. Wilkes-Barre, PA: N.P., 1891 ed.

Haygood, Atticus G. *Our Brother in Black: His Freedom and His Future*. Nashville, TN: M. E. Church, 1896.

Hedrick, Joan D. (ed.). *The Oxford Harriet Beecher Stowe Reader*. New York, NY: Oxford University Press, 1999.

Heidler, David S., and Jeanne T. Heidler. *Henry Clay: The Essential American*. New York, NY: Random House, 2010.

Helper, Hinton Rowan. *The Impending Crisis of the South: How to Meet It*. New York, NY: A. B. Burdick, 1860.

———. *Compendium of the Impending Crisis of the South*. New York, NY: A. B. Burdick, 1860.

———. *Nojoque: A Question for a Continent*. New York, NY: George W. Carleton, 1867.

———. *The Negroes in Negroland: The Negroes in America; and Negroes Generally*. New York, NY: George W. Carlton, 1868.

———. *Oddments of Andean Diplomacy and Other Oddments*. St. Louis, MO: W. S. Bryan, 1879.

Henderson, George Francis Robert. *Stonewall Jackson and the American Civil War*. 2 vols. London, UK: Longmans, Green, and Co., 1919.

Henry, Robert Selph (ed.). *The Story of the Confederacy*. 1931. New York, NY: Konecky and Konecky, 1999 ed.

———. *As They Saw Forrest: Some Recollections and Comments of Contemporaries*. 1956. Wilmington, NC: Broadfoot Publishing Co., 1991 ed.

———. *First with the Most: Forrest*. New York, NY: Konecky and Konecky, 1992.

Henson, Josiah. *Father Henson's Story of His Own Life*. Boston, MA: John P. Jewett and Co., 1858.

Herndon, William H., and Jesse W. Weik. *Abraham Lincoln: The True Story of a Great Life*. 2 vols. New York, NY: D. Appleton and Co., 1892.

Hertz, Emanuel. *Abraham Lincoln: A New Portrait*. 2 Vols. New York, NY: H. Liveright, 1931.

———. *The Hidden Lincoln*. New York, NY: Blue Ribbon Works, 1940.

Hervey, Anthony. *Why I Wave the Confederate Flag, Written By a Black Man: The End of Niggerism and the Welfare State*. Oxford, UK: Trafford Publishing, 2006.

Hesseltine, William B. *Lincoln and the War Governors*. New York, NY: Alfred A. Knopf, 1948.

Hey, David. *The Oxford Guide to Family History*. Oxford, UK: Oxford University Press, 1993.

Hickey, William. *The Constitution of the United States*. Philadelphia, PA: T. K. and P. G. Collins, 1853.

Highsmith, Carol M. and Ted Landphair. *Civil War Battlefields and Landmarks: A Photographic Tour.* New York, NY: Random House, 2003.

Hildreth, Richard. *The White Slave: Another Picture of Slave Life in America.* Boston, MA: Adamant Media Corp., 2001.

Hinkle, Don. *Embattled Banner: A Reasonable Defense of the Confederate Battle Flag.* Paducah, KY: Turner Publishing Co., 1997.

Hitler, Adolf. *Mein Kampf.* 2 vols. 1925, 1926. New York: NY: Reynal and Hitchcock, 1941 English translation ed.

Hoffman, Michael A., II. *They Were White and They Were Slaves: The Untold History of the Enslavement of Whites in Early America.* Dresden, NY: Wiswell Ruffin House, 1993.

Hofstadter, Richard. *The American Political Tradition, and the Men Who Made It.* New York, NY: Alfred A. Knopf, 1948.

Holland, Jesse J. *Black Men Built the Capitol: Discovering African-American History in and Around Washington, D.C.* Guilford, CT: The Globe Pequot Press, 2007.

Holland, Josiah Gilbert. *The Life of Abraham Lincoln.* Springfield, MA: Gurdon Bill, 1866.

Holland, Rupert Sargent (ed.). *Letters and Diary of Laura M. Towne: Written From the Sea Islands of South Carolina, 1862-1884.* Cambridge, MA: Riverside Press, 1912.

Holzer, Harold (ed.). *The Lincoln-Douglas Debates: The First Complete, Unexpurgated Text.* 1993. Bronx, NY: Fordham University Press, 2004 ed.

Hood, John Bell. *Advance and Retreat: Personal Experiences in the United States and Confederate States Armies.* New Orleans, LA: G. T. Beauregard, 1880.

Horn, Stanley F. *Invisible Empire: The Story of the Ku Klux Klan, 1866-1871.* 1939. Montclair, NJ: Patterson Smith, 1969 ed.

———. *The Decisive Battle of Nashville.* 1956. Baton Rouge, LA: Louisiana State University Press, 1991 ed.

Horwitz, Tony. *Confederates in the Attic: Dispatches From the Unfinished Civil War.* 1998. New York, NY: Vintage, 1999 ed.

House Documents, 64th Congress, 1st Session, December 6, 1915, to September 8, 1916, Vol. 145. Washington, D.C.: Government Printing Office, 1916.

Howe, Daniel Wait. *Political History of Secession.* New York, NY: G. P. Putnam's Sons, 1914.

Howe, Henry. *Historical Collections of Virginia.* Charleston, SC: William R. Babcock, 1852.

Howe, M. A. DeWolfe (ed.). *Home Letters of General Sherman.* New York, NY: Charles Scribner's Sons, 1909.

Hubbard, John Milton. *Notes of a Private.* St. Louis, MO: Nixon-Jones, 1911.

Hunt, John Gabriel (ed.). *The Essential Abraham Lincoln.* Avenel, NJ: Portland House, 1993.

Hurmence, Belinda (ed.). *Before Freedom, When I Can Just Remember: Twenty-seven Oral Histories of Former South Carolina Slaves.* 1989. Winston-Salem, NC: John F. Blair, 2002 ed.

Hurst, Jack. *Nathan Bedford Forrest: A Biography.* 1993. New York, NY: Vintage, 1994 ed.

Ingersoll, Thomas G., and Robert E. O'Connor. *Politics and Structure: Essential of American National Government*. North Scituate, MA: Duxbury Press, 1979.

Isaacson, Walter (ed.). *Profiles in Leadership: Historians on the Elusive Quality of Greatness*. New York, NY: W. W. Norton and Co., 2010.

Jaffa, Harry V. *Crisis of the House Divided: An Interpretation of the Issues in the Lincoln-Douglas Debates*. 1959. Chicago, IL: University of Chicago Press, 2009 ed.

Jahoda, Gloria. *The Trail of Tears: The Story of the American Indian Removals, 1813-1855*. 1975. New York, NY: Wings Book, 1995 ed.

Jaquette, Henrietta Stratton (ed.). *South After Gettysburg: Letters of Cornelia Hancock, 1863-1868*. Philadelphia, PA: University of Pennsylvania Press, 1937.

Jefferson, Thomas. *Notes on the State of Virginia*. Boston, MA: H. Sprague, 1802.

——. *Thomas Jefferson's Farm Book*. (Edwin Morris Betts, ed.). Charlottesville, VA: Thomas Jefferson Memorial Foundation, 1999.

Jenkins, John S. *The Life of James Knox Polk, Late President of the United States*. Auburn, NY: James M. Alden, 1850.

Jensen, Merrill. *The New Nation: A History of the United States During the Confederation, 1781-1789*. New York, NY: Vintage, 1950.

——. *The Articles of Confederation: An Interpretation of the Social-Constitutional History of the American Revolution, 1774-1781*. Madison, WI: University of Wisconsin Press, 1959.

Jimerson, Randall C. *The Private Civil War: Popular Thought During the Sectional Conflict*. Baton Rouge, LA: Louisiana State University Press, 1988.

Johannsen, Robert Walter. *Lincoln, the South, and Slavery: The Political Dimension*. Baton Rouge, LA: Louisiana State University Press, 1991.

Johnson, Adam Rankin. *The Partisan Rangers of the Confederate States Army*. Louisville, KY: George G. Fetter, 1904.

Johnson, Benjamin Heber. *Making of the American West: People and Perspectives*. Santa Barbara, CA: ABC-Clio, 2007.

Johnson, Clint. *The Politically Incorrect Guide to the South (and Why It Will Rise Again)*. Washington, D.C.: Regnery, 2006.

Johnson, Ludwell H. *North Against South: The American Iliad, 1848-1877*. 1978. Columbia, SC: Foundation for American Education, 1993 ed.

Johnson, Michael, and James L. Roark. *Black Masters: A Free Family of Color in the Old South*. New York, NY: W.W. Norton, 1984.

Johnson, Oliver. *William Lloyd Garrison and His Times*. 1879. Boston, MA: Houghton Mifflin and Co., 1881 ed.

Johnson, Robert Underwood (ed.). *Battles and Leaders of the Civil War*. 4 vols. New York, NY: The Century Co., 1884-1888.

Johnson, Thomas Cary. *The Life and Letters of Robert Lewis Dabney*. Richmond, VA: Presbyterian Committee of Publication, 1903.

Jones, Howard. *Abraham Lincoln and a New Birth of Freedom: The Union and Slavery in the Diplomacy of the Civil War*. Lincoln, NE: University of Nebraska Press, 1999.

Jones, John Beauchamp. *A Rebel War Clerk's Diary at the Confederate States Capital*. 2 vols. in 1. Philadelphia, PA: J. B. Lippincott and Co., 1866.
Jones, John William. *Personal Reminiscences, Anecdotes, and Letters of Gen. Robert E. Lee*. New York, NY: D. Appleton and Co., 1874.
Jones, Wilmer L. *Generals in Blue and Gray*. 2 vols. Westport, CT: Praeger, 2004.
Jordan, Don, and Michael Walsh. *White Cargo: The Forgotten History of Britain's White Slaves in America*. New York, NY: New York University Press, 2008.
Jordan, Ervin L. *Black Confederates and Afro-Yankees in Civil War Virginia*. Charlottesville, VA: University Press of Virginia, 1995.
Jordan, Thomas, and John P. Pryor. *The Campaigns of General Nathan Bedford Forrest and of Forrest's Cavalry*. New Orleans, LA: Blelock and Co., 1868.
Julian, George Washington. *Speeches on Political Questions*. New York, NY: Hurd and Houghton, 1872.
Kane, Joseph Nathan. *Facts About the Presidents: A Compilation of Biographical and Historical Data*. 1959. New York, NY: Ace, 1976 ed.
Katcher, Philip. *The Civil War Source Book*. 1992. New York, NY: Facts on File, 1995 ed.
——. *Brassey's Almanac: The American Civil War*. London, UK: Brassey's, 2003.
Kautz, August Valentine. *Customs of Service for Non-Commissioned Officers and Soldiers (as Derived from Law and Regulations and Practised in the Army of the United States)*. Philadelphia, PA: J. B. Lippincott and Co., 1864.
Keckley, Elizabeth. *Behind the Scenes, or Thirty Years a Slave, and Four Years in the White House*. New York, NY: G. W. Carlton and Co., 1868.
Kelly, Alfred H., Winfred A. Harbison, and Herman Belz. *The American Constitution: Its Origins and Development* (Vol. 2). 1965. New York, NY: W.W. Norton, 1991 ed.
Keneally, Thomas. *Abraham Lincoln*. New York, NY: Viking, 2003.
Kennedy, James Ronald, and Walter Donald Kennedy. *The South Was Right!* Gretna, LA: Pelican Publishing Co., 1994.
——. *Why Not Freedom!: America's Revolt Against Big Government*. Gretna, LA: Pelican Publishing Co., 2005.
——. *Nullifying Tyranny: Creating Moral Communities in an Immoral Society*. Gretna, LA: Pelican Publishing Co., 2010.
Kennedy, Walter Donald. *Myths of American Slavery*. Gretna, LA: Pelican Publishing Co., 2003.
Kennett, Lee B. *Sherman: A Soldier's Life*. 2001. New York, NY: HarperCollins, 2002 ed.
Kettell, Thomas Prentice. *History of the Great Rebellion*. Hartford, CT: L. Stebbins, 1865.
Kinder, Hermann, and Werner Hilgemann. *The Anchor Atlas of World History: From the French Revolution to the American Bicentennial*. 2 vols. Garden City, NY: Anchor, 1978.
King, Charles R. (ed.). *The Life and Correspondence of Rufus King*. 6 vols. New York, NY: G. P. Putnam's Sons, 1897.

King, Edward. *The Great South: A Record of Journeys.* Hartford, CT: American Publishing Co., 1875.

Kinshasa, Kwando Mbiassi. *Black Resistance to the Ku Klux Klan in the Wake of the Civil War.* Jefferson, NC: McFarland and Co., 2006.

Kirkland, Edward Chase. *The Peacemakers of 1864.* New York, NY: Macmillan, 1927.

Klingaman, William K. *Abraham Lincoln and the Road to Emancipation, 1861-1865.* 2001. New York, NY: Penguin, 2002 ed.

Knox, Thomas Wallace. *Camp-Fire and Cotton-Field: Southern Adventure in Time of War - Life With the Union Armies, and Residence on a Louisiana Plantation.* New York, NY: Blelock and Co., 1865.

Koger, Larry. *Black Slaveowners: Free Black Slave Masters in South Carolina, 1790-1860.* Columbia, SC: University of South Carolina Press, 1995.

Kunhardt, Philip B., Peter W. Kunhardt, and Peter W. Kunhardt, Jr. *Looking for Lincoln: The Making of an American Icon.* New York, NY: Borzoi, 2008.

Lamb, Brian, and Susan Swain (eds.). *Abraham Lincoln: Great American Historians on Our Sixteenth President.* New York, NY: PublicAffairs, 2010.

Lamon, Ward Hill. *The Life of Abraham Lincoln: From His Birth to His Inauguration as President.* Boston, MA: James R. Osgood and Co., 1872.

——. *Recollections of Abraham Lincoln: 1847-1865.* Chicago, IL: A. C. McClurg and Co., 1895.

Lang, J. Stephen. *The Complete Book of Confederate Trivia.* Shippensburg, PA: Burd Street Press, 1996.

Lanning, Michael Lee. *The African-American Soldier: From Crispus Attucks to Colin Powell.* 1997. New York, NY: Citadel Press, 2004 ed.

Lapsley, Arthur Brooks (ed.). *The Writings of Abraham Lincoln.* 8 vols. New York, NY: The Lamb Publishing Co., 1906.

Lawrence, William. *Life of Amos A. Lawrence.* Boston, MA: Houghton, Mifflin, and Co., 1899.

Leech, Margaret. *Reveille in Washington, 1860-1865.* 1941. Alexandria, VA: Time-Life Books, 1980 ed.

Lee, Robert E., Jr. *Recollections and Letters of General Robert E. Lee.* New York, NY: Doubleday, Page and Co., 1904.

Lehrman, Lewis E. *Lincoln at Peoria: The Turning Point.* Mechanicsburg, PA: Stackpole, 2008.

Lemay, J. A. Leo, and P. M. Zall (eds.). *Benjamin Franklin's Autobiography: An Authoritative Text, Backgrounds, Criticism.* 1791. New York, NY: W. W. Norton and Co., 1986 ed.

Lemire, Elise. *Black Walden: Slavery and Its Aftermath in Concord, Massachusetts.* Philadelphia, PA: University of Pennsylvania Press, 2009.

Lester, Charles Edwards. *Life and Public Services of Charles Sumner.* New York, NY: U.S. Publishing Co., 1874.

Lester, John C., and D. L. Wilson. *Ku Klux Klan: Its Origin, Growth, and Disbandment.* 1884. New York, NY: Neale Publishing, 1905 ed.

Lewis, Lloyd. *Myths After Lincoln.* 1929. New York, NY: The Press of the Reader's

Club, 1941 ed.
LeVert, Suzanne (ed.). *The Civil War Society's Encyclopedia of the Civil War*. New York, NY: Wings Books, 1997.
Levin, Mark R. *Liberty and Tyranny: A Conservative Manifesto*. New York, NY: Threshold, 2009.
Lincoln, Abraham. *The Autobiography of Abraham Lincoln* (selected from the *Complete Works of Abraham Lincoln*, 1894, by John G. Nicolay and John Hay). New York, NY: Francis D. Tandy Co., 1905.
Lincoln, Abraham, and Stephen A. Douglas. *Political Debates Between Abraham Lincoln and Stephen A. Douglas*. Cleveland, OH: Burrows Brothers Co., 1894.
Lind, Michael (ed.). *Hamilton's Republic: Readings in the American Democratic Nationalist Tradition*. New York, NY: Free Press, 1997.
Littell, Eliakim (ed.). *The Living Age*. Seventh Series, Vol. 30. Boston, MA: The Living Age Co., 1906.
Litwack, Leon F. *North of Slavery: The Negro in the Free States, 1790-1860*. Chicago, IL: University of Chicago Press, 1961.
———. *Been in the Storm So Long: The Aftermath of Slavery*. New York, NY: Vintage, 1980.
Livermore, Thomas L. *Numbers and Losses in the Civil War in America, 1861-65*. 1900. Carlisle, PA: John Kallmann, 1996 ed.
Livingstone, William. *Livingstone's History of the Republican Party*. 2 vols. Detroit, MI: William Livingstone, 1900.
Locke, John. *Two Treatises of Government* (Mark Goldie, ed.). 1924. London, UK: Everyman, 1998 ed.
Lodge, Henry Cabot (ed.). *The Works of Alexander Hamilton*. 12 vols. New York, NY: G. P. Putnam's Sons, 1904.
Logan, John Alexander. *The Great Conspiracy: Its Origin and History*. New York, NY: A. R. Hart, 1886.
Logsdon, David R. (ed.). *Eyewitnesses at the Battle of Franklin*. 1988. Nashville, TN: Kettle Mills Press, 2000 ed.
———. *Tennessee Antebellum Trail Guidebook*. Nashville, TN: Kettle Mills Press, 1995.
Long, David E. *The Jewel of Liberty: Abraham Lincoln's Re-election and the End of Slavery*. Mechanicsburg, PA: Stackpole, 2008.
Long, Everette Beach, and Barbara Long. *The Civil War Day by Day: An Almanac, 1861-1865*. 1971. New York, NY: Da Capo Press, 1985 ed.
Lonn, Ella. *Foreigners in the Confederacy*. 1940. Chapel Hill, NC: University of North Carolina Press, 2002 ed.
Lott, Stanley K. *The Truth About American Slavery*. 2004. Clearwater, SC: Eastern Digital Resources, 2005 ed.
Lowry, Don. *Dark and Cruel War: The Decisive Months of the Civil War, September-December 1864*. New York, NY: Hippocrene, 1993.
Lubbock, Francis Richard. *Six Decades in Texas, or Memoirs of Francis Richard Lubbock, Governor of Texas in War-Time, 1861-1863*. 1899. Austin, TX: Ben C. Jones, 1900 ed.
Ludlow, Daniel H. (ed.). *Encyclopedia of Mormonism: The History, Scripture, Doctrine, and*

Procedure of the Church of Jesus Christ of Latter-Day Saints. New York, NY: Macmillan, 1992.

Lytle, Andrew Nelson. *Bedford Forrest and His Critter Company*. New York, NY: G. P. Putnam's Sons, 1931.

MacDonald, William. *Select Documents Illustrative of the History of the United States 1776-1861*. New York, NY: Macmillan, 1897.

Mackay, Charles. *Life and Liberty in America, or Sketches of a Tour in the United States and Canada in 1857-58*. New York, NY: Harper and Brothers, 1859.

Madison, James. *Letters and Other Writings of James Madison, Fourth President of the United States*. 4 vols. Philadelphia, PA: J. B. Lippincott and Co., 1865.

Magness, Phillip W., and Sebastian S. Page. *Colonization After Emancipation: Lincoln and the Movement for Black Resettlement*. Columbia, MO: University of Missouri Press, 2011.

Maihafer, Harry J. *War of Words: Abraham Lincoln and the Civil War Press*. Dulles, VA: Brassey's, 2001.

Main, Jackson Turner. *The Anti-Federalists: Critics of the Constitution, 1781-1788*. 1961. New York, NY: W. W. Norton and Co., 1974 ed.

Malone, Laurence J. *Opening the West: Federal Internal Improvements Before 1860*. Westport, CT: Greenwood Press, 1998.

Mandel, Bernard. *Labor, Free and Slave: Workingmen and the Anti-Slavery Movement in the United States*. New York, NY: Associated Authors, 1955.

Manegold, Catherine S. *The Forgotten History of Slavery in the North*. Princeton, NJ: Princeton University Press, 2010.

Manning, Timothy D., Sr. (ed.) *Lincoln Reconsidered: Conference Reader*. High Point, NC: Heritage Foundation Press, 2006.

Marshall, Jessie Ames. *Private and Official Correspondence of General Benjamin F. Butler During the Period of the Civil War*. 5 vols. Norwood, MA: The Plimpton Press, 1917.

Marten, James. *The Children's Civil War*. Chapel Hill, NC: University of North Carolina Press, 1998.

Martin, Iain C. *The Quotable American Civil War*. Guilford, CT: Lyons Press, 2008.

Martineau, Harriet. *Retrospect of Western Travel*. 3 vols. London, UK: Saunders and Otley, 1838.

Martinez, James Michael. *Carpetbaggers, Cavalry, and the Ku Klux Klan: Exposing the Invisible Empire During Reconstruction*. Lanham, MD: Rowman and Littlefield, 2007.

Martinez, Susan B. *The Psychic Life of Abraham Lincoln*. Franklin Lakes, NJ: New Page Books, 2009.

Masur, Louis P. *The Real War Will Never Get In the Books: Selections From Writers During the Civil War*. New York, NY: Oxford University Press, 1993.

Mathes, Capt. J. Harvey. *General Forrest*. New York, NY: D. Appleton and Co., 1902.

Maury, Dabney Herndon. *Recollections of a Virginian in the Mexican, Indian, and Civil Wars*. New York, NY: Charles Scribner's Sons, 1894.

Mayer, David N. *The Constitutional Thought of Thomas Jefferson*. Charlottesville, VA:

University of Virginia Press, 1995.
Mayer, Henry. *All on Fire: William Lloyd Garrison and the Abolition of Slavery.* New York, NY: St. Martin's Press, 1998.
McAfee, Ward M. *Citizen Lincoln.* Hauppauge, NY: Nova History Publications, 2004.
McCabe, James Dabney. *Our Martyred President: The Life and Public Services of Gen. James A. Garfield, Twentieth President of the United States.* Philadelphia, PA: National Publishing Co., 1881.
McClintock, Russell. *Lincoln and the Decision for War: The Northern Response to Secession.* Chapel Hill, NC: University of North Carolina Press, 2008.
McClure, Alexander Kelly. *Abraham Lincoln and Men of War-Times: Some Personal Recollections of War and Politics During the Lincoln Administration.* Philadelphia, PA: Times Publishing Co., 1892.
——. *Our Presidents and How We Make Them.* New York, NY: Harper and Brothers, 1900.
McCullough, David. *John Adams.* New York, NY: Touchstone, 2001.
McDonald, Forrest. *States' Rights and the Union: Imperium in Imperio, 1776-1876.* Lawrence, KS: University Press of Kansas, 2000.
McDonough, James Lee, and Thomas L. Connelly. *Five Tragic Hours: The Battle of Franklin.* 1983. Knoxville, TN: University of Tennessee Press, 2001 ed.
McElroy, Robert. *Jefferson Davis: The Unreal and the Real.* 1937. New York, NY: Smithmark, 1995 ed.
McFeely, William S. *Yankee Stepfather: General O. O. Howard and the Freedmen - The Story of a Civil War Promise to Former Slaves Made—and Broken.* 1968. New York, NY: W. W. Norton, 1994.
McGehee, Jacob Owen. *Causes That Led to the War Between the States.* Atlanta, GA: A. B. Caldwell, 1915.
McGuire, Hunter, and George L. Christian. *The Confederate Cause and Conduct in the War Between the States.* Richmond, VA: L. H. Jenkins, 1907.
McHenry, George. *The Cotton Trade: Its Bearing Upon the Prosperity of Great Britain and Commerce of the American Republics, Considered in Connection with the System of Negro Slavery in the Confederate States.* London, UK: Saunders, Otley, and Co., 1863.
McIlwaine, Shields. *Memphis Down in Dixie.* New York, NY: E. P. Dutton, 1848.
McKissack, Patricia C., and Frederick McKissack. *Sojourner Truth: Ain't I a Woman?* New York: NY: Scholastic, 1992.
McManus, Edgar J. *A History of Negro Slavery in New York.* Syracuse, NY: Syracuse University Press, 1966.
——. *Black Bondage in the North.* Syracuse, NY: Syracuse University Press, 1973.
McMaster, John Bach. *Our House Divided: A History of the People of the United States During Lincoln's Administration.* 1927. New York, NY: Premier, 1961 ed.
McPherson, Edward. *The Political History of the United States of America, During the Great Rebellion (From November 6, 1860, to July 4, 1864).* Washington, D.C.: Philp and Solomons, 1864.
——. *The Political History of the United States of America, During the Period of Reconstruction, (From April 15, 1865, to July 15, 1870,) Including a Classified Summary of the*

Legislation of the Thirty-ninth, Fortieth, and Forty-first Congresses. Washington, D.C.: Solomons and Chapman, 1875.
McPherson, James M. *The Struggle for Equality: Abolitionists and the Negro in the Civil War and Reconstruction*. 1964. Princeton, NJ: Princeton University Press, 1992 ed.
———. *The Negro's Civil War: How American Negroes Felt and Acted During the War for the Union*. 1965. Chicago, IL: University of Illinois Press, 1982 ed.
———. *Battle Cry of Freedom: The Civil War Era*. Oxford, UK: Oxford University Press, 2003.
———. *The Atlas of the Civil War*. Philadelphia, PA: Courage Books, 2005.
McPherson, James M., and the staff of the *New York Times*. *The Most Fearful Ordeal: Original Coverage of the Civil War by Writers and Reporters of the New York Times*. New York, NY: St. Martin's Press, 2004.
McWhiney, Grady, and Judith Lee Hallock. *Braxton Bragg and Confederate Defeat*. 2 vols. Tuscaloosa, AL: University of Alabama Press, 1991.
McWhiney, Grady, and Perry D. Jamieson. *Attack and Die: Civil War Military Tactics and the Southern Heritage*. Tuscaloosa, AL: University of Alabama Press, 1982.
Melish, Joanne Pope. *Disowning Slavery: Gradual Emancipation and 'Race' in New England 1780-1860*. Ithaca, NY: Cornell University Press, 1998.
Meltzer, Milton. *Slavery: A World History*. 2 vols. in 1. 1971. New York, NY: Da Capo Press, 1993 ed.
Meriwether, Elizabeth Avery. *Facts and Falsehoods Concerning the War on the South, 1861-1865*. (Originally written under the pseudonym "George Edmonds.") Memphis, TN: A. R. Taylor, 1904.
Merry, Robert W. *A Country of Vast Designs: James K. Polk, the Mexican War and the Conquest of the American Continent*. New York, NY: Simon and Schuster, 2009.
Message of the President of the United States and Accompanying Documents to the Two Houses of Congress at the Commencement of the Third Session of the 40th Congress. Washington, D.C.: Government Printing Office, 1868.
Metzger, Bruce M., and Michael D. Coogan (eds.). *The Oxford Companion to the Bible*. New York, NY: Oxford University Press, 1993.
Miller, Francis Trevelyan. *Portrait Life of Lincoln*. Springfield, MA: Patriot Publishing Co., 1910.
Miller, John Chester. *The Wolf By the Ears: Thomas Jefferson and Slavery*. 1977. Charlottesville, VA: University Press of Virginia, 1994 ed.
Miller, Marion Mills (ed.). *Great Debates in American History*. 14 vols. New York, NY: Current Literature, 1913.
Miller, Nathan. *Star-Spangled Men: America's Ten Worst Presidents*. New York, NY: Touchstone, 1998.
Miller, William Lee. *Lincoln's Virtues: An Ethical Biography*. New York, NY: Vintage, 2003.
Min, Pyong Gap (ed.). *Encyclopedia of Racism in the United States*. 3 vols. Westport, CT: Greenwood Press, 2005.
Minor, Charles Landon Carter. *The Real Lincoln: From the Testimony of His Contemporaries*.

Richmond, VA: Everett Waddey Co., 1904.
Mirabello, Mark. *Handbook for Rebels and Outlaws*. Oxford, UK: Mandrake of Oxford, 2009.
Mish, Frederick C. (ed.). *Webster's Ninth New Collegiate Dictionary*. 1984. Springfield, MA: Merriam-Webster.
Mitchell, Margaret. *Gone With the Wind*. 1936. New York, NY: Avon, 1973 ed.
Mitgang, Herbert (ed.). *Lincoln As They Saw Him*. 1956. New York, NY: Collier, 1962 ed.
Mode, Peter George. *Source Book and Bibliographical Guide for American Church History*. Menasha, WI: Collegiate Press, 1921.
Mode, Robert L. (ed.). *Nashville: Its Character in a Changing America*. Nashville, TN: Vanderbilt University, 1981.
Montgomery, David Henry. *The Student's American History*. 1897. Boston, MA: Ginn and Co., 1905 ed.
Moore, Frank (ed.). *The Rebellion Record: A Diary of American Events*. 12 vols. New York, NY: G. P. Putnam, 1861.
Moore, George Henry. *Notes on the History of Slavery in Massachusetts*. New York, NY: D. Appleton and Co., 1866.
Moorhead, James H. *American Apocalypse: Yankee Protestants and the Civil War, 1860-1869*. New Haven, CT: Yale University Press, 1971.
Morel, Lucas E. *Lincoln's Sacred Effort: Defining Religion's Role in American Self-Government*. Lanham, MD: Lexington Books, 2000.
Morris, Benjamin Franklin (ed.). *The Life of Thomas Morris: Pioneer and Long a Legislator of Ohio, and U.S. Senator from 1833 to 1839*. Cincinnati, OH: Moore, Wilstach, Keys and Overend, 1856.
Morris, Roy, Jr. *The Long Pursuit: Abraham Lincoln's Thirty-Year Struggle with Stephen Douglas for the Heart and Soul of America*. New York, NY: HarperCollins, 2008.
Morris, Thomas D. *Free Men All: The Personal Liberty Laws of the North, 1780-1861*. Baltimore, MD: John Hopkins University Press, 1974.
Morton, John Watson. *The Artillery of Nathan Bedford Forrest's Cavalry*. Nashville, TN: The M. E. Church, 1909.
Moses, John. *Illinois: Historical and Statistical, Comprising the Essential Facts of Its Planting and Growth as a Province, County, Territory, and State* (Vol. 2). Chicago, IL: Fergus Printing Co., 1892.
Mullen, Robert W. *Blacks in America's Wars: The Shift in Attitudes From the Revolutionary War to Vietnam*. 1973. New York, NY: Pathfinder, 1991 ed.
Munford, Beverly Bland. *Virginia's Attitude Toward Slavery and Secession*. 1909. Richmond, VA: L. H. Jenkins, 1914 ed.
Murphy, Jim. *A Savage Thunder: Antietam and the Bloody Road to Freedom*. New York, NY: Margaret K. McElderry, 2009.
Napolitano, Andrew P. *The Constitution in Exile: How the Federal Government has Seized Power by Rewriting the Supreme Law of the Land*. Nashville, TN: Nelson Current, 2006.

———. *A Nation of Sheep*. Nashville, TN: Thomas Nelson, 2007.
Neely, Mark E., Jr. *The Fate of Liberty: Abraham Lincoln and Civil Liberties*. New York, NY: Oxford University Press, 1991.
Neilson, William Allan (ed.). *Webster's Biographical Dictionary*. Springfield, MA: G. and C. Merriam Co., 1943.
Neufeldt, Victoria (ed.). *Webster's New World Dictionary of American English* (3rd college ed.). 1970. New York, NY: Prentice Hall, 1994 ed.
Nevins, Allan. *The Evening Post: A Century of Journalism*. New York, NY: Boni and Liveright, 1922.
Nicolay, John G., and John Hay (eds.). *Abraham Lincoln: A History*. 10 vols. New York, NY: The Century Co., 1890.
———. *Complete Works of Abraham Lincoln*. 12 vols. 1894. New York, NY: Francis D. Tandy Co., 1905 ed.
———. *Abraham Lincoln: Complete Works*. 12 vols. 1894. New York, NY: The Century Co., 1907 ed.
Nivola, Pietro S., and David H. Rosenbloom (eds.). *Classic Readings in American Politics*. New York, NY: St. Martin's Press, 1986.
Norris, Mary Harriot (ed.). *Sir Walter Scott's Marmion*. Boston, MA: Leach, Shewell, and Sanborn, 1891.
Norwood, Thomas Manson. *A True Vindication of the South*. Savannah, GA: Citizens and Southern Bank, 1917.
Nye, Russel B. *William Lloyd Garrison and the Humanitarian Reformers*. Boston, MA: Little, Brown and Co., 1955.
Oakes, James. *The Radical and the Republican: Frederick Douglass, Abraham Lincoln, and the Triumph of Antislavery Politics*. New York, NY: W. W. Norton, 2008.
Oates, Stephen B. *Abraham Lincoln: The Man Behind the Myths*. New York, NY: Meridian, 1984.
———. *The Approaching Fury: Voices of the Storm, 1820-1861*. New York, NY: Harper Perennial, 1998.
O'Brien, Cormac. *Secret Lives of the U.S. Presidents: What Your Teachers Never Told You About the Men of the White House*. Philadelphia, PA: Quirk, 2004.
———. *Secret Lives of the Civil War: What Your teachers Never Told You About the War Between the States*. Philadelphia, PA: Quirk, 2007.
Oglesby, Thaddeus K. *Some Truths of History: A Vindication of the South Against the Encyclopedia Britannica and Other Maligners*. Atlanta, GA: Byrd Printing, 1903.
Olmsted, Frederick Law. *A Journey in the Seaboard Slave States, With Remarks on Their Economy*. New York, NY: Dix and Edwards, 1856.
———. *A Journey Through Texas; or a Saddle-Trip on the Western Frontier*. New York, NY: Dix and Edwards, 1857.
———. *A Journey in the Back Country*. New York, NY: Mason Brothers, 1860.
———. *The Cotton Kingdom: A Traveler's Observations on Cotton and Slavery in the American Slave States*. 2 vols. London, UK: Sampson Low, Son, and Co., 1862.
Olson, Ted (ed.). *CrossRoads: A Southern Culture Annual*. Macon, GA: Mercer University Press, 2004.

ORA (full title: *The War of the Rebellion: A Compilation of the Official Records of the Union and Confederate Armies*. (Multiple volumes.) Washington, D.C.: Government Printing Office, 1880.

ORN (full title: *Official Records of the Union and Confederate Navies in the War of the Rebellion*). (Multiple volumes.) Washington, D.C.: Government Printing Office, 1894.

Ostergard, Philip L. *The Inspired Wisdom of Abraham Lincoln: How Faith Shaped an American President and Changed the Course of a Nation*. Carol Stream, IL: Tyndale House, 2008.

Owsley, Frank Lawrence. *King Cotton Diplomacy: Foreign Relations of the Confederate States of America*. 1931. Chicago, IL: University of Chicago Press, 1959 ed.

Page, Thomas Nelson. *Robert E. Lee, Man and Soldier*. New York, NY: Charles Scribner's Sons, 1911.

Palin, Sarah. *Going Rogue: An American Life*. New York, NY: HarperCollins, 2009.

Paludan, Phillip Shaw. *The Presidency of Abraham Lincoln*. Lawrence, KS: University Press of Kansas, 1994.

Parker, Bowdoin S. (ed.). *What One Grand Army Post Has Accomplished: History of Edward W. Kinsley Post, No. 113*. Norwood, MA: Norwood Press, 1913.

Parry, Melanie (ed.). *Chambers Biographical Dictionary*. 1897. Edinburgh, Scotland: Chambers Harrap, 1998 ed.

Patrick, Rembert W. *Jefferson Davis and His Cabinet*. Baton Rouge, LA: Louisiana State University Press, 1944.

Paul, Ron. *The Revolution: A Manifesto*. New York, NY: Grand Central Publishing, 2008.

Pearson, Henry Greenleaf. *The Life of John A. Andrew, Governor of Massachusetts, 1861-1865*. 2 vols. Boston, MA: Houghton, Mifflin and Co., 1904.

Perkins, Henry C. *Northern Editorials on Secession*. 2 vols. D. Appleton and Co., 1942.

Perry, James M. *Touched With Fire: Five Presidents and the Civil War Battles That Made Them*. New York, NY: Public Affairs, 2003.

Perry, John C. *Myths and Realities of American Slavery: The True History of Slavery in America*. Shippenburg, PA: Burd Street Press, 2002.

Perry, Mark. *Lift Up Thy Voice: The Grimké Family's Journey From Slaveholders to Civil Rights Leaders*. New York, NY: Penguin, 2001.

Peter, Laurence J., and Raymond Hull *The Peter Principle: Why Things Always Go Wrong*. New York, NY: William Morrow and Co., 1969.

Peterson, Merrill D. (ed.). *James Madison, A Biography in His Own Words*. (First published posthumously in 1840.) New York, NY: Harper and Row, 1974 ed.

——. (ed.). *Thomas Jefferson: Writings, Autobiography, A Summary View of the Rights of British America, Notes on the State of Virginia, Public Papers, Addresses, Messages and Replies, Miscellany, Letters*. New York, NY: Literary Classics, 1984.

——. *Lincoln in American Memory*. New York, NY: Oxford University Press, 1994.

Peterson, Paul R. *Quantrill of Missouri: The Making of a Guerilla Warrior, The Man, the Myth, the Soldier*. Nashville, TN: Cumberland House, 2003.

Phillips, Michael. *White Metropolis: Race, Ethnicity, and Religion in Dallas, 1841-2001*.

Austin, TX: University of Texas Press, 2006.
Phillips, Robert S. (ed.). *Funk and Wagnalls New Encyclopedia.* 1971. New York, NY: Funk and Wagnalls, 1979 ed.
Phillips, Ulrich Bonnell. *American Negro Slavery: A Survey of the Supply, Employment and Control of Negro Labor as Determined by the Plantation Régime.* New York, NY: D. Appleton and Co., 1929.
Phillips, Wendell. *Speeches, Letters, and Lectures.* Boston, MA: Lee and Shepard, 1894.
Piatt, Donn. *Memories of the Men Who Saved the Union.* New York, NY: Belford, Clarke, and Co., 1887.
Piatt, Donn, and Henry V. Boynton. *General George H. Thomas: A Critical Biography.* Cincinnati, OH: Robert Clarke and Co., 1893.
Pickett, George E. *The Heart of a Soldier: As Revealed in the Intimate Letters of General George E. Pickett, CSA.* 1908. New York, NY: Seth Moyle, 1913 ed.
Pickett, William Passmore. *The Negro Problem: Abraham Lincoln's Solution.* New York, NY: G. P. Putnam's Sons, 1909.
Pike, James Shepherd. *The Prostrate State: South Carolina Under Negro Government.* New York, NY: D. Appleton and Co., 1874.
Pinsker, Matthew. *Lincoln's Sanctuary: Abraham Lincoln and the Soldiers' Home.* Oxford, UK: Oxford University Press, 2003.
Pollard, Edward A. *Southern History of the War.* 2 vols. in 1. New York, NY: Charles B. Richardson, 1866.
———. *The Lost Cause.* 1867. Chicago, IL: E. B. Treat, 1890 ed.
———. *The Lost Cause Regained.* New York, NY: G. W. Carlton and Co., 1868.
———. *Life of Jefferson Davis, With a Secret History of the Southern Confederacy, Gathered "Behind the Scenes in Richmond."* Philadelphia, PA: National Publishing Co., 1869.
Post, Lydia Minturn (ed.). *Soldiers' Letters, From Camp, Battlefield and Prison.* New York, NY: Bunce and Huntington, 1865.
Potter, David M. *The Impending Crisis: 1848-1861.* New York, NY: Harper and Row, 1976.
Powell, Edward Payson. *Nullification and Secession in the United States: A History of the Six Attempts During the First Century of the Republic.* New York, NY: G. P. Putnam's Sons, 1897.
Powell, William S. *North Carolina: A History.* 1977. Chapel Hill, NC: University of North Carolina Press, 1988 ed.
Pratt, Harry E. *Concerning Mr. Lincoln: As He Appeared to Letter Writers of His Time.* Springfield, IL: The Abraham Lincoln Association, 1944.
Pritchard, Russ A., Jr. *Civil War Weapons and Equipment.* Guilford, CT: Lyons Press, 2003.
Putnam, Samuel Porter. *400 Years of Free Thought.* New York, NY: Truth Seeker Co., 1894.
Quarles, Benjamin. *The Negro in the Civil War.* 1953. Cambridge, MA: Da Capo Press, 1988 ed.
———. *Lincoln and the Negro.* 1962. Cambridge, MA: Da Capo Press, 1990 ed.

Quintero, José Agustín, Ambrosio José Gonzales, and Loreta Janeta Velazquez (Phillip Thomas Tucker, ed.). *Cubans in the Confederacy*. Jefferson, NC: McFarland and Co., 2002.

Rable, George C. *The Confederate Republic: A Revolution Against Politics*. Chapel Hill, NC: University of North Carolina Press, 1994.

Ramage, James A. *Rebel Raider: The Life of General John Hunt Morgan*. Lexington, KY: University Press of Kentucky, 1986.

Randall, James Garfield. *Lincoln: The Liberal Statesman*. New York, NY: Dodd, Mead and Co., 1947.

Randall, James Garfield, and Richard N. Current. *Lincoln the President: Last Full Measure*. 1955. Urbana, IL: University of Illinois Press, 2000 ed.

Randolph, Thomas Jefferson (ed.). *Memoir, Correspondence, and Miscellanies, from the Papers of Thomas Jefferson*. 4 vols. Charlottesville, VA: F. Carr and Co., 1829.

Ransom, Roger L. *Conflict and Compromise: The Political Economy of Slavery, Emancipation, and the American Civil War*. Cambridge, UK: Cambridge University Press, 1989.

Rawle, William. *A View of the Constitution of the United States of America*. Philadelphia, PA: Philip H. Nicklin, 1829.

Rayner, B. L. *Sketches of the Life, Writings, and Opinions of Thomas Jefferson*. New York, NY: Alfred Francis and William Boardman, 1832.

Reaney, P. H., and R. M. Wilson. *A Dictionary of English Surnames*. 1958. Oxford, UK: Oxford University Press, 1997 ed.

Reid, Richard M. *Freedom for Themselves: North Carolina's Black Soldiers in the Era of the Civil War*. Chapel Hill, NC: University of North Carolina Press, 2008.

Remsburg, John B. *Abraham Lincoln: Was He a Christian?* New York, NY: The Truth Seeker Co., 1893.

Reports of Committees of the Senate of the United States (for the Thirty-eighth Congress). Washington, D.C.: Government Printing Office, 1864.

Report of the Joint Committee on Reconstruction (at the First Session, Thirty-ninth Congress). Washington, D.C.: Government Printing Office, 1866.

Reports of Committees of the Senate of the United States (for the Second Session of the Forty-second Congress). Washington, D.C.: Government Printing Office, 1872.

Report of the Joint Select Committee to Inquire into the Condition of Affairs in the Late Insurrectionary States. Washington, D.C.: Government Printing Office, 1872.

Reuter, Edward Byron. *The Mulatto in the United States*. Boston, MA: Gorham Press, 1918.

Rhodes, James Ford. *History of the United States from the Compromise of 1850 to the Final Restoration of Home Rule at the South in 1877*. 7 vols. 1895. New York, NY: Macmillan Co., 1907 ed.

Rice, Allen Thorndike (ed.). *The North American Review*, Vol. 227. New York, NY: D. Appleton and Co., 1879.

———. *Reminiscences of Abraham Lincoln, by Distinguished Men of His Time*. New York, NY: North American Review, 1888.

Rich, Burdett A., and Henry P. Farnham (eds.). *Lawyers' Reports, Annotated* (Book 22).

Rochester, NY: The Lawyers' Co-Operative Publishing, Co., 1894.

Richardson, James Daniel (ed.). *A Compilation of the Messages and Papers of the Confederacy.* 2 vols. Nashville, TN: United States Publishing Co., 1905.

Riley, Franklin Lafayette (ed.). *Publications of the Mississippi Historical Society.* Oxford, MS: The Mississippi Historical Society, 1902.

———. *General Robert E. Lee After Appomattox.* New York, NY: MacMillan Co., 1922.

Riley, Russell Lowell. *The Presidency and the Politics of Racial Inequality.* New York, NY: Columbia University Press, 1999.

Rives, John (ed.). *Abridgement of the Debates of Congress: From 1789 to 1856* (Vol. 13). New York, NY: D. Appleton and Co., 1860.

Roberts, Paul M. *United States History: Review Text.* 1966. New York, NY: Amsco School Publications, 1970 ed.

Roberts, R. Philip. *Mormonism Unmasked: Confronting the Contradictions Between Mormon Beliefs and True Christianity.* Nashville, TN: Broadman and Holman, 1998.

Robertson, James I., Jr. *Soldiers Blue and Gray.* 1988. Columbia, SC: University of South Carolina Press, 1998 ed.

Rockwell, Llewellyn H., Jr. "Genesis of the Civil War." Website: www.lewrockwell.com/rockwell/civilwar.html.

Rogers, Joel Augustus. *Africa's Gift to America: The Afro-American in the Making and Saving of the United States.* St. Petersburg, FL: Helga M. Rogers, 1961.

———. *The Ku Klux Spirit.* 1923. Baltimore, MD: Black Classic Press, 1980 ed.

Rosen, Robert N. *The Jewish Confederates.* Columbia, SC: University of South Carolina Press, 2000.

Rosenbaum, Robert A. (ed.). *The New American Desk Encyclopedia.* 1977. New York, NY: Signet, 1989 ed.

Rosenbaum, Robert A., and Douglas Brinkley (eds.). *The Penguin Encyclopedia of American History.* New York, NY: Viking, 2003.

Rothschild, Alonzo. *"Honest Abe": A Study in Integrity Based on the Early Life of Abraham Lincoln.* Boston, MA: Houghton Mifflin Co., 1917.

Rouse, Adelaide Louise (ed.). *National Documents: State Papers So Arranged as to Illustrate the Growth of Our Country From 1606 to the Present Day.* New York, NY: Unit Book Publishing Co., 1906.

Rowland, Dunbar (ed.). *Jefferson Davis, Constitutionalist: His Letters, Papers, and Speeches.* 10 vols. Jackson, MS: Mississippi Department of Archives and History, 1923.

Rozwenc, Edwin Charles (ed.). *The Causes of the American Civil War.* 1961. Lexington, MA: D. C. Heath and Co., 1972 ed.

Rubenzer, Steven J., and Thomas R. Faschingbauer. *Personality, Character, and Leadership in the White House: Psychologists Assess the Presidents.* Dulles, VA: Brassey's, 2004.

Ruffin, Edmund. *The Diary of Edmund Ruffin: Toward Independence: October 1856-April 1861.* Baton Rouge, LA: Louisiana State University Press, 1972.

Rutherford, Mildred Lewis. *Four Addresses.* Birmingham, AL: The Mildred Rutherford Historical Circle, 1916.

———. *A True Estimate of Abraham Lincoln and Vindication of the South.* N.p., n.d.

———. *Truths of History: A Historical Perspective of the Civil War From the Southern Viewpoint.* Confederate Reprint Co., 1920.

———. *The South Must Have Her Rightful Place In History.* Athens, GA, 1923.

Rutland, Robert Allen. *The Birth of the Bill of Rights, 1776-1791.* 1955. Boston, MA: Northeastern University Press, 1991 ed.

Sachsman, David B., S. Kittrell Rushing, and Roy Morris, Jr. (eds.). *Words at War: The Civil War and American Journalism.* West Lafayette, IN: Purdue University Press, 2008.

Salley, Alexander Samuel, Jr. *South Carolina Troops in Confederate Service.* 2 vols. Columbia, SC: R. L. Bryan, 1913 and 1914.

Salzberger, Ronald P., and Mary C. Turck (eds.). *Reparations For Slavery: A Reader.* Lanham, MD: Rowman and Littlefield, 2004.

Samuel, Bunford. *Secession and Constitutional Liberty.* 2 vols. New York, NY: Neale Publishing, 1920.

Sancho, Ignatius. *Letters of the Late Ignatius Sancho, an African.* 1782. New York, NY: Cosimo Classics, 2005 ed.

Sandburg, Carl. *Abraham Lincoln: The War Years.* 4 vols. New York, NY: Harcourt, Brace and World, 1939.

———. *Storm Over the Land: A Profile of the Civil War.* 1939. Old Saybrook, CT: Konecky and Konecky, 1942 ed.

Sargent, F. W. *England, the United States, and the Southern Confederacy.* London, UK: Sampson Low, Son, and Co., 1863.

Scharf, John Thomas. *History of the Confederate Navy, From Its Organization to the Surrender of Its Last Vessel.* Albany, NY: Joseph McDonough, 1894.

Schauffler, Robert Haven. *Our American Holidays: Lincoln's Birthday - A Comprehensive View of Lincoln as Given in the Most Noteworthy Essays, Orations and Poems, in Fiction and in Lincoln's Own Writings.* 1909. New York, NY: Moffat, Yard and Co., 1916 ed.

Schlüter, Herman. *Lincoln, Labor and Slavery: A Chapter from the Social History of America.* New York, NY: Socialist Literature Co., 1913.

Schurz, Carl. *Life of Henry Clay.* 2 vols. 1887. Boston, MA: Houghton, Mifflin and Co., 1899 ed.

Schwartz, Barry. *Abraham Lincoln and the Forge of National Memory.* Chicago, IL: University of Chicago Press, 2000.

Scott, Emmett J., and Lyman Beecher Stowe. *Booker T. Washington: Builder of a Civilization.* Garden City, NY: Doubleday, Page, and Co., 1916.

Scott, James Brown. *James Madison's Notes of Debates in the Federal Convention of 1787, and Their Relation to a More Perfect Society of Nations.* New York, NY: Oxford University Press, 1918.

Scruggs, *The Un-Civil War: Truths Your Teacher Never Told You.* Hendersonville, NC: Tribune Papers, 2007.

Seabrook, Lochlainn. *Britannia Rules: Goddess-Worship in Ancient Anglo-Celtic Society - An Academic Look at the United Kingdom's Matricentric Spiritual Past.* 1999. Franklin, TN: Sea Raven Press, 2007 ed.

——. *The Caudills: An Etymological, Ethnological, and Genealogical Study - Exploring the Name and National Origins of a European-American Family*. 2003. Franklin, TN: Sea Raven Press, 2010 ed.

——. *Carnton Plantation Ghost Stories: True Tales of the Unexplained From Tennessee's Most Haunted Civil War House!* 2005. Franklin, TN: Sea Raven Press, 2010 ed.

——. *Nathan Bedford Forrest: Southern Hero, American Patriot: Honoring a Confederate Hero and the Old South*. 2007. Franklin, TN: Sea Raven Press, 2010 ed.

——. *The McGavocks of Carnton Plantation: A Southern History - Celebrating One of Dixie's Most Noble Confederate Families and Their Tennessee Home*. 2008. Franklin, TN: Sea Raven Press, 2011 ed.

——. *Abraham Lincoln: The Southern View - Demythologizing America's Sixteenth President*. Franklin, TN: Sea Raven Press, 2009.

——. *Everything You Were Taught About the Civil War is Wrong, Ask a Southerner!* 2009. Franklin, TN: Sea Raven Press, 2012 ed.

——. *A Rebel Born: A Defense of Nathan Bedford Forrest, Confederate General, American Legend*. 2010. Franklin, TN: Sea Raven Press, 2011 ed.

——. *Lincolnology: The Real Abraham Lincoln Revealed In His Own Words*. Franklin, TN: Sea Raven Press, 2011.

——. *The Quotable Jefferson Davis: Selections From the Writings and Speeches of the Confederacy's First President*. Franklin, TN: Sea Raven Press, 2011.

——. *The Quotable Robert E. Lee: Selections From the Writings and Speeches of the Confederacy's Most Beloved Civil War General*. Franklin, TN: Sea Raven Press, 2011.

——. *The Unquotable Abraham Lincoln: The President's Quotes They Don't Want You To Know!* Franklin, TN: Sea Raven Press, 2011.

——. *The Quotable Nathan Bedford Forrest: Selections From the Writings and Speeches of the Confederacy's Most Brilliant Cavalryman*. Franklin, TN: Sea Raven Press, 2011.

——. *The Old Rebel: Robert E. Lee As He Was Seen By His Contemporaries*. Franklin, TN: Sea Raven Press, 2012.

——. *Give 'Em Hell Boys! The Complete Military Correspondence of Nathan Bedford Forrest*. Franklin, TN: Sea Raven Press, 2012.

——. *The Constitution of the Confederate States of America: Explained*. Franklin, TN: Sea Raven Press, 2012.

——. *Encyclopedia of the Battle of Franklin: A Comprehensive Guide to the Conflict That Changed the Civil War*. Franklin, TN: Sea Raven Press, 2012.

Segal, Charles M. (ed.). *Conversations with Lincoln*. 1961. New Brunswick, NJ: Transaction, 2002 ed.

Segars, J. H., and Charles Kelly Barrow. *Black Southerners in Confederate Armies: A Collection of Historical Accounts*. Atlanta, GA: Southern Lion Books, 2001.

Seligmann, Herbert J. *The Negro Faces America*. New York, NY: Harper and Brothers, 1920.

Semmes, Admiral Ralph. *Service Afloat, or the Remarkable Career of the Confederate Cruisers Sumter and Alabama During the War Between the States*. London, UK: Sampson Low, Marston, Searle, and Rivington, 1887.

Sewall, Samuel. *Diary of Samuel Sewall*. 3 vols. Boston, MA: The Society, 1879.

Sewell, Richard H. *John P. Hale and the Politics of Abolition*. Cambridge, MA: Harvard University Press, 1965.
Shenk, Joshua Wolf. *Lincoln's Melancholy: How Depression Challenged a President and Fueled His Greatness*. New York, NY: Houghton Mifflin, 2005.
Shenkman, Richard, and Kurt Edward Reiger. *One-Night Stands with American History: Odd, Amusing, and Little-Known Incidents*. 1980. New York, NY: Perennial, 2003 ed.
Sherman, William Tecumseh. *Memoirs of General William T. Sherman*. 2 vols. 1875. New York, NY: D. Appleton and Co., 1891 ed.
———. *Memoirs of Gen. W. T. Sherman*. 2 vols. 1875. New York, NY: Charles L. Webster and Co., 1892 ed.
Shillington, Kevin. *History of Africa*. 1989. New York, NY: St. Martin's Press, 1994 ed.
Shorto, Russell. *Thomas Jefferson and the American Ideal*. Hauppauge, NY: Barron's, 1987.
Shotwell, Walter G. *Life of Charles Sumner*. New York, NY: Thomas Y. Crowell and Co., 1910.
Siepel, Kevin H. *Rebel: The Life and Times of John Singleton Mosby*. New York, NY: St. Martin's Press, 1983.
Simkins, Francis Butler. *A History of the South*. New York, NY: Random House, 1972.
Simmons, Henry E. *A Concise Encyclopedia of the Civil War*. New York, NY: Bonanza Books, 1965.
Simon, James F. *Lincoln and Chief Justice Taney: Slavery, Secession, and the President's War Powers*. New York, NY: Simon and Schuster, 2006.
Simon, Paul. *Lincoln's Preparation for Greatness: The Illinois Legislative Years*. 1965. Chicago, IL: University of Illinois Press, 1971 ed.
Simpson, Lewis P. (ed.). *I'll Take My Stand: The South and the Agrarian Tradition*. 1930. Baton Rouge, LA: University of Louisiana Press, 1977 ed.
Slotkin, Richard. *No Quarter: The Battle of the Crater, 1864*. New York, NY: Random House, 2009.
Smelser, Marshall. *American Colonial and Revolutionary History*. 1950. New York, NY: Barnes and Noble, 1966 ed.
———. *The Democratic Republic, 1801-1815*. New York, NY: Harper and Row, 1968.
Smith, Hedrick. *Reagan: The Man, The President*. Oxford, UK: Pergamon Press, 1980.
Smith, Jean Edward. *Grant*. New York, NY: Touchstone, 2001.
Smith, John David (ed.). *Black Soldiers in Blue: African American Troops in the Civil War Era*. Chapel Hill, NC: University of North Carolina Press, 2002.
Smith, Joseph. *The Pearl of Great Price*. Salt Lake City, UT: George Q. Cannon and Sons, 1891.
Smith, Mark M. (ed.). *The Old South*. Oxford, UK: Blackwell Publishers, 2001.
Smith, Page. *Trial by Fire: A People's History of the Civil War and Reconstruction*. New York, NY: McGraw-Hill, 1982.
Smith, Philip D., Jr. *Tartan for Me!: Suggested Tartan for 13,695 Scottish, Scotch-Irish, Irish and North American Names with Lists of Clan, Family, and District Tartans*.

Bruceton, WV: Scotpress, 1990.

Smucker, Samuel M. *The Life and Times of Thomas Jefferson*. Philadelphia, PA: J. W. Bradley, 1859.

Snider, Denton J. *Lincoln at Richmond: A Dramatic Epos of the Civil War*. St. Louis, MO: Sigma, 1914.

Sobel, Robert (ed.). *Biographical Directory of the United States Executive Branch, 1774-1898*. Westport, CT: Greenwood Press, 1990.

Sorrel, Gilbert Moxley. *Recollections of a Confederate Staff Officer*. New York, NY: Neale Publishing Co., 1905.

Spaeth, Harold J., and Edward Conrad Smith. *The Constitution of the United States*. 1936. New York, NY: HarperCollins, 1991 ed.

Spence, James. *On the Recognition of the Southern Confederation*. Ithaca, NY: Cornell University Library, 1862.

Spooner, Lysander. *No Treason* (only Numbers 1, 2, and 6 were published). Boston, MA: Lysander Spooner, 1867-1870.

Stampp, Kenneth M. *The Peculiar Institution: Slavery in the Antebellum South*. New York, NY: Vintage, 1956.

Stanford, Peter Thomas. *The Tragedy of the Negro in America*. Boston, MA: published by author, 1898.

Stanton, Elizabeth Cady, Susan B. Anthony, and Matilda Joslyn Gage (eds.). *History of Woman Suffrage*. 2 vols. New York, NY: Fowler and Wells, 1881.

Starr, John W., Jr. *Lincoln and the Railroads: A Biographical Study*. New York, NY: Dodd, Mead and Co., 1927.

Staudenraus, P. J. *The African Colonization Movement, 1816-1865*. New York, NY: Columbia University Press, 1961.

Stebbins, Rufus Phineas. *An Historical Address Delivered At the Centennial Celebration of the Incorporation of the Town of Wilbraham, June 15, 1863*. Boston, MA: George C. Rand and Avery, 1864.

Stedman, Edmund Clarence, and Ellen Mackay Hutchinson (eds.). *A Library of American Literature From the Earliest Settlement to the Present Time*. 10 vols. New York, NY: Charles L. Webster and Co., 1888.

Steele, Joel Dorman, and Esther Baker Steele. *Barnes' Popular History of the United States of America*. New York, NY: A. S. Barnes and Co., 1904.

Steele, Shelby. *White Guilt: How Blacks and Whites Together Destroyed the Promise of the Civil Rights Era*. New York, NY: Harper Perennial, 2007.

Steers, Edward, Jr. *Lincoln Legends: Myths, Hoaxes, and Confabulations Associated With Our Greatest President*. Lexington, KY: University Press of Kentucky, 2007.

Stein, Ben, and Phil DeMuth. *How To Ruin the United States of America*. Carlsbad, CA: New Beginnings Press, 2008.

Steiner, Bernard. *The History of Slavery in Connecticut*. Baltimore, MD: Johns Hopkins University Press, 1893.

Steiner, Lewis Henry. *Report of Lewis H. Steiner: Inspector of the Sanitary Commission, Containing a Diary Kept During the Rebel Occupation of Frederick, MD, September, 1862*. New York, NY: Anson D. F. Randolph, 1862.

Stephens, Alexander Hamilton. *Speech of Mr. Stephens, of Georgia, on the War and Taxation.* Washington, D.C.: J & G. Gideon, 1848.

———. *A Constitutional View of the Late War Between the States; Its Causes, Character, Conduct and Results.* 2 vols. Philadelphia, PA: National Publishing, Co., 1870.

———. *Recollections of Alexander H. Stephens: His Diary Kept When a Prisoner at Fort Warren, Boston Harbour, 1865.* New York, NY: Doubleday, Page, and Co., 1910.

Stephenson, Nathaniel Wright. *Abraham Lincoln and the Union: A Chronicle of the Embattled North.* New Haven, CT: Yale University Press, 1918.

———. *Lincoln: An Account of His Personal Life, Especially of Its Springs of Action as Revealed and Deepened by the Ordeal of War.* Indianapolis, IN: Bobbs-Merrill, 1922.

Sterling, Dorothy (ed.). *Speak Out in Thunder Tones: Letters and Other Writings by Black Northerners, 1787-1865.* 1973. Cambridge, MA: Da Capo, 1998 ed.

Stern, Philip Van Doren (ed.). *The Life and Writings of Abraham Lincoln.* 1940. New York, NY: Modern Library, 2000 ed.

Stoddard, William O. *Inside the White House in War Times: Memoirs and Reports of Lincoln's Secretary.* Lincoln, NE: University of Nebraska Press, 2000.

Stonebraker, J. Clarence. *The Unwritten South: Cause, Progress and Results of the Civil War - Relics of Hidden Truth After Forty Years.* Seventh ed., n.p., 1908.

Stovall, Pleasant A. *Robert Toombs: Statesman, Speaker, Soldier, Sage.* New York, NY: Cassell Publishing, 1892.

Strain, John Paul. *Witness to the Civil War: The Art of John Paul Strain.* Philadelphia, PA: Courage, 2002.

Strode, Hudson. *Jefferson Davis: American Patriot.* 3 vols. New York, NY: Harcourt, Brace and World, 1955, 1959, 1964.

Strozier, Charles B. *Lincoln's Quest for Union: A Psychological Portrait.* Philadelphia, PA: Paul Dry Books, 2001.

Sturge, Joseph. *A Visit to the United States in 1841.* London, UK: Hamilton, Adams, and Co., 1842.

Summers, Mark W. *The Plundering Generation: Corruption and the Crisis of the Union, 1849-1861.* New York, NY: Oxford University Press, 1988.

Sumner, Charles. *The Crime Against Kansas: The Apologies for the Crime - The True Remedy.* Boston, MA: John P. Jewett, 1856.

Swanson, James L. *Bloody Crimes: The Chase for Jefferson Davis and the Death Pageant for Lincoln's Corpse.* New York, NY: HarperCollins, 2010.

Swint, Henry L. (ed.) *Dear Ones at Home: Letters From Contraband Camps.* Nashville, TN: Vanderbilt University Press, 1966.

Sword, Wiley. *The Confederacy's Last Hurrah: Spring Hill, Franklin, and Nashville.* New York, NY: HarperCollins, 1992.

———. *Southern Invincibility: A History of the Confederate Heart.* New York, NY: St. Martin's Press, 1999.

Tagg, Larry. *The Unpopular Mr. Lincoln: The Story of America's Most Reviled President.* New York, NY: Savas Beatie, 2009.

Tarbell, Ida Minerva. *The Life of Abraham Lincoln.* 4 vols. New York, NY: Lincoln History Society, 1895-1900.

Tatalovich, Raymond, and Byron W. Daynes. *Presidential Power in the United States.* Monterey, CA: Brooks/Cole, 1984.

Taylor, Richard. *Destruction and Reconstruction: Personal Experiences of the Late War in the United States.* New York, NY: D. Appleton, 1879.

Taylor, Susie King. *Reminiscences of My Life in Camp With the 33rd United States Colored Troops Late 1st S. C. Volunteers.* Boston, MA: Susie King Taylor, 1902.

Taylor, Walter Herron. *General Lee: His Campaigns in Virginia, 1861-1865, With Personal Reminiscences.* Norfolk, VA: Nusbaum Book and News Co., 1906.

Tenney, William Jewett. *The Military and Naval History of the Rebellion in the United States.* New York, NY: D. Appleton and Co., 1865.

Terkel, Studs. *Hard Times: An Oral History of the Great Depression.* New York, NY: Avon, 1970.

Testimony Taken By the Joint Select Committee to Inquire Into the Condition of Affairs in the Late Insurrectionary States. 13 vols. Washington, D.C.: Government Printing Office, 1872.

Thackeray, William Makepeace. *Roundabout Papers.* Boston, MA: Estes and Lauriat, 1883.

Thatcher, Marshall P. *A Hundred Battles in the West: St. Louis to Atlanta, 1861-1865.* Detroit, MI: Marshall P. Thatcher, 1884.

The American Annual Cyclopedia and Register of Important Events of the Year 1861. New York, NY: D. Appleton and Co., 1868.

The American Annual Cyclopedia and Register of Important Events of the Year 1862. New York, NY: D. Appleton and Co., 1869.

The American Annual Cyclopedia and Register of Important Events of the Year 1863. New York, NY: D. Appleton and Co., 1864.

The Congressional Globe, Containing Sketches of the Debates and Proceedings of the First Session of the Twenty-Eighth Congress (Vol. 13). Washington, D.C.: The Globe, 1844.

The Great Issue to be Decided in November Next: Shall the Constitution and the Union Stand or Fall, Shall Sectionalism Triumph? Washington, D.C.: National Democratic Executive Committee, 1860.

The National Almanac and Annual Record for the Year 1863. Philadelphia, PA: George W. Childs, 1863.

The Oxford English Dictionary. Compact edition, 2 vols. 1928. Oxford, UK: Oxford University Press, 1979 ed.

The Quarterly Review (Vol. 111). London, UK: John Murray, 1862.

Thomas, Emory M. *The Confederate Nation: 1861-1865.* New York, NY: Harper and Row, 1979.

Thomas, Gabriel. *An Account of Pennsylvania and West New Jersey.* 1698. Cleveland, OH: Burrows Brothers Co., 1903 ed.

Thompson, Frank Charles (ed.). *The Thompson Chain Reference Bible* (King James Version). 1908. Indianapolis, IN: B. B. Kirkbride Bible Co., 1964 ed.

Thompson, Neal. *Driving With the Devil: Southern Moonshine, Detroit Wheels, and the Birth of NASCAR.* Three Rivers, MI: Three Rivers Press, 2006.

Thompson, Robert Means, and Richard Wainwright (eds.). *Confidential Correspondence*

       of *Gustavus Vasa Fox, Assistant Secretary of the Navy, 1861-1865*. 2 vols. 1918. New York, NY: Naval History Society, 1920 ed.
Thorndike, Rachel Sherman (ed.). *The Sherman Letters*. New York, NY: Charles Scribner's Sons, 1894.
Thornton, Brian. *101 Things You Didn't Know About Lincoln: Loves and Losses, Political Power Plays, White House Hauntings*. Avon, MA: Adams Media, 2006.
Thornton, Gordon. *The Southern Nation: The New Rise of the Old South*. Gretna, LA: Pelican Publishing Co., 2000.
Thornton, John. *Africa and Africans in the Making of the Atlantic World, 1400-1800*. 1992. Cambridge, UK: Cambridge University Press, 1999 ed.
Thornton, Mark, and Robert B. Ekelund, Jr. *Tariffs, Blockades, and Inflation: The Economics of the Civil War*. Wilmington, DE: Scholarly Resources, 2004.
Tilley, John Shipley. *Lincoln Takes Command*. 1941. Nashville, TN: Bill Coats Limited, 1991 ed.
——. *Facts the Historians Leave Out: A Confederate Primer*. 1951. Nashville, TN: Bill Coats Limited, 1999 ed.
Tocqueville, Alexis de. *Democracy in America*. 2 vols. 1836. New York, NY: D. Appleton and Co., 1904 ed.
Tourgee, Albion W. *A Fool's Errand By One of the Fools*. London, UK: George Routledge and Sons, 1883.
Tracy, Gilbert A. (ed.). *Uncollected Letters of Abraham Lincoln*. Boston, MA: Houghton Mifflin Co., 1917.
Traupman, John C. *The New College Latin and English Dictionary*. 1966. New York, NY: Bantam, 1988 ed.
Trumbull, Lyman. *Speech of Honorable Lyman Trumbull, of Illinois, at a Mass Meeting in Chicago, August 7, 1858*. Washington, D.C.: Buell and Blanchard, 1858.
Truth, Sojourner. *Sojourner Truth's Narrative and Book of Life*. 1850. Battle Creek, MI: Sojourner Truth, 1881 ed.
Tucker, St. George. *On the State of Slavery in Virginia, in View of the Constitution of the United States, With Selected Writings*. Indianapolis, IN: Liberty Fund, 1999.
Turner, Edward Raymond. *The Negro in Pennsylvania, Slavery, Servitude, Freedom, 1639-1861*. Washington, D.C.: American Historical Association, 1911.
Tyler, Lyon Gardiner. *The Gray Book: A Confederate Catechism*. Columbia, TN: Gray Book Committee, SCV, 1935.
——. *The Letters and Times of the Tylers*. 3 vols. Williamsburg, VA: N.P., 1896.
——. *Propaganda in History*. Richmond, VA: Richmond Press, 1920.
Upshur, Abel Parker. *A Brief Enquiry Into the True Nature and Character of Our Federal Government*. Philadelphia, PA: John Campbell, 1863.
Vallandigham, Clement Laird. *Speeches, Arguments, Addresses, and Letters of Clement L. Vallandigham*. New York, NY: J. Walter and Co., 1864.
Vanauken, Sheldon. *The Glittering Illusion: English Sympathy for the Southern Confederacy*. Washington, D.C.: Regnery, 1989.
Van Buren, G. M. *Abraham Lincoln's Pen and Voice: Being a Complete Compilation of His Letters, Civil, Political, and Military*. Cincinnati, OH: Robert Clarke and Co.,

1890.

Ver Steeg, Clarence Lester, and Richard Hofstadter. *A People and a Nation.* New York, NY: Harper and Row, 1977.

Villard, Henry. *Memoirs of Henry Villard, Journalist and Financier, 1835-1900.* 2 vols. Boston, MA: Houghton, Mifflin and Co., 1904.

Voegeli, Victor Jacque. *Free But Not Equal: The Midwest and the Negro During the Civil War.* Chicago, IL: University of Chicago Press, 1967.

Wade, Wyn Craig. *The Fiery Cross: The Ku Klux Klan in America.* 1987. New York, NY: Touchstone, 1988 ed.

Walker, Barbara G. *The Woman's Encyclopedia of Myths and Secrets.* New York, NY: Harper and Row, 1983.

Wallcut, R. F. (pub.). *Southern Hatred of the American Government, the People of the North, and Free Institutions.* Boston, MA: R. F. Wallcut, 1862.

Wallechinsky, David, Irving Wallace, and Amy Wallace. *The People's Almanac Presents The Book of Lists.* New York, NY: Morrow, 1977.

Walsh, George. *"Those Damn Horse Soldiers": True Tales of the Civil War Cavalry.* New York, NY: Forge, 2006.

Ward, John William. *Andrew Jackson: Symbol for an Age.* 1953. Oxford, UK: Oxford University Press, 1973 ed.

Waring, George Edward, Jr. *Whip and Spur.* New York, NY: Doubleday and McClure, 1897.

Warner, Ezra J. *Generals in Gray: Lives of the Confederate Commanders.* 1959. Baton Rouge, LA: Louisiana State University Press, 1989 ed.

——. *Generals in Blue: Lives of the Union Commanders.* 1964. Baton Rouge, LA: Louisiana State University Press, 2006 ed.

Warren, Robert Penn. *Who Speaks for the Negro?* New York, NY: Random House, 1965.

Waugh, John C. *Reelecting Lincoln: The Battle for the 1864 Presidency.* Cambridge, MA: Da Capo Press, 1997.

——. *Lincoln and McClellan: The Troubled Partnership Between a President and His General.* New York, NY: Palgrave Macmillan, 2010.

Washington, Booker T. *Up From Slavery: An Autobiography.* 1901. Garden City, NY: Doubleday, Page and Co., 1919 ed.

Washington, Henry Augustine. *The Writings of Thomas Jefferson.* 9 vols. New York, NY: H. W. Derby, 1861.

Watkins, Samuel Rush. *"Company Aytch," Maury Grays, First Tennessee Regiment; or, A Side Show of the Big Show.* 1882. Chattanooga, TN: Times Printing Co., 1900 ed.

Watson, Harry L. *Andrew Jackson vs. Henry Clay: Democracy and Development in Antebellum America.* New York, NY: St. Martin's Press, 1998.

Watts, Peter. *A Dictionary of the Old West.* 1977. New York, NY: Promontory Press, 1987 ed.

Waugh, John C. *Surviving the Confederacy: Rebellion, Ruin, and Recovery - Roger and Sara Pryor During the Civil War.* New York, NY: Harcourt, 2002.

Weber, Jennifer L. *Copperheads: The Rise and Fall of Lincoln's Opponents in the North.*

New York, NY: Oxford University Press, 2006.
Weintraub, Max. *The Blue Book of American History*. New York, NY: Regents Publishing Co., 1960.
Welles, Gideon. *Diary of Gideon Welles, Secretary of the Navy Under Lincoln and Johnson* (Vol. 1). Boston, MA: Houghton Mifflin, 1911.
Wheeler, Joe L. *Abraham Lincoln, a Man of Faith and Courage: Stories of Our Most Admired President*. New York, NY: Howard Books, 2008.
Wheeler, Tom. *Mr. Lincoln's T-Mails: How Abraham Lincoln Used the Telegraph to Win the Civil War*. New York, NY: HarperCollins, 2008.
White, Charles Langdon, Edwin Jay Foscue, and Tom Lee McKnight. *Regional Geography of Anglo-America*. 1943. Englewood Cliffs, NJ: Prentice-Hall, 1985 ed.
White, Henry Alexander. *Robert E. Lee and the Southern Confederacy, 1807-1870*. New York, NY: G. P. Putnam's Sons, 1897.
White, Reginald Cedric. *A. Lincoln: A Biography*. New York, NY: Random House, 2009.
White, Ronald C., Jr. *The Eloquent President: A Portrait of Lincoln Through His Words*. New York, NY: Random House, 2006.
Whitman, Walt. *Leaves of Grass*. 1855. New York, NY: Modern Library, 1921 ed.
——. *Complete Prose Works*. Boston, MA: Small, Maynard, and Co., 1901.
Wilbur, Henry Watson. *President Lincoln's Attitude Towards Slavery and Emancipation: With a Review of Events Before and Since the Civil War*. Philadelphia, PA: W. H. Jenkins, 1914.
Wilder, Craig Steven. *A Covenant With Color: Race and Social Power in Brooklyn*. New York, NY: Columbia University Press, 2000.
Wiley, Bell Irvin. *Southern Negroes: 1861-1865*. 1938. New Haven, CT: Yale University Press, 1969 ed.
——. *The Life of Johnny Reb: The Common Soldier of the Confederacy*. 1943. Baton Rouge, LA: Louisiana State University Press, 1978 ed.
——. *The Plain People of the Confederacy*. 1943. Columbia, SC: University of South Carolina, 2000 ed.
——. *The Life of Billy Yank: The Common Soldier of the Union*. 1952. Baton Rouge, LA: Louisiana State University Press, 2001 ed.
Wilkens, J. Steven. *America: The First 350 Years*. Monroe, LA: Covenant Publications, 1998.
Williams, Charles Richard. *The Life of Rutherford Birchard Hayes, Nineteenth President of the United States*. 2 vols. Boston, MA: Houghton Mifflin Co., 1914.
Williams, George Washington. *History of the Negro Race in America: From 1619 to 1880, Negroes as Slaves, as Soldiers, and as Citizens*. New York, NY: G. P. Putnam's Sons, 1885.
——. *A History of the Negro Troops in the War of the Rebellion 1861-1865*. New York, NY: Harper and Brothers, 1888.
Williams, James. *The South Vindicated*. London, UK: Longman, Green, Longman, Roberts, and Green, 1862.

Williams, William H. *Slavery and Freedom in Delaware, 1639-1865*. Wilmington, DE: Scholarly Resources, 1996.

Wills, Brian Steel. *The Confederacy's Greatest Cavalryman: Nathan Bedford Forrest*. Lawrence, KS: University Press of Kansas, 1992.

Wills, Gary. *Lincoln At Gettysburg: The Words that Remade America*. New York, NY: Touchstone, 1992.

Wilson, Charles Reagan, and William Ferris. *Encyclopedia of Southern Culture* (Vol. 1). New York, NY: Anchor, 1989.

Wilson, Clyde N. *Why the South Will Survive: Fifteen Southerners Look at Their Region a Half Century After I'll Take My Stand*. Athens, GA: University of Georgia Press, 1981.

———. (ed.) *The Essential Calhoun: Selections From Writings, Speeches, and Letters*. New Brunswick, NJ: Transaction Publishers, 1991.

———. *A Defender of Southern Conservatism: M.E. Bradford and His Achievements*. Columbia, MO: University of Missouri Press, 1999.

———. *From Union to Empire: Essays in the Jeffersonian Tradition*. Columbia, SC: The Foundation for American Education, 2003.

———. *Defending Dixie: Essays in Southern History and Culture*. Columbia, SC: The Foundation for American Education, 2005.

Wilson, Douglas L. *Honor's Voice: The Transformation of Abraham Lincoln*. New York, NY: Vintage, 1998.

———. *Lincoln's Sword: The Presidency and the Power of Words*. New York, NY: Vintage, 2006.

Wilson, Henry. *History of the Rise and Fall of the Slave Power in America*. 3 vols. Boston, MA: James R. Osgood and Co., 1877.

Wilson, Joseph Thomas. *The Black Phalanx: A History of the Negro Soldiers of the United States in the Wars of 1775-1812, 1861-'65*. Hartford, CT: American Publishing Co., 1890.

Wilson, Woodrow. *Division and Reunion: 1829-1889*. 1893. New York, NY: Longmans, Green, and Co., 1908 ed.

———. *A History of the American People*. 5 vols. 1902. New York, NY: Harper and Brothers, 1918 ed.

Wood, W. J. *Civil War Generalship: The Art of Command*. 1997. New York, NY: Da Capo Press, 2000 ed.

Woodard, Komozi. *A Nation Within a Nation: Amiri Baraka (LeRoi Jones) and Black Power Politics*. Chapel Hill, NC: University of North Carolina Press, 1999.

Woodburn, James Albert. *The Life of Thaddeus Stevens*. Indianapolis, IN: Bobbs-Merrill, 1913.

Woods, Thomas E., Jr. *The Politically Incorrect Guide to American History*. Washington, D.C.: Regnery, 2004.

Woodson, Carter G. (ed.). *The Journal of Negro History* (Vol. 4). Lancaster, PA: Association for the Study of Negro Life and History, 1919.

Woodward, William E. *Meet General Grant*. 1928. New York, NY: Liveright Publishing, 1946 ed.

Woodworth, Steven E. *Jefferson Davis and His Generals: The Failure of Confederate Command in the West.* Lawrence, KS: University Press of Kansas, 1990.

Wright, John D. *The Language of the Civil War.* Westport, CT: Oryx, 2001.

Wyeth, John Allan. *Life of General Nathan Bedford Forrest.* 1899. New York, NY: Harper and Brothers, 1908 ed.

Young, John Russell. *Around the World With General Grant.* 2 vols. New York, NY: American News Co., 1879.

Zaehner, R. C. (ed.) *Encyclopedia of the World's Religions.* 1959. New York, NY: Barnes and Noble, 1997 ed.

Zall, Paul M. (ed.). *Lincoln on Lincoln.* Lexington, KY: University Press of Kentucky, 1999.

Zavodnyik, Peter. *The Age of Strict Construction: A History of the Growth of Federal Power, 1789-1861.* Washington, D.C.: Catholic University of America Press, 2007.

Zinn, Howard. *A People's History of the United States: 1492-Present.* 1980. New York, NY: HarperCollins, 1995.

The Battle of Fort Sumter, where Lincoln tricked the South into firing the first shot!

INDEX

Adler, Adolphus H. 213
Ammen, Jacob 27
Anderson, Robert 28, 97, 98
Astor, John Jacob 36
Baldwin, John B. 193
Bate, William B. 217
Bates, Edward 127, 198
Beauregard, Pierre 22, 110, 114
Bell, Mary 215
Bell, Molly 215
Benjamin, Judah P. 80, 197, 211
Birney, David B. 28
Birney, William 28
Blair, Francis P., Jr. 28
Blair, Montgomery 127, 199
Blakely, Alexander 202
Blalock, Malinda 215
Bonaparte, Louis Napoleon 181
Booth, John Wilkes 224
Boyd, Belle 215, 218
Boyle, Jeremiah T. 28
Bragg, Braxton 22, 119, 137
Bragg, Thomas 198
Breckinridge, John C. 198
Brown, John 61, 62
Buchanan, Franklin 113
Buchel, Augustus 213
Buckner, Simon B. 112
Buell, Don Carlos 114
Buford, John 28
Buford, Napoleon B. 28
Burbridge, Stephen G. 27
Burns, Anthony 43

Butler, Benjamin F. 133, 226
Calhoun, John C. 195
Cameron, Simon 160, 198
Campbell, William B. 28
Canby, Edward R. S. 28
Carter, Samuel P. 27
Castro, Fidel 90
Cavenish, Charles 213
Chase, Salmon P. 127, 198
Chesnut, Mary 54
Chetlain, Augustus L. 28
Clarke, Amy 215
Clay, Cassius M. 28
Cleburne, Patrick R. 218, 225
Cleveland, Grover 175
Conkling, James C. 121
Cooke, Philip St. George 27
Cooper, Douglas H. 212
Cooper, Joseph A. 28
Cooper, Samuel 240
Crittenden, Thomas L. 28
Crittenden, Thomas T. 28
Davis, George 198
Davis, Jefferson . 6, 11, 12, 19, 22, 25, 79, 86, 96, 98, 101, 111, 147, 151, 161, 167, 181, 194, 197, 209, 211, 217, 224, 228-230, 233, 236
Davis, Varina (Howell) 229
de Polignac, Prince 213
Dean, Henry C. 164
Degataga, Chief 212
Dennison, William 199
Dicey, Edward 52
Douglas, Stephen A. 148
Douglass, Frederick 207, 233, 236
Estran, Bela 213

Ewell, Richard S.	27, 137, 218
Farragut, David G.	28
Fessenden, William P.	198
Finn, Huckleberry	226
Floyd, John B.	112
Foote, Andrew H.	112
Forrest, Mary Ann (Montgomery)	242
Forrest, Nathan Bedford	12, 112, 114, 146, 180, 200, 204, 206, 217, 218, 241, 243, 258
Franco, Francisco	90
Franklin, William	115
Fremantle, Arthur	213
Frémont, John C.	160
French, Samuel G.	27
Frost, Daniel M.	27
Gardner, Franklin	26
Garrison, William Lloyd	43, 45-48, 54-56
Gingrich, Newt	18
God	49, 61, 224, 245
Gordon, George	213
Gordon, John B.	22
Gordon, Nathaniel	41
Gorgas, Josiah	26
Gracie, Archibald	36
Grant, Ulysses S.	112, 114, 115, 144, 145, 152, 153, 199, 201, 226
Gray, Thomas R.	55
Greenhow, Rose O'Neal	215
Griffith, Richard	27
Grimké, Angela	41
Grimké, Sarah	41
Halleck, Henry W.	233
Hamlin, Hannibal	198
Hampton, Wade	22, 219
Hardee, William J.	22

Harpootlian, Richard 18, 19
Hatch, Edward 227
Hatton, Robert H. 27
Henningson, Karl F. 213
Henry, Margaret 215
Henry, Patrick 70, 246
Herndon, William H. 232
Hill, Ambrose P. 22, 137
Hitler, Adolf 89, 90
Hood, John Bell 22, 149-152
Hooker, Joseph 134
Houston, Sam 242
Hunter, David 160, 227
Hunter, Robert M. T. 197
Hussein, Saddam 90
Jackson, Stonewall . 22, 111, 115, 116, 134, 135, 192, 205, 206,
217, 219
James, Jesse 224
Jefferson, Thomas 38, 39, 41, 60, 69, 70, 100, 246
Jesus 39, 88
Johnson, Adam R. 218
Johnson, Andrew 198
Johnston, Albert S. 22, 114, 218
Johnston, Joseph E. 12, 22, 110
Jones, Arnold E. 26
Jones, Catesby R. 113
Jong-il, Kim 90
King, Horatio 199
King, Martin Luther 18
Lane, Jim 160
Leadbetter, Danville 27
Lee, Fitzhugh 218, 240
Lee, Francis Lightfoot 240
Lee, George W. 240
Lee, Henry "Light Horse Harry" 240

Lee, Mary Anne (Custis) 238
Lee, Richard Henry 240
Lee, Robert E.   6, 22, 80, 115-117, 134-136, 144, 145, 150, 152, 153, 169, 176, 198, 201, 217, 218, 225, 230, 238, 240, 243, 245, 250
Lee, Samuel P. 240
Lee, William H. F. 239, 240
Lehman Brothers 36
Lenin, Vladimir I. 90
Lincoln, Abraham . 11, 18, 19, 26, 41, 63, 64, 66, 71, 72, 74, 76, 79, 81-83, 85, 86, 88, 90, 91, 95, 97-99, 101, 103, 105-108, 111, 117, 118, 120-122, 124, 125, 127, 129-133, 137, 139, 140, 142, 144, 147, 148, 151, 157-164, 171, 176, 178, 179, 181, 183, 193, 197, 198, 200, 205, 207, 208, 212, 219, 220, 224-227, 230, 232, 235, 236, 240, 243, 246, 257, 258
Little Irish 217
Longstreet, James 22, 116, 137
Madison, James 38, 41, 70, 246
Magruder, John 115
Mallory, Stephen R. 80, 198
Marshall, Louis 28
Marx, Karl 67
Mason, George 70, 246
McClellan, George B. 111, 115, 117, 119, 148
McComb, William 27
McCulloch, Hugh 198
McDowell, Irvin 110, 111
McIntosh, John B. 27
McLean, Wilmer 153
Meade, George G. 135, 144, 145
Memminger, Christopher G. 79, 197
Milroy, Robert H. 227
Moore, Thomas O. 205
Morgan, John H. 22, 205

Morgan, Pierpont	36
Mugabe, Robert	90
Mussolini, Benito	89
Nelson, Louis N.	206
Obama, Barack	74, 76, 77
Olmsted, Frederick L.	52
O'Reilly, Bill	18
Page, Richard L.	240
Pemberton, John C.	26
Phelps, John W.	160
Pickett, George E.	136
Pierce, Franklin	228
Pillow, Gideon	112
Pinckney, Charles	70
Polk, Leonidas	22
Pope, John	116, 227
Porter, Fitz J.	115, 116
Porter, William D.	28
Price, Sterling	22
Quantrill, William C.	27
Rains, Gabriel J.	183
Randolph, George W.	198
Rasin, William I.	218
Reagan, John H.	80, 198
Reagan, Ronald	67
Richardson, John A.	192
Robertson, Felix H.	220
Robertson, John	216
Roosevelt, Franklin D.	66
Rosecrans, William S.	119, 137
Ross, Lawrence S.	27
Ruffin, Edmund	194
Ruggles, Daniel	26
Santorum, Rick	18
Scheibert, Justus	213

Schofield, John M.	149, 150
Scott, Winfield	223
Sears, Claudius W.	27
Seddon, James A.	198
Seward, William H.	105, 106, 124, 127, 198
Sheridan, Philip H.	226
Sherman, William T.	218, 226, 227, 233
Shoup, Fancis A.	27
Slidell, John	27
Smith, Caleb B.	127, 198
Smith, Edmund K.	22
Smith, Gustavus W.	198
Smith, John	69
Smith, Martin L.	27
Speed, James	198
St. Leger, George	213
Stalin, Joseph	89
Stanley, Morton	213
Stanton, Edwin M.	118, 127, 198, 207
Steele, William	26
Stephens, Alexander H.	12, 22, 79, 162, 197
Stevens, Clement H.	27
Stevens, Walter H.	27
Stowe, Harriet Beecher	54, 56
Strahl, Otho F.	27
Stuart, Jeb	22, 137, 217
Sturgis, Samuel D.	146
Sumner, Edwin	115
Taney, Roger B.	163
Taylor, Richard	12, 151
Taylor, Sarah K.	151
Taylor, Zachary	151
Terrill, James	240
Terrill, William R.	240
Thomas, George H.	28, 137, 150, 233

Thompson, M. Jeff 217
Tiffany, Charles 36
Tilghman, Lloyd 27
Tito, Josip 90
Tocqueville, Alexis de 42, 52
Tompkins, Sally 216
Toombs, Robert A. 79, 197
Trenholm, George A. 197
Truth, Sojourner 122
Turner, Nat 55, 56
Twain, Mark 226
Usher, John P. 198
Vallandigham, Clement L. 158
Van Dorn, Earl 212
Velasquez, Loreta J. 215
von Borcke, Heros 213
Walker, LeRoy P. 80, 197
Walker, William S. 27
Ward, William T. 28
Washington, George 38, 41, 70, 238, 246
Watie, Stand 212
Watts, Thomas H. 198
Welles, Gideon 127, 198
West, Joseph R. 28
Wheaton, Frank 240
Williams, Laura J. 215
Williams, Walter W. 220
Williamson, James A. 27
Winbush, Nelson W. 204, 206
Winder, John H. 26
Winthrop, Theodore 205
Woolson, Albert 220
Worden, John L. 113
Wright, Mary 215
York, Zebulon 26

MEET THE AUTHOR

LOCHLAINN SEABROOK, winner of the prestigious Jefferson Davis Historical Gold Medal for his "masterpiece," *A Rebel Born: A Defense of Nathan Bedford Forrest,* is one of the world's leading pro-South writers. He is an unreconstructed Southern historian, award-winning author, Nathan Bedford Forrest scholar, and traditional Southern Agrarian of Scottish, English, Irish, Welsh, German, and Italian extraction. An encyclopedist, lexicographer, musician, artist, graphic designer, genealogist, and photographer, as well as an award-winning poet, songwriter, and screenwriter, he has a thirty year background in historical nonfiction writing and is a member of the Sons of Confederate Veterans, the Civil War Trust, and the National Grange.

(Illustration © Tracy Latham)

Due to similarities in their writing styles, ideas, and literary works, Seabrook is referred to as the "American ROBERT GRAVES," after his cousin, the prolific English writer, historian, mythographer, poet, and author of the classic tomes *The White Goddess* and *The Greek Myths.*

The grandson of an Appalachian coal-mining family, Seabrook is a seventh-generation Kentuckian, co-chair of the Jent/Gent Family Committee (Kentucky), founder and director of the Blakeney Family Tree Project, and a board member of the Friends of Colonel Benjamin E. Caudill. Seabrook's literary works have been endorsed by leading authorities, museum curators, award-winning historians, bestselling authors, celebrities, noted scientists, well respected educators, renown military artists, esteemed Southern organizations, and distinguished academicians from around the world.

As a published writer, Seabrook has authored some thirty popular adult books specializing in the following topics: the American Civil War, pro-South studies, Confederate biography and history, the anthropology of religion, genealogical monographs, Goddess-worship (thealogy), ghost stories, the paranormal, family histories, military encyclopedias, etymological dictionaries, ufology, social issues, comparative analysis of the origins of Christmas, and cross-cultural studies of the family and marriage.

Seabrook's eight children's books include a guide to the Civil War for

Southern children, a dictionary of religion and myth, a rewriting of the King Arthur legend (which reinstates the original pre-Christian motifs), two bedtime stories for preschoolers, a naturalist's guidebook to owls, a worldwide look at the family, and an examination of the Near-Death Experience.

Of blue-blooded Southern stock through his Kentucky, Tennessee, Virginia, West Virginia, and North Carolina ancestors, he is a direct descendant of European royalty via his 6th great-grandfather, the EARL OF OXFORD, after which London's famous Harley Street is named. Among his celebrated male Celtic ancestors is ROBERT THE BRUCE, King of Scotland, Seabrook's 22nd great-grandfather. The 21st great-grandson of EDWARD I "LONGSHANKS" PLANTAGENET), King of England, Seabrook is a thirteenth-generation Southerner through his descent from the colonists of Jamestown, Virginia (1607).

The 2nd, 3rd, and 4th great-grandson of dozens of Confederate soldiers, one of his closest connections to the War for Southern Independence is through his 3rd great-grandfather, ELIAS JENT, SR., who fought for the Confederacy in the Thirteenth Cavalry Kentucky under Seabrook's 2nd cousin, Colonel BENJAMIN E. CAUDILL. The Thirteenth, also known as "Caudill's Army," fought in numerous conflicts, including the Battles of Saltville, Gladsville, Mill Cliff, Poor Fork, Whitesburg, and Leatherwood.

Seabrook is also related to the following Confederates and other 19th-Century luminaries: ROBERT E. LEE, STEPHEN DILL LEE, JOHN SINGLETON MOSBY, STONEWALL JACKSON, NATHAN BEDFORD FORREST, JAMES LONGSTREET, JOHN HUNT MORGAN, JEB STUART, P. G. T. BEAUREGARD (designed the Confederate Battle Flag), JOHN BELL HOOD, ALEXANDER PETER STEWART, ARTHUR M. MANIGAULT, JOSEPH MANIGAULT, CHARLES SCOTT VENABLE, THORNTON A. WASHINGTON, JOHN A. WASHINGTON, ABRAHAM BUFORD, EDMUND W. PETTUS, THEODRICK "TOD" CARTER, JOHN B. WOMACK, JOHN H. WINDER, GIDEON J. PILLOW, STATES RIGHTS GIST, EDMUND WINCHESTER RUCKER, HUGH ALFRED GARLAND JR., HENRY R. JACKSON, JOHN C. BRECKINRIDGE, LEONIDAS POLK, ZACHARY TAYLOR, SARAH KNOX TAYLOR (the first wife of JEFFERSON DAVIS), RICHARD TAYLOR, DAVY CROCKETT, DANIEL BOONE, MERIWETHER LEWIS (of the Lewis and Clark Expedition) ANDREW JACKSON, JAMES K. POLK, ABRAM POINDEXTER MAURY (founder of Franklin, TN), WILLIAM GILES HARDING, ZEBULON VANCE, THOMAS JEFFERSON, GEORGE WYTHE RANDOLPH (grandson of Jefferson), FELIX K. ZOLLICOFFER, FITZHUGH LEE,

(Photo © Lochlainn Seabrook)

NATHANIEL F. CHEAIRS, JESSE JAMES, FRANK JAMES, ROBERT BRANK VANCE, CHARLES SIDNEY WINDER, JOHN W. MCGAVOCK, CARRIE (WINDER) MCGAVOCK, DAVID HARDING MCGAVOCK, LYSANDER MCGAVOCK, JAMES RANDAL MCGAVOCK, RANDAL WILLIAM MCGAVOCK, FRANCIS MCGAVOCK, EMILY MCGAVOCK, WILLIAM HENRY F. LEE, LUCIUS E. POLK, MINOR MERIWETHER (husband of noted pro-South author Elizabeth Avery Meriwether), ELLEN BOURNE TYNES (wife of Forrest's chief of artillery, Captain John W. Morton), South Carolina Senators PRESTON SMITH BROOKS and ANDREW PICKENS BUTLER, and famed South Carolina diarist MARY CHESNUT.

Seabrook's modern day cousins include: PATRICK J. BUCHANAN (conservative author), REBECCA GAYHEART (Kentucky-born actress), SHELBY LEE ADAMS (Letcher County, Kentucky, portrait photographer), BERTRAM THOMAS COMBS (Kentucky's fiftieth governor), EDITH BOLLING (wife of President Woodrow Wilson), and actors ROBERT DUVALL, REESE WITHERSPOON, LEE MARVIN, and TOM CRUISE.

Born with music in his blood, Seabrook is an award-winning, multi-genre, BMI-Nashville songwriter and lyricist who has composed some 3,000 songs (250 albums), and whose original music has been heard on TV and radio worldwide. A musician, producer, multi-instrumentalist, and renown performer—whose keyboard work has been variously compared to pianists from HARGUS ROBBINS and VINCE GUARALDI to ELTON JOHN and LEONARD BERNSTEIN—Seabrook has opened for groups such as the EARL SCRUGGS REVIEW, TED NUGENT, and BOB SEGER, and has performed privately for such public figures as President RONALD REAGAN, BURT REYNOLDS, and Senator EDWARD W. BROOKE.

Seabrook's cousins in the music business include: JOHNNY CASH, ELVIS PRESLEY, BILLY RAY and MILEY CYRUS, PATTY LOVELESS, TIM MCGRAW, LEE ANN WOMACK, DOLLY PARTON, PAT BOONE, NAOMI, WYNONNA, and ASHLEY JUDD, RICKY SKAGGS, the SUNSHINE SISTERS, MARTHA CARSON, and CHET ATKINS.

Seabrook lives with his wife and family in historic Middle Tennessee, the heart of Forrest country and the Confederacy, where his conservative Southern ancestors fought valiantly against liberal Lincoln and the progressive North in defense of Jeffersonianism, constitutional government, and personal liberty.

LOCHLAINNSEABROOK.COM

316 ❧ Honest Jeff & Dishonest Abe

Parents, if you enjoyed Mr. Seabrook's *Honest Jeff and Dishonest Abe*, you will be interested in his adult works, including:

Everything You Were Taught About the Civil War is Wrong, Ask a Southerner!
The Quotable Jefferson Davis
Abraham Lincoln: The Southern View
A Rebel Born: A Defense of Nathan Bedford Forrest

Available from Sea Raven Press and wherever fine books are sold.

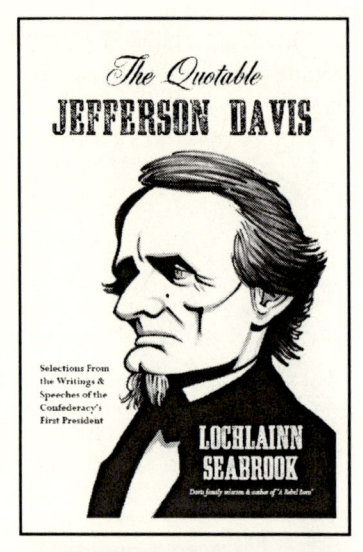